BERING SEA
BLUES

OTHER BOOKS BY JOE UPTON

Alaska Blues: A Fisherman's Journal (1977)

Amaretto (1986)

Journeys Through the Inside Passage: Seafaring Adventures Along the Coast of British Columbia and Alaska (1992)

The Coastal Companion (1994)

The Alaska Cruise Companion (1997)

Runaways on the Inside Passage (2002)

The Alaska Cruise Handbook (2005)

BERING SEA BLUES

A Crabber's Tale of FEAR in the Icy North

JOE UPTON

EPICENTER PRESS

For Dave Kennedy, Rick Nelson, Jim Odegaard,
friends lost at sea

Epicenter Press is a regional press publishing nonfiction books about the arts, history, environment, and diverse cultures and lifestyles of Alaska and the Pacific Northwest.

Publisher: Kent Sturgis
Acquisitions Editor: Lael Morgan
Editor: Ellen Wheat
Designer: Elizabeth M. Watson, Watson Graphics
Indexer: Sherrill Carlson
Mapmaker: Joe Upton
Printer: Thomson-Shore

Copyright © 2011 Joe Upton
All photographs copyright © 2011 Joe Upton except for those indicated otherwise.

No part of this publication may be reproduced, stored in a retrieval system, or transmitted in any form or by any means, electronic, mechanical, photocopying, recording, or otherwise, without the prior written permission of the publisher. Permission is given for brief excerpts to be published with book reviews in newspapers, magazines, newletters, catalogs, and online publications.

Photos: Front cover, crabbing in the Bering Sea, copyright © 1999, Daryl Binney; back cover, the *Flood Tide* collects ice in the Bering Sea; page 6, *Flood Tide* running before a southerly gale, Hecate Strait, British Columbia, March 1971.

Library of Congress Control Number: 2010943443
ISBN 978-1-935347-11-8

Trade paperback, First Edition
First Printing, 2010
10 9 8 7 6 5 4 3 2 1

Printed in the United States of America

To order single copies of *Bering Sea Blues*, mail $17.85 plus $6 for shipping (WA residents add $2.10 state sales tax) to Epicenter Press, PO Box 82368, Kenmore, WA 98028; call us day or night at 800-950-6663, or visit www.EpicenterPress.com. MC, Visa accepted. Contact info@EpicenterPress.com about volume discounts.

Acknowledgments

So MANY TIMES, in big boats and small, when the wind blew, we'd anchor up, and the rum and the stories would flow. Part of the Northwest fishing lore that I have shared here came from such evenings. Additionally, many Northwest fishermen have been kind enough to share their stories with me: John Enge, my old superintendent at Whitney Fidalgo Seafoods, Petersburg, Alaska, and my old boss at Marco, canneryman Eldon Grimes, both had wonderful tales, as did Bob and Ann Holmstrand of the tender *Frigidland*. Bob Thorstensen of Icicle Seafoods, Peter Schmidt, president of Marco, Richard Phillips of Commercial Fisherman's News, John van Amerongen of *Alaska Fishermen's Journal* and Jerry Fraser of *National Fisherman* magazine were all excellent sources of historical material. My first Alaska skipper, Lloyd Whaley, shared some great old photos, and Bruce Whittemore, designer of the *Flood Tide* and the long line of fine Marco crabbers that came before and after her, was very instrumental in giving me a clearer sense of stability issues. My friends Chuck and Diane Bundrant at Trident Seafoods were generous in allowing me to access their company's fine photos. Kaare Ness, another legendary crab fisherman, shared his history with me, as did crabber Bart Eaton, whose fine pictures also grace these pages. George and Russell Fulton both taught me the intricacies of crabbing as well as sharing their colorful pasts. Shipmates Johnny Nott and Bob Mason: if you're still out there, I hope I got it right. Walter Kuhr, now deceased, was a treasure trove of great stories. Crabber Mike Jackson, who went overboard twice in the Bering Sea before starting Stormy Seas to make inflatable vests just for such accidents, shared his years in the crab fishery. Special thanks to my wise and patient wife, Mary Lou, for putting up with another long project. But most of all, thanks to my first Alaska deck boss, Mickey Hansen, of the old salmon tender *Sidney*, for taking a green teenager under his wing forty-five years ago and showing him the ways of the North.

Contents

PAGE 21

PAGE 182–183

PAGE 153

PAGE 275

Crabber *Alma* at Seattle Fishermen's Terminal, around 1960. Before steel boats took over, many older wooden boats entered the crab fishery. Fishermen simply took the boat they had, put in a steel crab tank, and headed north with a load of pots into the winter conditions of the Bering Sea. It wouldn't take much of a sea to knock the pilothouse windows out of this boat. LLOYD WHALEY PHOTOGRAPH.

Prologue

"The weather in the Bering Sea is generally bad and very changeable. Good weather is the exception and it does not last long when it does occur. Wind shifts are both frequent and rapid. Late fall and early winter is the time of almost continuous storminess."
—*United States Coast Pilot, Vol. 9: Pacific and Arctic Coasts of Alaska from Cape Spencer to the Beaufort Sea*

THE BERING SEA is a bad place, the meanest sea that washes any shore. To the west is Siberia, to the north the Arctic, to the south the North Pacific, and to the east the vast tundra coast of Alaska. All are weather breeders. Calm days are rare. The boundary between the Bering Sea and the North Pacific is the Aleutian Islands, nicknamed "the Birthplace of the Winds." Every six hours, hundreds of cubic miles of water force their way through the narrow passes between the islands, resulting in currents that when opposed by the frequent strong winds, create seas big enough to wash forty-foot containers off the decks of 700-foot freighters.

In the winter, much of the Bering Sea freezes, the ice pack often reaching south of the Pribilof Islands. The action of the ice scours the shore along the shallow Alaska coast, making the construction of permanent harbor facilities difficult. Humans are scarce on the coast, their settlements even scarcer. Except for Dutch Harbor in the Aleutians, Nome near the Arctic Circle, and a few scattered Native villages, the land is empty and treeless, bleak and daunting.

The mountains that border the coast to the south are the meeting place of two of the gigantic plates that make up the earth's crust. Many of these peaks are active volcanoes, some regularly burping ash, steam, and lava in places so remote the eruptions are seldom noticed, except perhaps by crewmen on a trawler or crabber, nudging each other as a thousand tons of glowing ash and steam lights up the night sky with a spectacular show so far away no sound reaches them.

On the south side of the Bering Sea, along the Alaska Peninsula, a particular weather phenomenon occurs that has caused the loss of numerous vessels and crews. In the bitter depths of Alaskan winters, the air in the Interior valleys becomes unusually cold and dense. When circumstances are right, it roars down into the bays, picking up water and creating an ice fog that freezes instantly to any part of a boat it touches, forming ice so heavy that vessels at anchor can capsize before their crews know what's happening. Once a helicopter trying to locate a sinking vessel in one of these bays found itself icing up so badly with saltwater ice a thousand feet up, it had to abandon the search.

Yet, like the shallow banks of the western Atlantic that have proved so rich for generations of East Coast fishermen, the Bering Sea is also unusually productive. Upwelling currents sweep nutrients in from the depths of the Aleutian Trench to the south and from the mile-deep basin to the west, resulting in an immense fishery resource.

But because of its remoteness and the severity of the weather, even by Alaskan standards, it has long been a Last Frontier for commercial fishing, attracting only the hardiest, most entrepreneurial of fishermen. The first non-Native fishermen to come were the American whaling fleet, beginning in the 1850s and 1860s. Within a few decades, over a hundred big sail and steam whalers traveled the Bering Sea, seeking bowhead and right whales.

And the ice was always waiting for the careless, the unwary, or simply the unlucky. Many whaling ships were crushed when the ice trapped them.

THE CRABBER *Key West* sinking, Bering Sea, 1978. The Bering Sea is always probing, trying to find a vessel's weakness. The *Key West* was brand new, and jogging into a strong Bering Sea gale. A pot broke loose on the back deck and started slamming around, but it was so rough no one was able to go out and tie it down. Eventually it found the weak spot in the design: a 12-inch-diameter vent pipe for the lazarette. Unbeknownst to the crew, the pot broke the vent pipe off at the deck, and the water rolling across the deck in the heavy seas filled the lazarette, sinking the boat. Fortunately there were other crabbers nearby and all hands were rescued safely. BART EATON PHOTO

But what they did—travel for years at a time, half a world away from home, braving the cold and the ice in wooden boats—makes even the battles of the hardiest king crabbers today seem modest.

Next was the salmon boom starting in the late 1890s, when entrepreneurs from California and the Columbia River sent square-rigged ships filled with cannery building materials, fishing boats and gear, plus carpenters, cannery workers, and fishermen up to remote Bristol Bay in the eastern Bering Sea. The ships would anchor and all hands would turn to unloading, driving piling for docks, building canneries, and installing machinery before the fish run began.

When the salmon run started, the small fishing boats would be rigged with masts, sails, and gill nets, and then launched. For the fishermen, the challenges were immense: the tidal and river currents were strong, the wind gusty. But when the salmon arrived, they came by the tens of millions, the largest run on the entire coast, so the rewards for fishermen and cannery owners were great.

Then, starting in the 1940s, the foreign fleets came—200- to 300-foot processors and factory trawlers from Japan, Korea, Poland, Russia, and other countries—to harvest the immense resource of so-called bottom-fish, primarily pollock, haddock, and cod.

For the Americans, it was mostly the hardiest of the hardy—a few fishermen in halibut boats that were renowned up and down the coast for their seaworthiness—seeking their catch in the remote Bering Sea. And the tales they brought back with them, of below-zero temperatures and hurricane winds springing up without notice, of icing up so fast the crew couldn't keep up with it, didn't make other fishermen eager to go.

THE KING CRAB, a large, slow-moving, spider-like creature with thick legs loaded with tasty meat, was largely ignored by foreigners and Americans alike until second-generation Alaska seafood processor Lowell Wakefield developed a mechanical process to extract the leg meat from king crab in the mid-1950s. With this breakthrough, Wakefield began widely marketing frozen crab.

Wakefield's first big crab catcher-processor was the 140-foot *Deep Sea*, a trawler that towed a funnel-shaped net along the bottom, scraping up crab and depositing them in the tail of the net, called a cod end. The *Deep Sea*'s net caught a lot of crabs, but many were crushed by being jammed together when dragged and then hoisted aboard the *Deep Sea*. Because of this waste, trawling for king crab was banned in 1961.

Today, crab fishermen use large pots, which look like cages and are sometimes eight feet by eight feet by three feet and weigh 600 to 700 pounds empty. These king crab pots evolved from Dungeness crab traps, which were round with steel frames and nylon or stainless steel netting. The design was first expanded to a six-foot-diameter round trap about thirty inches high, but the rectangular pot was quickly adopted since it could be stacked with

TOP: THE *DEEP SEA*, Wakefield Fisheries pioneer crab dragger, around
1955. Entrepreneur Lowell Wakefield invested in the boat on the bet that
the U.S. market would buy tasty frozen king crab sections. He was right, and the
fishery eventually grew into a major Alaska industry. COURTESY *FISHERMEN'S NEWS.*
BOTTOM: KING CRAB PILED up near the big trawl winches of the trawler *Deep
Sea*, around 1955. The *Deep Sea* caught an impressive amount of crab, but as the
funnel-shaped trawl net was pulled to the surface, many crab were crushed, and
eventually this style of harvesting king crab was banned by the state of Alaska.
COURTESY *FISHERMEN'S NEWS.*

less wasted space on deck and it had more volume; fishermen were discovering that there were a lot of king crab on the bottom.

Early on, crab fishermen discovered that king crab exhibited a behavior unlike any other crab they had known: they often traveled in immense groups of hundreds of thousands of individual crabs. And it appeared that at certain times, the pods or herds would segregate themselves by size and gender. This habit allowed crab fishermen to "prospect" with their crab gear, by setting pots over a wide area to discover the composition of herds. For instance, a big herd might cover several acres, and one part might be females, another part might be small males, and another part of the herd might be mostly large males. The females are illegal and the smaller males are "sublegal." By targeting the large-male part of the herd and trying to stay on it (the herds also move), a savvy crab fisherman could spare his crew much of the tedious job of sorting out the mature males, or keepers, with big meaty legs from the others.

By the late 1950s, salmon fishermen in the Kodiak Island area looking for a good winter fishery for their boats were beginning to fish king crab in the bays around that big island. Today's crab boats keep their crab alive by putting them in tanks of circulating seawater. But in the early 1960s when the crab fishery was getting under way, most of the fleet in Kodiak were salmon seiners and other wooden boats, usually smaller than seventy feet, and were generally unsuited for installing the watertight tanks needed to keep king crab alive.

But Kodiak was an island with dozens of sheltered bays that were close enough to town for the smaller boats to fish without a tank and deliver every day. Fishing the bays close to Kodiak and returning to town to deliver each night was fine when the crab were close, but it became quickly apparent that with the fishery rapidly growing, crab fishermen would have to travel farther with larger boats equipped with flooded crab tanks. With a very large salmon fleet and a population of talented and aggressive fishermen, Kodiak was an ideal place for king crabbing to first take off. The fleet grew rapidly: 183 boats participated in 1965, leaping to 258 just a year later.

Harvests jumped from 11 million pounds in 1958 to a huge 158 million pounds in 1966. At an average price of ten cents a pound, it averaged out to something like $60,000 per boat, and a "highliner," or top fisherman, might double or triple that. Dollars were worth way more back then: the average crab boat working in the winter would make what an average summer salmon season brought in, doubling the income for the year, a very exciting prospect.

It was immediately apparent to Kodiak's crab fishermen that this was a very strong resource: some boats were catching as much as 3,000 ten- to twelve-pound crabs a day—huge numbers. So those with the money sought larger boats that could be equipped with steel crab tanks. At the time, there were few suitable steel boats available on the West Coast, so many wooden boats were purchased and refitted with steel crab tanks. These crab conversions were not a marriage made in heaven: rigid water-filled steel tanks and limber old wooden boats are not a great combination. But fishermen go with what is available and what they can afford, so the nasty waters around Kodiak Island saw the loss of numerous boats and crews.

Crabbing, unlike salmon fishing, was in the winter. And winter around Kodiak meant snow and ice. The smaller boats used in the early Kodiak fishery weren't built for the rigors of crabbing, with 700-pound pots slamming around on deck. Furthermore, when the bitter winds of winter blew, the flying spray would quickly freeze to any exposed surfaces, building up weight and putting vessels in danger of capsizing. Icing, and the decreasing stability that comes with it, is a continuing challenge for crab fishermen.

It didn't take long for crabbers to think steel, and by 1966, Northwest shipbuilders' books began to fill with orders for what were essentially the first modern steel crabbers. Some were conversions, steel vessels built for other uses and converted to crabbers. Particularly popular and available were U.S. Navy surplus YOs and YFs, big 150-foot yard oilers and yard freighters.

One of the first crabbers to be designed and built from the ground up as a crabber, and which essentially served as a model for the hundreds of house-forward (with the pilothouse in the front of the boat) crabbers that followed, was the *Peggy Jo*, built for Oscar Dyson, a well-known Kodiak fisherman. Built by the Martinolich yard in Tacoma, Washington, she was a hundred feet long by twenty-eight feet wide by twelve feet deep, and could carry 10,000 king crab alive for a week or more in her two big crab tanks. Delivered in the spring of 1966, she was an eye opener for Kodiak fishermen. Compared to the smaller boats that often had dry holds, which were the mainstay of the crab fleet then, the *Peggy Jo* was truly a vision of what the future looked like, and fishermen liked what they saw.

The forward quarter, or third, of the boat was accommodations—galley and crew quarters—on the same level as the main deck, with the pilothouse and the skipper's cabin behind it on the upper deck. On the smaller wooden boats that had been the core of the fleet, the deckhouse, holding the galley aft and the steering area forward with crew's bunks usually below decks, was narrow with room on either side to walk up to the bow. In heavy weather, waves would come over the bow and wash along the side decks and often back into the deck area where the crew worked, but the *Peggy Jo's* design with a deckhouse that stretched the full width of the boat (access to the bow was through the pilothouse on the upper deck) created a more sheltered and therefore safer crew area. Plus, the working deck seemed almost the size of a football field compared to the cramped and cluttered back deck of the typical Kodiak crabber then.

Another critical feature was flush decks. Most other fishing boats of that era had large raised hatches, perhaps as large as eight by ten feet, which provided access to the fish holds as well as keeping water out of the holds when the boat was heavily loaded in rough conditions. On a fifty-foot boat with the forward third taken up by the deckhouse and bow, a big hatch was in the way, especially when manipulating heavy, awkward crab pots. On the *Peggy Jo* and essentially all crabbers that followed her, hatches were set flush to the deck, with sliding doors for loading crab. And for unloading, the huge steel hatch cover, maybe fifteen feet by fifteen feet on a big crabber, could be unbolted, lifted up, and placed out of the way. Sometimes a portable steel or aluminum chute, perhaps two feet high, was inserted into whichever sliding

THE CRABBER *Shishaldin*, converted from a U.S. navy ship, around 1960. Before shipyards like Marco started building new crabbers in the late 1960s, fishermen often purchased old military hulls and converted them by putting in crab tanks and pot handling gear. Note her smoking engines, probably surplus as well, but never a good sign, and barrels of lube oil lashed to the upper deck. COURTESY MARCO.

door was being used, to load crab into the tank and prevent female or sub-legal male crabs from accidentally getting into the tank. And since the *Peggy Jo* and other new crabbers were built with crab tanks designed to be filled with seawater, there was no longer a need for a hatch to keep the sea out.

At the same time that the *Peggy Jo* and other house-forward steel crab-bers were being built, the Pacific Fishermen Shipyard in Seattle launched an unusual boat for Seattle crabber Axel Buholm. Designed by Seattle naval architect Bill Jensen as a house-aft crabber, Buholm's *Sea Ern* became the first of many boats of essentially the same design, eighty-eight by twenty-six by ten feet, with a raised bow (bait freezer and storage underneath) that pro-vided some protection to the crew, and a two-story pilothouse that was aft, or at the back of the vessel. This configuration allowed the skipper to closely observe the crew without having to turn around all the time like on a conventional house-forward vessel.

The new fleet of steel crab boats electrified the Northwest fishing community. Previously, almost all fishing boats were wooden. Not only did these new boats provide a bigger working platform than other crabbers, but they offered amazing luxury as well: electric kitchens, electric heat, showers, flush toilets, multiple crew cabins, and, most amazing of all, a washer and dryer so you could have nice toasty rubber gloves whenever you wanted.

THE LATE 1960s were truly heady days for crabbers and Northwest shipyards. Each month, the cover of *Fishermen's News*, the Northwest's fishing trade magazine, featured a big photo of yet another large crabber getting launched and headed north. Anxious crabbers were ordering boats from as far away as Alabama in order to get delivery before the next crab season.

Almost all of these new big boats were headed for the Bering Sea, because in the mid-1960s it was clear that the Bering Sea was the place to crab. The crab resource in Kodiak was in decline, and the small Kodiak boats were unable to fish in the more challenging environment of the Bering Sea.

In the 1960s, the Bering Sea was the wild, wild west. While the town of Kodiak had bars, restaurants, hotels, and numerous stores, Dutch Harbor on Unalaska Island in the Aleutians was the only real port in the Bering Sea, an area the size of New England. And Dutch had one bar, one store, one church, and two public phones. Transport in and out in the winter, by Reeve Aleutian Airways, was spotty. If your boat broke down and you needed a part flown in, you could be out of business for a week or more.

The little fleet of nine boats that fished the first Bering Sea king crab season in 1966 included Soren Sorenson's new steel eighty-six footer *Denali*, Ed Grabowski's seventy-eight-foot wooden *North Sea*, Knute Franklin's wooden *Honey B*, and six others. They rocked the Northwest fishing community with their tales of huge fishing: 200 to 300 keepers in a single pot. A new gold rush was on.

Before king crabbing, salmon was the major commercial fishery in Alaska. The fleet was large and the harvests and prices were pretty stable. People could do well at salmon fishing. But as early reports trickled in from the Bering Sea king crab fleet, it was clear that this opportunity was something new even for Alaska—a wide-open fishery where, for those with the resources and will to gear up and get out there, the rewards could be huge. The only trouble was that the best crab fishing was in the middle of winter, and as even the most hardened veterans of Alaska fishing were to find out, Bering Sea winter fishing put strains on boats and crews that few had experienced.

This was the exciting environment into which I stepped as deckhand on the new steel 104-foot crabber *Flood Tide* in the late winter of 1971. I was twenty five.

 THE CREW OF *Officina de la Patria*, Chile, 1965. I (far right) worked as second engineer aboard a tuna seiner in the summer after high school. The bleak desert coast of northern Chile can be seen behind us.

1. Beginnings

THE STORY OF MY JOURNEY TO Alaska on the *Flood Tide* began in the bleak north Chilean town of Iquique in 1965. A few months out of high school and hoping to find an interesting job and make some money for college, through a family friend who had connections with a Chilean fishing company I got work as a fleet mechanic, and struggled with my high school Spanish in a very different world from my East Coast home.

Around the dusty town at the foot of a bluff on the edge of the great Atacama Desert were signs of a prosperous past: the late 1800s and early 1900s when ships from all over the world came to load nitrates—bags of brownish white power from mines in the great desert, used for fertilizer and gunpowder. There were photos of the wide harbor full of square-riggers, waiting their turn, sometimes for months, to load. Then came World War I, the Germans invented artificial nitrate, the ships abruptly stopped coming, and just like that, Iquique was *abajo* (down).

Then in the early 1960s came another sort of boom: anchovies. Fish meal for animal food and fertilizer was big business worldwide, and the vast anchovy schools eddying close to the coast there were a perfect source. The big fish meal companies from South Africa and the southern United States came to town to built plants and fleets.

Two new shipyards were building seiners as fast as they could, and already there were 300 plus in the harbor. Seiners set a net in a circle around the fish, then pull in a wire laced through steel rings along the bottom of the

OUR TUNA SEINER, anchored off the abandoned town of Caleta Buena, Chile, 1965. Towns like this were totally dependent on the big nitrate clippers, square-riggers that came from Germany loaded with food, supplies, even water, to take away the powdered nitrates that came from the mines in the desert behind the coast. When World War I started, the clippers stopped coming and the people in these towns had to leave or starve.

net to draw, or "purse," the net into a basket shape from which the fish cannot escape. Amazingly enough, in those heady days, the problem wasn't catching the fish, but rather the opposite: catching too many fish. The anchovy schools were so dense you could wrap so much with your net that the fish would smother and sink, bending your boom or capsizing your boat. The big steel skiffs that aided in the process of setting the net had an engine-driven water pump and a couple of empty fifty-five-gallon drums. As soon as the skiff hooked onto the net—the skiff held part of the net up while the seiner was pumping the fish out—the skiff operator hooked the drums to the skiff's opposite rail and pumped them full of water to counter the pull of the net.

Some of my ship- and workmates had come from essentially feudal living conditions in the farms of southern Chile, four days by dusty bus with their families to live in oven-hot shacks built of flattened fifty-five-gallon drums. But a job on a good seiner was a step on a path that could lead to

better lives, and there was work for the women as well in the fish meal plants. The combination made for new lives with hope.

This was the eye-opening world I entered, green and very wet behind the ears. I got off the plane and found a room in a pension, which once had been a large, elegant home but had fallen on hard times and the many rooms were rented out.

My first job was in the shop of a fishing company. Of course I wanted to get out on the boats where the action was. The graduation test from our little mechanic's shop was being able to take apart and reassemble the complex workings of the inertia starters used for the small diesel engines in the big metal skiffs that the seiners used in the fishing process. In my first attempts, I always had parts left over when I was done—never a good thing. But eventually I got it right and moved on to be crewman on a seventy-five-foot steel anchovy seiner. Things were pretty crude. One of the cook's jobs as we sat around the galley table playing cards was to occasionally reach up and swat

OUR TUNA SEINER, *Officina de la Patria*, Iquique, Chile, 1965. We would make one- to two-week trips offshore, fishing for bonita, a small species of tuna.

the pesky flies off the big pieces of meat swaying from hooks over his head; there was neither ice nor refrigeration. I had never even been out on a fishing boat before and so to be part of the process of loading the boat deep in the water with a single set of the net was fascinating.

Eventually, I graduated to assistant engineer on one of our company's tuna seiners, the largest boats in Iquique then. These were big 140 footers with ten-man crews and real staterooms. Instead of a quick overnight out to the grounds and back that the anchovy boats did, the tuna seiner had refrigerated holds and we'd be out for three or four weeks at a time, often out of sight of land for days or weeks.

As crewmen on a tuna boat, we each got two frozen bonita after each trip. The local men would take them up to the poor sections of town to share with their families and friends—a wonderful treat. For men like myself, a nice ten-pound bonita was worth a night on the town: including dinner, drinks, and company.

The Americans in Iquique hung out at the old Hotel Pratt, on the main plaza. In the hotel lobby hung wonderful old photos of Iquique in the nitrate days. Sometimes I'd nurse a beer in the bar and listen, because often the talk was of Alaska. There was a sizeable group of skippers from Alaska and Puget Sound, who had come, some with their boats, on contracts to demonstrate fishing methods to the Chilean fishermen. I'd hear snippets of conversation about places with intriguing names, spoken, it seemed to me, with awe. Names like Seymour Narrows, False Pass, Whirlpool Rapids, Ford's Terror. In time, I understood these were all in Alaska or along the Inside Passage, the winding waterway through the mountainous coast of British Columbia up to Alaska. So even before I ever went up to Alaska, it had become this mythic place to me: a land of big catches but with hidden dangers lurking to snare the careless or inattentive.

George Fulton was there, a big, brash, hard-drinking man who was popular with the Chilean skippers. He had an unusual job, demonstrating a new method of trawl fishing to Chilean fishermen up and down that long coast. A Seattle company, Marine Construction and Design (Marco), had a shipyard in Iquique, building and launching seiners as fast as it could, but also providing technical fisheries assistance to the government of Chile. As part of that program, Marco had built a small stern trawler, the *Gringo*, with a drum to roll the net back onboard. At that time, all Chilean trawlers were side trawlers, a less efficient design. Wherever George and the *Gringo* went, he amazed the local Chilean fishermen with the boat's efficiency, at the same time setting catch records for such a small boat.

George befriended me and introduced me around to other American skippers. I was an anomaly to them—an American working for Chilean wages, about $50 a month.

"Go to Alaska," George said one night. "You can make big bucks there with the experience you're getting here."

It seemed like a faraway dream, and I said so.

"There's a boat leaving next month for Seattle. I can get you on it," George said, just like that. "Then you pound the docks, asking all the skippers, until you get a job."

I could feel goose bumps rising on my arms. A ride up to Seattle, the possibility of fishing in Alaska. A whole new world was opening up to me.

I thought I'd run it by my parents back home in Virginia. Phone calls were undependable and expensive in Chile, but one of the engineers at Marco had a ham radio set up in his dining room, so one night I sat with him and he tuned up and finally connected with a ham radio operator in Alabama, who called my parents collect, and then put me on.

THE *GRINGO*, in Chile, 1965. Marco built this pioneering stern trawler to demonstrate new fishing techniques to Chilean fishermen. Her skipper, George Fulton, encouraged me to seek work in Alaska and eventually hired me on his king crabber *Flood Tide*. Courtesy Marco.

It went like this: "Hey, Mom and Dad, it's Joe, still down in Iquique. Can you hear me . . . over? You have to say 'over' when you're done talking."

Long pause, then, "Hello . . . Joe. Where are you? . . Over."

"I'm still down in Iquique, but I want to get a fishing job in Alaska this summer, and I think I've got a ride on a boat that's heading up there next month. What do you think? Over."

Long, long pause, and then, "Could you say that one more time? We're not sure we really understand."

Decades later, when our own son would tell me and my wife things like how he was going to go to Croatia for a month to climb, and my reaction would be to discourage it, I would recall that long-ago phone call from Iquique to my parents, and I would admire their equanimity.

I explained the best I could, and their reply was "be careful," the same one I use today with our son.

AND SO, IN JUNE OF 1965, after a forty-five-day voyage from Chile in a seventy-foot wooden seiner, I began to pound the docks at Seattle's Fishermen's Terminal, looking for my first job on an Alaska-bound fishing boat. The feeling among the young men like myself, walking the docks day after day, was electric. When our paths crossed, we'd share what information we had gathered: "The *Johnny H* might need a man; skipper will be back tomorrow," or "I heard that there's a guy on the *Prospector* that might not work out. It might be worth talking to the skipper." The guys who found jobs seemed to walk with a new bounce in their step.

It was exhilarating to think that a great job was just a tip or a conversation away, but at the same time it was deeply discouraging to see the freshly painted boats assemble their gear and crews, have one last evening party on the dock, and then be gone in the morning, up the northern marine highway that was the Inside Passage.

Steve Trutich, the owner of the boat I had traveled on from Chile, had kindly allowed me to stay aboard. We were tied up at the edge of the fresh-water waterway that led from the inland lakes and channels to the salt water of Puget Sound and the beginning of the Inside Passage. It was great to have a place to stay, but it was also bittersweet. On those fine, warm, June evenings as I sat eating in the galley or out on the back deck with a beer, boats would pass that I knew were headed up to Alaska, and I could clearly hear their crews chatting about all the things that they would do when they got "up North."

After I walked the docks each day, I'd hang out at Seattle Ship Supply, a big dockside store that smelled of tar and paint. The rough-faced, suspender-wearing customers seemed to ooze Alaska. So I'd pretend to be studying the instructions on the paint cans and eavesdrop on their conversations, which were sprinkled with some of the same names that I had heard in the bar back in Iquique. When there was a break between customers, I'd cautiously approach the clerks to ask them if they had heard of any boats that needed a man. And they always had time to suggest or encourage, knowing perhaps that the young men seeking jobs today might be the prosperous skippers of tomorrow.

"The *Sidney* needs an engineer," the cashier said one day without fanfare. "You were on a tuna boat as engineer, weren't you?"

"Second engineer," I corrected him. "I was just basically a helper, but I learned the basics."

"Well, she's tied up at the West Wall, loading."

I thanked that man, you bet, and beat feet over to the West Wall, the place in Fishermen's Terminal where the big boats load their Alaska freight just before departing. The *Sidney* was big, easily twenty feet bigger than the fifty-eight-foot seiners I had been trying for. I knew from being around the waterfront that such boats were used for fish buying and were called tenders or packers. They would buy fish from fishing boats in the remote fishing areas and take them to the canneries. Their crews were paid by the day and generally had better living conditions than those on the smaller seiners, where you were paid a crew share or part of the catch.

A big man was standing on the back of the upper deck, above the main deck, using a set of levers that I quickly realized were winch controls, used to unload pallets of boxed freight from a truck on the dock. As I watched, the pallets disappeared through the square hatch and into the hold below. From what I had seen on the docks, these bigger boats usually left for Alaska heavily loaded with freight for the cannery they worked for. When the last pallet dropped into the hold, I called to the winch operator, who hopefully was the skipper.

"Hello. I hear you might be looking for an engineer."

He looked me up and down before finally responding. "You look a little young. What boat were you engineer on before?"

"Well, it was a tuna boat down in Chile."

"Chile?" My answer seemed to set him back. "I didn't know there was any tuna down there."

"Oh, yeah," I answered confidently, "lots. This was a big seiner . . . "

"What kind of refrigeration?" he asked.

"Ammonia," I answered. "Big systems . . ."

He waved toward the hold. "Well, we got a big Freon system . . . different from those big tuna boat ammonia systems. Think you can handle it? I got a guy who'll show you the ropes."

"Same principle. I can figure it out," I said, with more confidence than I felt.

"How about gas engines?" he asked. "Almost all our boats are gas. Big Chrysler straight-eight Royals. They always need a little help . . . "

"I know the basics," I said, beginning to wonder what I was getting myself into.

Another big flatbed truck loaded with pallets of freight appeared.

"Well, you sound okay," the skipper said, "but who can I talk with that you worked with before?"

"Uhh . . . okay, how about Steve Trutich? He owns the *Nick C II*. He knows me." And I gave him my name.

"Okay, kid, I'll call Steve tonight. Check in with me tomorrow." With that, he turned back to the winch levers.

I didn't sleep that night, going over in my mind what the man had said. I think I could figure out the refrigeration, especially if he had someone who

THE *SIDNEY*, rigged for fish buying, Southeast Alaska, 1965. My first Alaska job was as engineer aboard her. Such vessels play an important role, buying salmon from gillnetters and seiners and putting them in refrigerated seawater holds until they can be delivered to the cannery, often several hundred miles away.

could go over the systems with me. I was a little nervous about the Chrysler Royals or whatever they were. About all I knew about gas engines came from changing spark plugs on our lawn mower at home. But I could get a book or something.

Finally the morning came, and I made what I hoped would be my last breakfast aboard the *Nick C II*, and headed over the Ballard Bridge to Fishermen's Terminal. Another truck was already backed up to the edge of the dock by the *Sidney* and the skipper was at the winch controls again. He waved me aboard and up to the boat deck, as soon as he saw me.

"Hey kid, you're hired," he said right off, and stuck out his hand. "Steve said you were pretty sharp, and that's good enough for me. "A thousand bucks a month and a bonus at the end of the season if everything goes okay. How does that sound?"

"Great," I managed to say confidently, barely able to hide my excitement and amazement.

"Okay, done deal." A shake from a calloused hand, and a new life opened up ahead of me.

FOR ME, THAT SUMMER OF 1965, when I was just nineteen and engineer on the *Sidney*, was ALASKA in capital letters. We worked for a cannery in Metlakatla, an Indian village in Southeast. There were totem poles on the docks and bald eagles in the trees. The sixty-year-old mate, Mickey Hansen, was an old Alaska hand, a Norwegian with fifty seasons "up North," having fished for about everything that swam or crawled in the waters of Alaska. Mickey took me, a greenhorn, under his wing, showed me the intricacies of fish buying, navigation, diesel mechanics, and refrigeration. But most of all, he shared with me a lifetime of fishing in Alaska.

MICKEY HANSON (right), the mate of the *Sidney*, and me, Southeast Alaska, 1965. Mick took me under his wing and shared his fifty years of experience in Alaska, in many jobs, aboard many boats. It was this man's kindness, patience, advice, and wonderful stories that helped set me on the path of becoming an Alaska fisherman and writer.

In August, we'd bought fish in an exquisite little cove in the Inian Islands, just south of Glacier Bay in Icy Strait. Snow still lay on the north-facing slopes of the forests around us, and occasionally at night, icebergs from Glacier Bay would drift into the cove and bump into us. We'd usually finish up unloading our last boats for the week around 7 p.m. and start running for our cannery, a fourteen-hour run to the south. After we picked up the anchor and started steaming, I'd clean up the back deck with Old Mick. Then, after a big supper, I'd spend an hour or so in the engine room, getting the refrigeration to run right, checking all the fluids, putting my tools away, and wiping everything down.

By the time it was my watch, it would be almost dark, and we'd have made the turn into Chatham Strait—a wide, lonely canyon with steeply forested islands on both sides. The high-latitude twilight would linger, illuminating the haunting landscapes with a pale, dying light. Our skipper would show me the penciled line that was our route, straight down the middle, then slap me on the back and retire to his stateroom just behind the wheelhouse.

Sometimes, if conditions were right, I could even find a radio station—usually some 10,000-watt boomer from the South or Midwest—broadcasting evangelism and country western all mixed together. I'd sit there in the big chair, marveling at the vast and mysterious land sliding past, listening to the country music fading in and out on the radio. The automatic pilot did all the work. Every fifteen minutes or so, I'd look at the radar and the chart, measure off some distances with a divider, and put a pencil tick where we were. That was before GPS, so it was navigation the old-fashioned way—look at the radar, look out with the binoculars, look at the fathometer (depth sounder), and then compare what you see with the information on the chart. Those old charts were rich with information—old course tracks, little notations like "bear on beach 9/22/59"—and when I penciled in our positions and times, I felt part of a grand tradition. Every hour on the dot, I'd go down for my engine room tour—checking all the gauges and looking for leaking hoses or any other indication of possible problems. Then it was out on the back deck to pull up the thermometer, hanging into the middle of the fish hold, and make sure it was still dropping. The last stop at the galley was for another mug up of coffee and a donut, and then back to that big seat again, watching the amazing landscape sliding past, and thinking about how grand life was just then.

And if Old Mick were up with me, hardly a bay or a cove would we pass without him telling me a story, like: "We picked our way into there in a snowstorm in '39 aboard the old *Patty A*. There wasn't no radar then, so we used the steam whistle, listening for the echo off the rocks."

That first season in Southeast Alaska filled me up in a way nothing else had. Working that boat, meeting that collection of rough characters, seeing all that amazing country instilled in me what turned out to be a lifelong fascination with the North. When it was over, all I wanted to do was to get up there in my own boat.

I TRIED COLLEGE FOR A WHILE, but Alaska called. I figured I'd better learn something useful before trying for a job again, and spent a year at the University of Rhode Island's commercial fishing program, one of the first in the country. There were just a dozen or so of us, working out of a building on a harbor on Narragansett Bay. In the morning we would learn about diesel engines, navigation, refrigeration, splicing wire, and making nets. In the afternoons we would take off in our fifty-foot commercial fishing vessel and work the different nets we had built, and take home the catch to eat. My classmates ranged from a young Maine lobstermen to an East African sent by his government to learn skills he could bring back.

And one guy, Dave Kennedy, had fished salmon with a gillnetter in Southeast Alaska and painted a grand picture for me of what it had been like for him and his wife on their fine boat, making steady money, exploring that vast country on the long weekends when the fishing was closed. He wanted to try to get a skipper's job on a big Gulf of Mexico shrimper after graduation, and offered generously to lease me his gillnetter, which was sitting at Fishermen's Terminal in Seattle. He didn't have a photograph, but sketched out this great boat, complete with a flying bridge. I figured it had to be a forty footer, and pretty soon I was envisioning myself and my girlfriend sitting up on the flying bridge, sharing a bottle of wine as we headed up that glorious Inside Passage to start our new lives as salmon fishermen in Alaska.

So as soon as school was out, I packed up my tools and gear, said goodbye to my parents, and headed out to Seattle. My dad had told me to get a maritime surveyor to look at the boat before I went, but I pooh-poohed the idea. Dave had made it to Alaska, put in a season, and returned with money in his pocket, and I was sure I could too.

I took a taxi straight to Fishermen's Terminal, loaded my stuff into a dock cart, and started rolling it down dock 6, where I had trudged up and down many times just a few years before, trying to get that first job. And now I had a boat there! I was the captain. We were going to Alaska! There was a real bounce in my step as I came to the slip.

And stopped. I took the piece of paper out of my pocket again with the information written on it. That joke of a boat couldn't be the *Denise*. But I walked out to the end of the pier finger and there it was on the bow: *Denise*. Listing, neglected, obviously rotten in places, it was all of maybe twenty-six feet. It did have a flying bridge, but it was clear it was only for looks and storage of light articles. Had I tried to climb up on it, the *Denise* probably would have capsized. Then I remembered Dave had never actually said how long the boat was, and in my excitement I had never asked him.

There was a really nice boat tied up next to it, actually what I had expected to find: a fine thirty-eight footer, beautifully painted and rigged, obviously ready to head up North. As I stood on the dock looking at the *Denise*, my head spinning, a husky man came down the dock with his cartload of stuff and stopped at the thirty-eight footer and started putting boxes and duffel bags aboard. When he was done, he looked over at me and my cart, then slowly over at the *Denise*. Then back at me again.

"Hey, kid. You're not planning to head up North in that rig," he said. It wasn't even a question.

"I think I am," I said, but without much conviction.

THE ILL-FATED *DENISE*, Lopez Island, Washington, 1970. Would you go to Alaska in this boat? Blinded by the desire to go to Alaska in my own boat, I tried with the *Denise*. Had we ever made it into some of the rougher stretches of the Inside Passage, she probably would have sunk.

"Well, let me give you a little tip. Forget it. That piece of shit'd be lucky to get out of the locks, much less to Alaska. I wouldn't even let my kids *swim* off that boat."

I should have taken his advice. Should have just swallowed my pride and walked away. The seine fleet was gearing up, and the *Sidney* was around. I should have started to beat the docks again. With my URI Fisheries School experience, I should have been able to get a really good job.

But I didn't. I wanted to go to Alaska in my own boat, so badly. I was so stubborn and determined and foolish, I realize in retrospect, that I plunged all my savings into a boat that should have been taken up some grassy slough and beached to slowly rot away.

I redid the wiring, rebuilt the steering, then when I discovered that the engine was way too tired to ever make it to Alaska, I hired a mechanic to rebuild it. While he was doing that, I built a net for Southeast Alaska (thanks to the net skills I learned at URI Fisheries), checked over the charts and radio, finished up the painting, so as to be all ready to head North as soon as the engine was put in.

And all the time that I worked on the *Denise*, I could not help but notice a gillnetter on the opposite side of the dock. It was all aluminum, a real no-nonsense boat, a husky thirty-six footer, and the only thing that I could see on it that was painted was the bottom and a little piece of wood trim around the cabin door. It had current Alaska registration stickers, but as I worked away, seven days a week getting the *Denise* ready, no one ever came down to work on the aluminum boat.

Then one day a dark haired fellow, maybe forty, appeared with a little paper bag. He nodded to me in passing, and as I watched furtively, he pulled a single piece of sandpaper out of the bag, sanded that whole piece of trim in maybe ten minutes, dusted the trim off with a piece of cloth, then pulled a small paint brush and a hobby-sized can of paint from the bag, and painted the trim, humming a little tune as he did. When he was done, he threw paint, brush, and sandpaper into the dock dumpster and disappeared up the dock. The next day he showed up with a couple of dock carts of supplies and a youngster, maybe twelve, and a nice looking woman, obviously his wife. They all chatted away happily as they stowed their supplies. And when they were done, they started up, threw off the lines, and headed out toward the locks, just like that.

"Wow," I said to myself, "I really like that guy's style."

And finally on the fairest sort of day, with the docks of Fishermen's Terminal a beehive of activity as literally hundreds of boats and crews hustled to get ready for the opening of the Alaska salmon season in a few weeks, we finished installing the rebuilt engine and took *the Denise* out into the channel for a quick test run. I had already bought my groceries and hoped to leave the next morning. I would be traveling alone, but I had made some friends among the gillnet fleet and would have other boats to travel with. Words could hardly do justice to the excitement that was building up inside me: it was finally happening, I was finally heading up to Alaska in my own (leased) boat.

Fifteen minutes into our test run, the engine threw a connecting rod through the side of the block, totally ruining it. At approximately the same

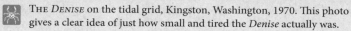 THE *DENISE* on the tidal grid, Kingston, Washington, 1970. This photo gives a clear idea of just how small and tired the *Denise* actually was.

JOE AND DOGFISH aboard the *Denise*, 1970. After the engine of the *Denise* blew up, I tried to put a season together near the Canadian border. I found that if you weren't careful where you set your net, you'd end up with more dogfish than salmon.

time, the boat caught fire when the exhaust pipe went through the cabin roof. After I'd put out the fire and we were waiting glumly for a tow back to the dock, the mechanic turned to me and said, "I don't understand it. The last engine I rebuilt did that too." My dream of going to Alaska in my own boat evaporated.

With the last of my money I slammed a tiny used engine into the *Denise*, and headed up to salvage my season by fishing salmon in Washington State waters. I ended up in Blaine, on the border with British Columbia, where a congenial bunch of fellows with older boats fished on Canadian salmon that had strayed over the border. Many of the guys had good winter jobs as long-shoremen on the Seattle docks and viewed their summers gillnetting out of Blaine as a chance to catch a few fish and drink a lot of beer with their buddies. They were welcoming and free with their advice and experience. And whenever two or three of us would get together after fishing to share few beers, the talk would always be of Alaska.

I reluctantly realized that had I headed to Alaska in the *Denise*, she would have probably sunk and drowned me. Fishing school taught me nets, hydraulics, diesel, electronics, and half a dozen different ways to find your position, but not the common sense to just walk away from an unsafe boat.

WHEN THE SEASON WOUND DOWN, I had learned more about gillnetting, but was still deeply in debt and a long ways from sailing to Alaska in my own boat. When I got back down to Seattle, I stopped in at the Marco office to say hello to the owner, whom I had met in Iquique, and to my surprise, he offered me a job working on some of their fishing gear development projects, and I jumped at it. I remember getting introduced around the Marco staff, as "Joe's been in the production side." It took me a moment to get it. Oh, yeah, the production side. That means I catch 'em.

Our shop was on a barge tied up in the Marco shipyard, where they were busy building what would turn out to be another in a long line of very successful king crabbers. And out the back windows of the barge passed all manner of fishing boats coming back from or headed up to Alaska.

My work had to do with developing a more automated way to catch halibut than the traditional and very labor-intensive method then used. But the real action around the waterfront that winter was king crab—boats and crews gearing up for the big action in the Bering Sea.

And George Fulton was in town, getting his *Flood Tide* ready for the king crab fishery. I knew him from Iquique days. Alaska and the "production side" of fishing were calling me. When he offered me a job, I jumped at it. Who wouldn't have? George was known to be a highliner, and I saw the job as a way to make enough money to get my own salmon boat and return to the waters of Southeast Alaska, where Mickey Hansen had showed me so much.

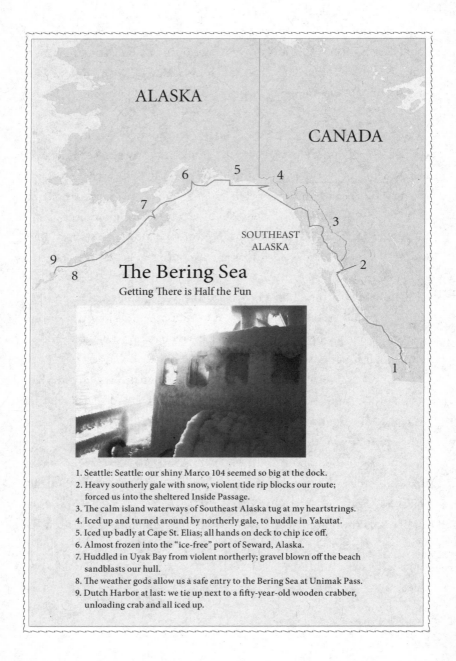

ALASKA

CANADA

SOUTHEAST
ALASKA

The Bering Sea

Getting There is Half the Fun

1. Seattle: Seattle: our shiny Marco 104 seemed so big at the dock.
2. Heavy southerly gale with snow, violent tide rip blocks our route; forced us into the sheltered Inside Passage.
3. The calm island waterways of Southeast Alaska tug at my heartstrings.
4. Iced up and turned around by northerly gale, to huddle in Yakutat.
5. Iced up badly at Cape St. Elias; all hands on deck to chip ice off.
6. Almost frozen into the "ice-free" port of Seward, Alaska.
7. Huddled in Uyak Bay from violent northerly; gravel blown off the beach sandblasts our hull.
8. The weather gods allow us a safe entry to the Bering Sea at Unimak Pass.
9. Dutch Harbor at last: we tie up next to a fifty-year-old wooden crabber, unloading crab and all iced up.

2. Trouble on the Inside Passage

H EY, KID, IT'S SEYMOUR. You gotta see this."

Russell's voice intruded on my dreams, and the words instantly registered in my brain: *Seymour Narrows*! The place where the tidal current can run up to almost twenty miles an hour—legendary among Northwest mariners. I pulled on my clothes and went up the steps into the wheelhouse. When I'd taken my eight to midnight wheel watch for the first time in my new job as deckhand on the *Flood Tide*, bound for the Bering Sea, we'd been steaming up Georgia Strait, a wide inland channel north of Vancouver, British Columbia. But now, in the thin light of the February dawn, the shores had drawn closer, the dark forest was clad in wisps of fog and low clouds and was pressing in from both sides. And most alarming, whirlpools surrounded us in the channel—from the tide, I assumed—and our heavy boat lurched from side to side. I'd seen Seymour once before in daylight, the summer I'd worked on the fish-packer *Sidney*. It was an awesome sight you never got used to.

Off our port side, in a clearing in the dark, thick forest, a sawmill emitted steam or smoke from every opening and stack. Around the mill were piles of freshly cut lumber, and at the docks in front sat barges laden deep with yellow sawdust. To the starboard side was a small cove with fishing boats moored peacefully, and the warm lights of cabins could be seen through the trees onshore.

ONE OF THE FIRST Marco crabbers, the *Rosie G*, shortly after launching in 1968. This boat started a dynasty. She was one of the first Marco 94 footers. She has a railroad boom, common before the use of the hydraulic "knuckle crane" that replaced it. This design was stretched to create the 104-foot *Flood Tide*, launched in 1971, then stretched, widened, and modified to create the very popular 108 footers like the *Northwestern* and her many sister ships. The *Rosie G* sank in 1997, but all aboard were rescued from the life raft.

The *Flood Tide* swayed slightly in the current as we swung to port and entered a steep-sided canyon with dark walls that pressed in around us. For a moment, it looked like we were headed for a dead end, but just then, on the right, a misty and forbidding passage through the mountains opened up unexpectedly, giving me a glimpse of a different landscape. Behind had been settlements on the shore; ahead were wild, impenetrable forests growing right down to the water's edge, the hand of man nowhere to be seen. I stepped out onto the deck behind the pilothouse to see more clearly and the cold, misty air wrapped around me with the smell of the sea and the forest. At the same time, the first snow we'd seen began to swirl softly around our little ship.

An invisible hand seemed to take hold of the *Flood Tide* and swirl us sideways. I grabbed the rail to hold on and looked down as we maneuvered between whirlpools the size of baseball diamonds, their vortexes choked with kelp and driftwood, spinning faster and faster. Suddenly, I felt uneasy out on deck alone and stepped back into the comforting warmth of the pilot-house. George, our skipper, was steering by hand. He had switched off the automatic pilot and was moving the short jog stick back and forth, trying to keep us out of the whirlpools that were swirling in the channel ahead. Like many large modern fishing boats, the automatic pilot on the *Flood Tide* had a jog stick, a short lever that was used for steering the boat manually. We also had a steering wheel, but that was only for use if the autopilot/jog stick system failed.

"That's the kind of crap you don't want to hit, kid." He pointed with his chin to what looked like the top of a telephone pole sticking up out of one of the whirlpools just to port. As I looked, it disappeared out of sight. It didn't come up again.

"You get these big logs, we call 'em deadheads, and they get water-logged, and settle in the water so just one end is sticking up, three or four feet in diameter. They must weigh tons, sometimes they're so waterlogged they bob up only every few minutes. If we hit one of those, it would only dent our hull, but if it came up under our propeller, it'd mean a trip to the shipyard. And where we're going, there aren't any shipyards."

I looked back to where the log had been. How could you see something like that to avoid it? An upwelling of current suddenly erupted from the water ahead of us, seeming to boil and surge, full of driftwood logs that obviously had been sucked under just a few minutes before. George moved the jog stick all the way to starboard this time to miss them.

"It used to be worse." It was Russell this time, George's brother, a hard-bitten but kind-hearted fisherman, who nudged me to the window as George steered us over to the east side of the channel. We were truly in a canyon, the walls rising steeply from the churning waters and so narrow that just ahead power lines crossed the channel high in the air. "Look right there," said Russell, pointing ahead and to our left. "See that big swirl, that's Old Rip, Ripple Rock, or what's left of it." I peered into the gloom and saw what he was pointing at, a place where the biggest whirlpool yet was rotating, taking up at least half the width of the channel. The surface of the water clearly dipped down at least six feet at the center of the whirl. "There used to be a rock right there, just below the surface. It would sink one or two big boats each year, sometimes even a big steamer that got swung into it by the current. And that wasn't the worst of it—Old Rip would make whirlpools large enough to suck down fifty or sixty footers if they weren't careful."

The somber sight of that huge whirlpool and Russell's words chilled me. And I knew, from previous conversations, that we had timed our departure from Seattle to arrive at Seymour around the time of slack water. I knew the story of Old Rip: it was part of the lore of the Northwest waterfront, one of the first things greenhorns heard about from other young men, proud of their Alaska seasons, proud of having been "through Seymour."

Each year Old Rip claimed at least one large vessel and numerous smaller ones, whose operators misread their tide books, underestimated the power of the currents, or were careless, stupid, or both.

As vessels grew larger and traffic increased heading to Alaska and farther up the B.C. coast, it became an intolerable situation, and attempts were made to drill and blast the Old Rip rock from barges anchored with four concrete moorings, each weighing 250 tons. It didn't work. Despite the moorings, the barges moved so much in the current that accurate drilling was impossible. A work crew drowned when their boat was caught in a whirlpool, and the effort was abandoned in favor of an ambitious scheme to tunnel from the east shore of the narrows.

Crews sank a shaft some 900 feet vertically, then tunneled under the bottom of the narrows, and carefully upward again, exploring with small-diameter, diamond-tipped drills until they broke through to the water, plugging the holes, measuring, creating a three-dimensional map so there was always at least thirty feet of rock between the tunnels and the angry rushing water of the narrows.

They honeycombed the insides of Old Rip with tunnels and side drifts like coal miners. Tugboats pushed bargeloads of Dupont Nitromex 2-H dynamite packed into fifty-pound canisters to the loading dock, where cranes lowered the heavy pallets into the shaft to be packed into the tunnels. Finally, on the morning of April 17, 1958, patrol boats pushed fishing boats and spectators a mile back. No one knew how far the rock would be flung by such an immense quantity of explosives.

And in a dramatic moment, watched by thousands on television all across Canada, Ripple Rock filled the air above Seymour Narrows with its remains and disappeared. What was left, forty feet under, was renamed Ripple Shoal.

We passed under the big swooping power lines just then, strung from the top of the cliffs above the narrows, and I looked back. You could still see a few houses in the trees a half-mile back from where Old Rip had guarded the channel. Ahead, in the increasing swirl of the snow, I could see that the land was very different—dark and wild, even unfriendly. I remembered what Mickey had told me about Seymour, Yuculta Rapids, and the other places where the tide raged through the narrow passages between islands in the Inside Passage. He said that the waterways to the south were all busy with homes on all the shores, with a friendly twinkle of lights at night. But that anyone traveling to the north coast of British Columbia or on to Alaska, big boat or small, had to proceed cautiously, waiting for slack water, before going on to the wilder land beyond.

"It was beyond them rapids, beyond Seymour and the Yucultas that I always felt the true North began," Old Mick, back on the *Sidney*, had told me. "Where there were hardly any towns, where a fellow was really on his own. But it was like this: it was as if nature had set these obstacles, right in that place where the busy south coast ends and the true North begins. It was like a warning to the traveler to be careful of the very different land and water that lay beyond."

OUR COOK ABOARD the *Flood Tide* was Missouri Bob Mason, a southerner with a slow drawl and seemingly endless stories about his years working on shrimpers in the Gulf of Mexico, before he came to Seattle seeking the Holy

Grail of a job on a crab boat. Our engineer was Johnny Nott, a feisty redhead, who'd been an amateur boxer and had fished with George on other boats for years. George's brother, Russell, was the mate, and I, the youngest, was a relative greenhorn. That was it: a skipper and a four-man crew.

No wives with children in arms came down to the dock to wish us well the night before we left Seattle, to drink to our luck in the long season ahead. Except for George and Russell, we were single guys with no kids yet. And this: there seemed to be an air of tension about our departure. In June, when the salmon fleet leaves, the days are warm and long, the trip up through the picturesque waterways of the Inside Passage something to be savored. But I sensed from George and the Marco shipyard staff, which had built the *Flood Tide*, that a winter passage up the coast, even in a vessel as well built, fitted out, and crewed as the *Flood Tide*, was not to be taken lightly. And we were traveling alone; if we got in a jam, there would be no one to help us.

The second to last day of February had come nasty, a cold rain turning to sleet. By mid-morning the last things had come aboard, and I went ashore to call my parents on the East Coast and tell them that we were off. They wished me luck, but I sensed anxiety in their voices. Their friends' children had regular jobs and phones at home on bedside tables so they could be reached at night. This business of going to Alaska, to the Bering Sea, in winter, was out of their realm of experience, and they were uncomfortable with it.

A day out of Seattle, I was already focused on the job at hand and on the exciting season ahead. Russell and I worked on the deck, in the narrow rectangle of space between the back of the pilothouse and the first row of huge 700-pound crab pots that filled our back deck. Our job was to drill dozens of holes in each of the hundreds of screw-top plastic quart jars that were to be filled with chopped herring to attract crabs. Each had to be rigged with a short piece of heavy nylon twine tied to a stainless steel spring clasp that would be clipped inside our crab pots.

We didn't say much. At cruising speed the sharp bark of the engine exhaust over our heads was loud enough to discourage all but the most important exchanges of information. The snow squalls came and went.

When they came, we traveled in a white cocoon that swirled around the boat, chilling us, even through our long underwear, wool shirts and sweaters, sweatshirts, insulated heavy coveralls, boots, and gloves. When the snow stopped, we peered out beyond the spray flung by the bow to the steep forest shore of Johnstone Strait, unbroken by the hand of man—no roads, phone poles, docks, or settlements.

The next day brought even more snow. By mid-morning, the wind had heaved up such a steep and confused sea that we could no longer work on deck, so we retreated inside to the refuge of the northern seaman—a comfortable bunk and a good book. At noon, I took over for my four-hour steering watch—essentially monitoring our position while the automatic pilot steered our heavily laden craft north before a southerly gale. The seas were large, and getting larger, but they were behind us so we had an easy ride. George was asleep in his stateroom. I was sure it was the first time he had been able to get in a good sleep since the frenzy of last-minute preparations for our season had begun a month or so earlier.

We were traveling up thirty-mile-wide Hecate Strait in northern British Columbia, about sixty miles south of the Alaska border. If the *Flood Tide* had been a smaller boat, like one of the several thousand thirty to sixty footers that traveled up the coast each spring for the Alaska salmon season, we would have taken a route through the narrower, winding channels forty miles east. Those water-filled canyons penetrate the steep coastal mountains of British Columbia and make for sheltered traveling. It was those sheltering channels that comprise the Inside Passage—the 1,000-mile route from Seattle to the historic Klondike gold rush port of Skagway, Alaska—that allowed even the smallest craft, by carefully watching the tides and the weather in the wider sections, to travel safely up the coast.

Threading through narrow channels and among numerous reefs, however, required the highest level of diligence from a vessel's crew. Rarely was a course leg more than a few miles long, so the position of the vessel had to be monitored constantly because a turn not made at just the right time might put the vessel in peril. Our parallel route up Hecate Strait allowed our skipper to relax without worrying about whether the person on watch was making the myriad precise course changes required in the narrower channels. The strait, however, exposed vessels to the wind from any direction, and was a notoriously bad place. The southern end was called Queen Charlotte Sound, a place dreaded by small craft headed up and down the coast, even in the good weather months.

At around 3 p.m., alone in the wheelhouse while the rest of the crew slept, I noticed an odd, blotchy-looking target on our radar where no land was supposed to be. Outside the thick windows that stretched all the way across the wide front of the pilothouse, I saw nothing but swirling white. I fiddled with the radar controls, and studied the chart carefully again, but there was only open water surrounding us. Yet the radar showed something—something that was growing closer as we swept northward, pushed by the growing seas of the building storm behind us. Inside the wheelhouse all was peaceful and quiet except for the muted hum of the engine. But I began to feel very uneasy, and finally pulled the engine throttle controls to the half-speed position, a move that I knew George would quickly react to.

He was out of his cabin in an instant, quickly scanning the radar display and the chart, pulling the throttle back to idle and speaking into the intercom. "Johnny, flood both crab tanks, quick as you can." We had been traveling with our two big holds, or crab tanks, empty, to give us a bit more speed. Filling them would make us travel a bit slower, but most important, it would lower our center of gravity, making the vessel more stable in heavy seas—an important factor, considering the heavy load of crab pots we were carrying on deck. Soon we heard the big diesel generator in the engine room change tone as the massive pumps came to life.

While the crab tanks filled, we idled slowly ahead. Sensing something was happening, the rest of the crew filed up into the pilothouse, peering forward into the snowy dusk. Finally Johnny came up and gave us the word— the tanks were full and overflowing, the condition for maximum stability. George throttled up to two-thirds, and we moved toward whatever was out there.

For a long while we saw nothing but the big gray-bearded seas marching past us in the thickly falling snow. Then there was what seemed like a lightening in the snow and gloom ahead, and we all peered intently, pressing our faces against the thick glass, trying to get a glimpse of what the radar was seeing, now less than a half-mile ahead of us. Then, briefly, a frightening sight, glimpsed quickly through the gloom and as quickly gone—the backs of great seas, breaking, the spume from their crests thrown back like the manes of wild horses, covering a wide area ahead.

"Shit, hang on, guys." George swiveled to look out the back window at the seas behind us, then throttled up, and in a break between seas, pushed the jog stick all the way to starboard. As we swung into our turn, our boat, that had seemed so big tied to the dock in Seattle, dropped suddenly and rolled alarmingly to port for what seemed a very long moment as a huge sea plowed into our side. Time seemed to stand still. Dishes crashed in the galley below, an alarm bell rang shrilly, and only then did we finish our turn, slowly come back upright. The alarm stopped ringing.

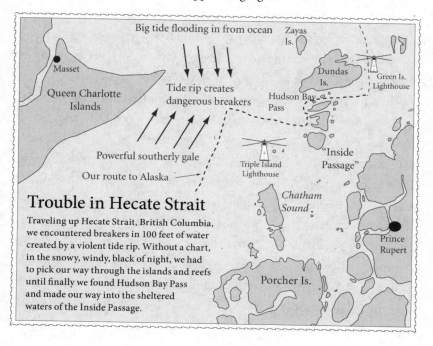

Big tide flooding in from ocean

Zayas Is.

Masset

Queen Charlotte Islands

Tide rip creates dangerous breakers

Dundas Is.

Green Is. Lighthouse

Hudson Bay Pass

Powerful southerly gale

Triple Island Lighthouse

"Inside Passage"

Our route to Alaska

Chatham Sound

Trouble in Hecate Strait

Traveling up Hecate Strait, British Columbia, we encountered breakers in 100 feet of water created by a violent tide rip. Without a chart, in the snowy, windy, black of night, we had to pick our way through the islands and reefs until finally we found Hudson Bay Pass and made our way into the sheltered waters of the Inside Passage.

Prince Rupert

Porcher Is.

George stood at the chart, shaking his head, and pointed to the north end of the strait, where it narrowed slightly. "Look at this, breaking here, in a hundred feet of water . . . breaking, for Christ sake. I heard about it once before but never really believed it."

The seas created by the gale blowing from the south were meeting the tidal current flooding in from the north, producing breaking seas all the way across the relatively shallow shelf that was 100 feet deep at the north end of the strait. Given the conditions, these were seas we'd be foolish to risk, even in our rugged steel 104 footer.

Somewhere there was a narrow gully of much deeper water, where we thought the seas wouldn't be breaking. But we jogged back and forth in that windy wasteland of angry churning water and hissing snow, and couldn't find it. The wind came on stronger still, and it began to get dark. The seas grew even bigger as the tidal current increased. So we reluctantly headed east, looking for a way through a maze of islands and breaking reefs to the sheltered waters of the Inside Passage.

But having planned to travel up wide Hecate Strait, George didn't have a detailed chart of the islands that surrounded it, and we had to rely on Russell's hazy memory of a passage through, several decades earlier, in good clear weather. The area we had to transit was full of islands, winding channels, and hidden rocks—no place to be on that wild night without a chart.

I was the youngest and least experienced member of the crew, and just stood back, taking it all in. Then I felt something unexpected, unspoken, but something that settled over us all—fear—even in the pilothouse of the finest and most rugged boat that the best shipyard in the Northwest could produce. The daylight fled away to the west and the blowing, snowy blackness swallowed us up. The flying snow and spray were so thick that our radar could barely penetrate them. Three times Russell said, "That way . . . ," and we proceeded cautiously into a narrow channel bounded by rock and snow-blasted trees. We were led into three dead ends: our crab lights high on the mast turned the night into snow-thick day and revealed only the sea beating violently against three rocky cul-de-sacs, one after the other. One was so narrow there wasn't even room to turn around, so we had to back out cautiously.

Finally the fourth channel opened into another passage, and yet another after that. The sea died down and the water stayed deep, and sometime after midnight we found our way into the sheltered waters of the Inside Passage. It was still snowing hard and it was inky dark, but we were back on our charts. But my confidence in our powerful boat and experienced skipper and mate had been shaken, something I hadn't expected on just the third day of our trip, and I slept uneasily.

In the early dusk of the next day, as we went through Wrangell Narrows, a winding channel between two large islands, we passed a Norman Rockwell scene that tugged strongly at my heartstrings—a single cabin in a little clearing on the shore with two small outboard boats drawn up on the bank before it. Wood smoke rose from the chimney. Snow-covered trees stood all around. And from each window, a cheery warm light shone out into the wild landscape. Even though I was excited and proud to be on the *Flood Tide* and headed north to an already legendary fishery, I yearned for the kind of fishing and living that could be had among those islands of Southeast Alaska where I had spent that wonderful season on the *Sidney*.

As a crew, we had no illusions about what we would face in the months ahead. None of us had fished the Bering Sea, the vast storm-breeding body of water between Alaska and Russia, yet we'd heard enough tales to know that it didn't take kindly to the folks and boats that came to wrest a living from her waters.

In the dark, a few hours later, we met the first ice—just small bergs, perhaps the size of a dump truck—drifting west with the current and the wind from LeConte Glacier, the most southerly place on the coast that the great glaciers meet the salt water and break off icebergs. The snowstorm had blown off to the west, and a half moon infused the bergs with an eerie light. We stood on deck, taking in the sobering sight—the black water, the glowing icebergs, and beyond, the snowy ice and rock spires of the Coast Range. We

were then some 800 miles north of Seattle. Between us and Dutch Harbor
where we would begin our crab season lay almost 1,200 miles more of an
increasingly brutal and unforgiving seascape.

"Hey guys, listen to this." The next morning we were in the galley, taking
a warm-up and coffee break from the deck work, when George came over the
intercom, switching the speaker over to the single-sideband radio (a shortwave radio with long-range capabilities, favored by mariners). " . . . Position
. . . west of . . . Spencer . . . iced up heavy, antennas broken . . ." The transmission
faded in and out and then faded out entirely.

The Coast Guard, with its higher antenna, must have received the signal more clearly: "Roger, we understand you are fifty miles northwest of Cape
Spencer, have suffered broken windows and have lost your main antennas from
icing and sea conditions, but require no assistance at this time. Please call
every hour with your status and we will be standing by on this frequency."

The speakers went silent, and a moment later our somber-faced skipper
came down the stairs from the pilothouse to fill us in.

"It's a Martinolich boat, a year old, smaller than us, an eighty-six footer,
but husky, built for anything the Bering Sea and North Pacific can dish out.
She'd been fishing south of Kodiak when it started to blow cold from the
northwest, blowing down off the glaciers and icy mountains and valleys of
the Alaska Range. She was headed back into town, and blew out two pilothouse windows bucking into the seas, and making ice so heavy their only
hope of survival was to turn around and run with the wind behind them
away from the land. By the time the storm blew itself out, they'd been blown
all the way across the Gulf."

Ice. No one said much as we nursed our coffees. "Making ice" was the
single greatest danger that boats working the Alaska coast faced in winter.
When the air temperature dropped into the twenties and below, sea spray
thrown up by the waves froze instantly upon contacting the cold steel rigging and hull of any boat. For crab boats, traveling with their loads of heavy
pots stacked many layers high, it was a double whammy: the pots offered a
huge amount of surface area on which ice could form, and with such loads,

boats had a reduced capacity to survive heavy icing since their center of gravity was raised by the weight of the pots.

By 1971, enough boats had had close calls with icing that fishermen and mariners were becoming more aware of the problem. But for the unsuspecting, especially at night, the effect was sinister. A boat with a high level of stability, meaning a low center of gravity, would have a quick, almost uncomfortably quick, motion in a seaway. But when such a vessel began to accumulate ice on her decks and rigging, her center of gravity would rise. This would have the effect of making the vessel's motion easier— the rolling and pitching occurred more slowly. To the uninformed, the change in the vessel's motion might bring a sense of security. In reality, the vessel's stability was diminished and was having a harder and harder time bringing the vessel back upright after each roll because of the increased weight of the ice. If nothing was done to break the cycle and the ice kept accumulating, the rolls would become slower and slower and more and more "comfortable," and eventually the vessel would, without warning, roll completely over.

In the afternoon, we worked on deck preparing for the next phase of our journey—the Gulf of Alaska. Following our incident with the breakers two evenings before in Hecate Strait, we'd been traveling up the sheltered waterways of Southeast Alaska, where our route passed among hundreds of islands and bays. The route offered many places to anchor up and wait, safe and secure, until weather improved. But once we passed Cape Spencer in the evening, our route for the next 250 miles would be along Southcentral Alaska's unforgiving coast, where most harbors were shallow river mouths, guarded by breaking seas, accessible only to small craft in good weather. If a storm found us along this route, we would have many miles of hard traveling to get to a safe harbor. If the weather had been more settled, we might have taken the straight route from Cape Spencer to Kodiak across the Gulf, saving several hundred miles, but in winter, the prudent fishing vessel traveled a few miles off the coast. So we retightened the chain binders that held our pots securely to the steel rails on the bulwarks, because we knew that once we got out into the rough waters of the Gulf, making those adjustments would be difficult or impossible.

We were passing then through Icy Strait, with Glacier Bay and the austere 12,000- and 15,000-foot peaks of the Fairweather Range (definitely not named for the weather) to our north. Now and then we would pass an errant iceberg, and that, along with the more and more unforgiving landscape, provided a reminder of what lay ahead.

The wan afternoon sun had worked its way to the southwest and we all were up in the pilothouse with our coffees when a strange sight appeared on the water in the distance to the west. At first, as we scanned it with the binoculars, we thought we were seeing some odd ice creation, spawned from the bowels of the great tidewater glaciers to our north, perhaps an iceberg with odd shining protrusions. Then, as we got closer, we realized what it was, shining in the rays of the setting sun: the iced-up king crabber we had heard talking on the radio to the Coast Guard.

That she had survived her battle with the ice was incredible. She was totally sheathed in it, from the stubs of her broken radio antennas to the dark water streaming along her iced hull. As she got closer, we could see her crew, breaking the ice off the anchor winch and railings around the bow with baseball bats and shoveling it over the side. Two others were on the back deck, breaking ice off the few remaining crab pots. A single pilothouse window had been cleared of ice, and two plywood patches on the others were battle scars of a storm at sea. As we passed about forty yards apart, the back door of the pilothouse opened and a figure emerged, waving. Humbled by the sight, we waved back. Probably the boat was headed to Juneau, fifty miles to the east, the nearest town with good marine supplies, to lick her wounds before heading out again.

The mood in the pilothouse after supper was subdued. Astern was the sweeping beam of the light at Cape Spencer, the entrance to the sheltered waters of the Inside Passage. Ahead lay the immense Gulf of Alaska. The night was hazy, dark, and cloudless. The bow rose and fell with the long Pacific swells, and there was neither star nor horizon to guide us.

Just before midnight, I rose, made coffee, and went up into the pilot-house to relieve Russell and take my midnight to 4 a.m. "graveyard watch." The pilothouse was illuminated only by the dim numbers from the loran, radar, and instrument displays. A half-moon had come up, shining starkly on the wall of ice and snow that rose from the shore ten miles east of us.

Russell's stubby forefinger punched down on the chart and he said: "Lituya Bay. You don't want to go in there unless you really have to. All that water in them fjords and this bay have to pour in and out through that narrow entrance. You can go in if the tide's flooding or slack if it's not blowing heavy, but on the ebb that current stacks up the seas and it's a boat-killer. That's the hell about this part of the coast." His finger traced the entrances to some other bays, Dry Bay and Dangerous River. "You get in a jam with some engine problem or bad weather and you need a harbor, and there's no place to go. I've seen breakers out here, two full miles from shore. You want to give this coast a good berth."

Twenty miles north of Yakutat, one of the few good harbors along that coast, a wind came up. After five minutes it was blowing seventy. The temperature was fifteen degrees. The first spray over the bow froze instantly on the wheelhouse windows. George Fulton turned the *Flood Tide* around with hardly a discussion.

As we entered Yakutat Bay, all of us in the wheelhouse witnessed a sobering sight. The 140-foot trawler *Deep Sea*, pioneer of the king crab fishery, lay at anchor with a big covered barge in tow. She had iced up bad, as had her barge, all the corners and sharp angles softened by the smooth, sinister contours of thick ice. But the sobering part was the barge. The whole front of the structure built on it, a long metal warehouse of a building, was crumpled in, the top and sides mangled for a third of the way back and in places the aluminum sheeting had been ripped off like paper. George got the story over the radio: The barge was a floating shrimp cannery, headed for Kodiak, 400 miles to the west. They had gotten within ten miles of the shelter of Cape St. Elias, 130 miles north of Yakutat, when the wind came up. Two hours later, the seas had punched in the front of the barge, forcing the *Deep Sea*

THE *FLOOD TIDE* at a cannery dock, Yakutat, March 1971. Yakutat in those days was a remote Native village with a cannery. When we tied up to the cannery dock on a stormy March evening, there were few signs of life and we felt as if we had come to the edge of the known world.

skipper to turn around and run before the storm, icing as they went, all the way back to Yakutat.

We tied our frozen lines to a silent cannery wharf, and I walked up to the village with Johnny and Missouri Bob in the blowing, drifting snow that was knee-deep. In all of Yakutat, we saw only two lighted windows, and nowhere a footprint or car track. We trudged back to the boat. With the bark of her diesel generator filling the night, our boat seemed like a visitor from another planet.

A blizzard swept in from the Canadian Yukon after midnight. At the head of the harbor, in the lee of the great mountains, we lay sheltered from its force, but morning showed a gray and chilling world. Outside the windows of the pilothouse, a steady plume of snow settled on us, drifting down from the wharf above. By noon, the deck was almost waist deep with snow. It was as if we'd come to the edge of the world as we knew it. And we still had some 1,000 miles more to go.

That night, sometimes even over the reassuring hum of our diesel generator, we could hear the wind, screeching through the trees and cannery buildings above us. At 4 a.m., when we got up to sniff the air, to see if it was "a chance," as mariners sometimes call a window of good weather, the storm had blown out to sea. So we drew in our stiff and frozen lines and headed out of the still bay and into the Gulf of Alaska.

The dawn, when it came, was truly awesome—first a faint yellow line, then a dozen peaks tinged with pink. The sun when it rose was red and angry, lighting up thousands of square miles of bleak ice and rock with its strange long-shadowed light before it disappeared into thin, hazy, cloud cover.

All day we steamed northwest, a few miles off the beach. The wind was offshore and light, our ride easy, but there was something about the day and place that made us all sober. The land to the north and east was a strip of beach, rising to ice fields and mountains as far as the eye could see, range after range of cold, white peaks. The coast was broken here and there by little bays, ice-choked and shallow, offering no shelter.

The night came early and inky black and without a breath of wind. It seemed as if we were traveling through a featureless void. We ate early, then gathered in the darkened pilothouse, anxious to make Cape Hinchinbrook, the end of the most exposed passage. The tension in the air was thick, and finally I went below to an uneasy sleep.

ICE ON THE *Flood Tide*, 1971. Icing is a terrible problem in wintertime in Alaskan waters because it reduces stability of the vessel. We encountered a violent cold wind off remote Cape St. Elias, and iced up so badly that had we not found shelter quickly, we might have capsized.

3. The Struggle at Cape St. Elias

SOMETIME AFTER MIDNIGHT I woke up suddenly. The engine was only rumbling at an idle, but it was something else that had awakened me—the boat's motion. She took a roll, slow and logy, seeming to hesitate at the end. I stumbled up into the pilothouse. Outside the window was a terrible sight—the two-inch-thick pipe rails around the foredeck were swollen into foot-thick bloated ice sausages, and in a few places they already had grown together into a solid ice wall. The anchor winch was an unrecognizable white mound. I took a quick look out the back windows, and just as quickly looked away. What had been a neat stack of big crab pots was now a lumpy hill of white ice, broken here and there by the black steel edges of the pots.

It was easy to see how vessels went down. In just a couple of hours, we'd accumulated enough ice to make the boat dangerously top-heavy, and we were only carrying fifty pots in a single layer on deck. Some larger vessels traveled north with their pots stacked three or four layers high.

Within moments, the others had joined us. Without a word, Russell and I suited up with rain gear over insulated coveralls. We grabbed a baseball bat and a hammer and edged cautiously out onto the foredeck, while Johnny and Bob did the same on the back deck. Footing was treacherous; if we slipped, there was a good chance we'd slide under the bottom rail to icy death, so we clipped short safety lines from our waists to the rails and started to cautiously knock off the ice. The ice popped off easily, but it was awkward work—the boat was rolling and pitching with that ominous slow motion, the deck was a sheet of ice, and the bitter wind turned the spray to slush on our oilskins. Once a "queer one," a wave larger than the others, loomed suddenly out of the night and solid, black water rose right up over the bow. It tugged at our knees and then was gone.

But it was an ominous feeling—the bow sinking, the water swirling around us, clutching at our legs, our hands grabbing the icy rail. We could see George's strained, white face in the window, and then the bow rose sluggishly and the water cleared from the deck.

When we'd knocked off the tons of ice from the bow and shoveled it overboard, we worked aft, knocking the ice off the rails as we went. After an hour's work, clearing the bow and boat deck area, our little ship seemed to ride a little higher, roll a little quicker, feel a little safer.

The back deck was another story. Even the nylon mesh of the pots had swollen with the ice and the stacked pots had grown into a seamless white frozen mound. Much of what we chipped fell on deck and had to be shoveled over the rails. And all the while the wind picked the water off the sea and froze it to every surface we had just uncovered. It was blowing perhaps twenty-five knots. We all knew that it would only take another twenty knots of wind to make ice faster than we could chip it off, and then it would only be a matter of time before we'd have to turn around and try to run out to sea with the wind behind us before we became too top heavy and simply rolled over. We had to find shelter and soon, and get as many pots below deck, into our holds, to reduce the area and height where ice could accumulate. At least here, I thought, we were near the land. If worse came to worst, I supposed, we could run the *Flood Tide* into the shore and try to find a sandy spot to beach her. Even that lonely shore would be a better place to walk home from than the Gulf of Alaska.

"It's the Copper River wind, boy," Russell told me in the galley when we had finished and were warming up. "All that ocean air just gets frozen up there, and suddenly decides to roll back to the sea, down the river valley. I

PREPARING TO LOWER pots into our hold, off Katala. We had iced so heavily that we needed to lower our center of gravity quickly. We found some sheltered water in the lee of an island off the abandoned boom town of Katala, opened our holds, and lowered as many crab pots as would fit into them.

told that guy down in Seattle to put the pots into the hold when we loaded them. 'Oh, no,' he said. 'We won't have to do that.' Those guys don't even know what ice is except when they see it in their drinks. They think these new super boats can take anything."

Even at less than a quarter throttle, we iced up again badly before we found a few acres of sheltered water behind a tiny dot of an island off the abandoned town of Katalla. We hoisted up the boom, lifted and set aside the heavy hatch covers, and loaded as many of the heavily iced pots into the hold as would fit. We laid the remaining dozen flat on the deck, then lowered the boom and chained it to the stern rail. The icy wind still clawed at us, but there was no sea. When we were finally done I looked around. Except perhaps for the Coast Guard lighthouse keepers at Cape St. Elias, we were probably the only humans within fifty miles. The vista was unspeakably bleak—frozen islands, frozen shore, and frozen mountains, now hidden, now revealed, clouds racing past the moon.

When I awoke, I stepped through the vestibule from the galley onto the back deck and peered out at the daunting world beyond. With our boom lashed down and the crab pots tied securely to the side rails, our center of gravity was as low as we could make it. Yet the wind still howled past us, the powerful gusts shaking the boat at times, even in the shelter of the island. I knew the sea and the ice and the howling gales of the Gulf of Alaska were probing again, looking for any chink in our armor. And we hadn't even reached the Bering Sea, which was considered to be much rougher and meaner than the Gulf. In Seattle, the *Flood Tide* had seemed so big and so powerful. But the farther north we got, the smaller and more vulnerable she seemed. I felt humbled by the grim landscape and the bitter winds that tore at us.

The wind eased at midnight on our sixth day out of Seattle, and George sent Russell and me forward to pick up the anchor. But first we had to break the ice off the anchor winch. We'd been anchored in the sheltered lee of the island, but enough sea spray had reached our bow to make the winch a lumpy mound of white, and it took forty-five minutes with hammers and baseball bats to clear the ice so that we could use the controls.

Westward we traveled, following the arc of that lonely coast. A frigid, arctic high had settled over the Alaska mainland, and when the wind came, it was out of the north and bitterly cold, making ice quickly. So we had learned to be prudent. When the wind blew, we anchored. When it eased, we traveled. If we needed help along that remote coast, it would be a long time in coming.

We finally entered the supposedly ice-free harbor at Seward, one of the few settlements along that coast. The ice was so thick on the water that we had to use the boat like a battering ram to get in close enough to tie up at the dock, and even then we had to walk across the ice to step onto the float, pushed up here and there by the pressure of the frozen harbor. We were met at the head of the dock by a friend of George's in his Cadillac, whose heater struggled without any noticeable success to melt the heavy frost on the windows.

In the Harbor Bar we were the only customers, and George's friend leaned forward and spoke intently of the riches to be had in the waters of the Bering Sea, now only 500 miles to the west. The weather had been bad, he said, but for the few boats still fishing, it was big money. You could load your boat in four or five days and the crab plants were crying for product. This was music to a crab fisherman's ears. Yet our enthusiasm was tempered by the difficulties we had faced so far. We'd expected a smooth voyage up to Dutch—Dutch Harbor, on Unalaska Island, in the Aleutians—but the trip had been a far more rigorous one than we had anticipated. And we still had a long way to go.

Seward, and indeed, the whole state of Alaska, were different places in that March of 1971 than they would be a few decades later. The oil rush of the mid-1970s and the cruise ship rush of the 1980s and '90s were still in the future, and the state was a hardscrabble place where a person made a dollar wherever he could. Along the coast, commercial fishing was pretty much the only game in town.

Though Seward was connected to Anchorage by a road, one of only six to penetrate the rugged ice wall of the Coastal Range in its entire 2,000-mile stretch along the Canada and Alaska coast, the town was small: in 1971, just 2,300 folks, and concentrated on the shores of its natural harbor, hemmed in by steep mountains. To the west, where we were headed, the coast was as rugged as any in the northern hemisphere. In the mountains directly behind the coast, an ice sheet the size of New Hampshire fed the many glaciers that dropped icebergs into the bays. In many places the land dropped sheer and bold into the ocean. This time of year, those parts of the coast would be a shining ice wall. Tucked into a few widely scattered coves that offered a modicum of protection were canneries and other fish-processing facilities. But in winter, the harbors and bays would be frozen over out to a half-mile or more from shore, and the only inhabitants were a watchman and perhaps

his family if he was lucky, getting by as best they could. To call the coast unfriendly was a considerable understatement.

We stumbled out of the Harbor Bar and into the night, warmed by alcohol and numbed to what lay ahead of us. Yet at the float, that future was all too clear. We had hoped for a quiet night tied to the dock before heading out in the morning, with at least the thin high latitude daylight of March as we started the next phase of our journey. It was not to be. In the few hours we'd been in Seward, the seawater had frozen, well out past our boat to the edge of the breakwater perhaps fifty yards away. Frozen hard, with little snow devils

As we worked in the lee of a tiny island off the ruins of an abandoned town, putting pots into the hold to make us more stable, we could hear the wind howling past the boat, a reminder of what awaited us.

whirling around on it, visible in the harsh glare of the dock security lights. Already it looked solid as an ice rink. If we waited until morning, we surely would be trapped. But getting out would be an iffy proposition. Instantly sobered by our situation, we clambered aboard, took in the frozen dock lines, and went up into the pilothouse to see whether George and our 1,200-horsepower GM diesel could break us free from the ice's grasp.

The skipper moved the jog stick that controlled the rudder fully to the right, and throttled up to a quarter, normally more than enough power to kick our stern away from the dock. The engine throbbed and the boat shuddered slightly, but the stern held fast in the ice. Half throttle gave the same result. Only when George pushed the throttle to three-quarters speed did we start to shudder forward, finally giving us enough room to swing slowly around and crunch our way toward open water. The upended pieces of ice beside us were about two inches thick—and that in just a few hours. We'd heard the weather in the bar: wind and bitter cold for as far as the forecaster could see. If we'd stayed another few hours we'd have been trapped, perhaps for weeks.

ANXIOUSLY WE CREPT west, closely paralleling the coast. Dawn revealed the austere and forbidding ice and rock mountain wall of the Kenai Peninsula to our north. There were no other boats, no smoke of towns on shore, no sign of humans. Our conversations in the pilothouse were hushed. We wanted to put this part of the coast behind us as soon as possible.

The bitter wind rushing down off the heights turned the water to froth a half-mile to the south of us, so we tried to stay in the lee of the land as much as possible. But each time we passed the mouth of a fjord or open bay where the wind had a longer fetch, it lifted spray and quickly froze on our hull and rigging. With the temperature at 10°F and the wind in the bays a good twenty-five miles per hour, working on deck wasn't possible. So for the most part, we stayed up in the cozy pilothouse and watched the moving landscape out the windows.

"It's here, boys, where you have to watch out." George's finger traced our route on the chart for the next 450 miles: across the mouth of Cook Inlet, where the north wind has 150 miles of open water to build up a big sea, and down Shelikof Strait, between Kodiak Island and the Alaska Peninsula, reputed to be the coldest and windiest of Alaska passages. His forefinger tapped the area where 20,320-foot Denali, 17,400-foot Mount Foraker, and her icy sisters provided a vast breeding ground for the dangerous north wind that funneled down the inlet. "When a norther' comes in winter, all you can do is run before it and hope you find shelter before you make too much ice," George told us.

Even in summer the waters of Cook Inlet are forbidding and unforgiving. Its funnel shape creates tides in the Anchorage area that rival those in the Bay of Fundy. In Turnagain Arm, named by Captain Cook as he searched for the Northwest Passage in 1780 and had to turn around, the advancing flood tide came as a low wall of water across the muddy flats—a bore tide. At low tide, the wide, muddy flats become vast areas of quicksand. Each year, unwary clammers are trapped and drowned by the incoming tide, their legs held fast while the water rises around them. Alaskans are avid boaters. Yet few use their boats in upper Cook Inlet, near Anchorage, preferring instead to drive two hours to Whittier, or four hours to Seward, where the tides are smaller, the sea and landscape friendlier.

But the sea gods smiled down on us that March, sending only moderate air as we gingerly crossed the mouth of Cook Inlet, and kindly waited until we were halfway down Shelikof Strait before hitting us with an eighty-mile-an-hour gust that sent us scurrying into the shelter of lonely Uyak Bay on the southwest of Kodiak Island with the very last light of the day. We dropped our anchor off a low gravel spit on the west side of the bay. The spit protected us from the hungry seas that were quickly building out in the strait but not from the wind. As we ate in the galley that night, now and again our conversation would stop as a particularly violent gust slammed into the boat, heeled us over at anchor, and moaned and whined through our steel pipe rigging that supported the mast, clearly audible through the steel walls and the hum of the diesel generator below us.

ICE ON DECK ON the *Flood Tide*, 1971. With our remaining pots lashed flat on deck and the railroad boom lowered and lashed to stern, lowering our center of gravity as much as possible, we were ready for whatever the North Pacific and Bering Sea could throw at us (we hope).

4. "Come Into My Icy Chamber," said the Sea God

WE'D BEEN A CONFIDENT bunch on the dock in Seattle, fitting out and loading our little ship, a product of the best small shipyard on the West Coast, maybe even in the whole United States. In the panoply of Alaska fisheries we were the chosen —the crew of what was then the largest new boat yet built for the king crab fishery, headed north to put that big Alaska money into our pocket. Except for George and perhaps his brother Russell, I don't think the rest of us—myself, engineer Johnny, and Bob, our easy-going cook, had looked on the trip north as anything more than a drive up the coast to get to the main event—Dutch Harbor, our new home in the Aleutian Islands and the Bering Sea king crab fishery.

The last ten days had changed all that. We had been battered by the ice, wind, and cold but most of all by the forbidding land and seascapes through which we had traveled. It was a subdued group that gathered around the galley table for the tasty, filling meals that Bob made. We still had almost 400 miles to go before we reached Unimak Pass, the entrance to the Bering Sea. After supper we played a few hands of cribbage, the board an antique ivory walrus tusk with a carved scrimshaw scene of the American whaling fleet in the ice off Point Barrow in 1901. They'd been "nipped"—caught between the pack ice and the shore—when an unexpected onshore wind pushed the ice in before they could get their anchors up and escape to the south. A half-dozen ships had been crushed, their crews forced onto the ice and finally to that inhospitable shore, and were rescued only after months of suffering. It was a good board to have, to remind us, as we pegged the points and slapped the cards, of the truly iron men who had come before us, lest we think we were tough.

After supper I retired to my bunk and my book. I drifted off eventually, lulled by the motion of the boat, as we sailed back and forth on our anchor chain, pushed by the relentless wind. Later I awoke and sat up quickly, bumping the bottom of the bunk above me. Something had hit our boat, sounding like an insistent hammer knocking against our hull. Outside I could hear the wild screech of the wind, angrier and wilder than it had been at supper. I quickly climbed the stairs to the pilothouse. Everyone was there, looking out at the stark, wild scene etched in the harsh light of our big crab lights high on the mast. Perhaps one eighth of a mile ahead of us was the sand and gravel spit that protected us from the violent seas flung by the churning strait against its opposite side. Beyond the spit was a violent maelstrom of wind and water where no boat could possibly survive. The water around us was covered with low white caps, but when I looked astern, I could see that they grew larger behind us. Another big angry gust slammed us, and nervously I looked at the anemometer: eighty-five, ninety, ninety-three miles an hour, before sagging back into just hurricane range, fifty to sixty mph.

Then it came again: the angry rattle of something hammering against our hull.

"It's rocks and gravel, boys," declared George, breaking our suspense, "picked up off the beach by the wind and carried all the way out to us, and we're 800 feet out! I've heard of boats that anchored too close to the beach here and had the paint sandblasted completely off their bows by flying gravel. It's our little welcome to Shelikof Strait."

I peered into the night again. I watched another furious gust churn the sea beyond the spit to a frenzy, and a moment later I could see what looked like a dust cloud erupting from the spit. And a moment after that it hit us, rattling insistently against the bow, ten feet below where we stood.

The *Big Sea*, 1990, an old wooden seiner, rerigged for crabbing with the addition of a new upper pilothouse and pot-handling gear. She is rigged for fish buying as evidenced by the bucket-style elevator for unloading the hold and by the fuel tank and hoses on the stern for selling fuel to the boats they are buying fish from. This vessel was previously the *Nick C II*, owned by Steve Trutich, one of the Americans hired to show Chileans how to seine. I crewed on this boat from Chile to Seattle, and then lived aboard her in Fishermen's Terminal while I was looking for my first Alaska fishing job. Lloyd Whaley Photo

"Is there another place to anchor?" I queried cautiously. "This is getting old."

"Look at the chart," George said. "If there's a better place to be in a howling norther' like this one, I don't know where it would be."

I looked. George was right, the shape of the bay and the depth of the water pretty much dictated where there was the best protection from the north.

"Besides," he said, as he pointed out the window and then at the temperature readout dial on the instrument panel that said 5°F, "you want to go out in that?"

At first, I didn't understand. I'd been looking at the spit and the angry strait rather than at our boat. But then I understood. The anchor winch. You couldn't see the controls at all any more. It was just sort of an amorphous luminous white shape with the edge of the brake wheel protruding in one place, totally iced over from just the spray thrown up by the wind while we were anchored.

FOUR DAYS WE LAY anchored in Uyak Bay. Each afternoon, the wind in Shelikof Strait would ease a bit, we'd break the ice off the anchor winch, and head out carefully around the end of the spit, to see if we could venture ever so cautiously southwest, even just ten or fifteen miles to the next secure anchorage. And each time, after just a half-hour, the sea would start to smoke again—frozen water vapor that rises from the sea on bitter, still days—the wind would throw up spray, and the icing would start. Our pilothouse windows were heated, designed to give clear visibility even in the worst conditions. But in fifteen minutes or less, they'd be opaque with the ice, except for a little circle directly in front of the starboard steering station, where George had rigged a fan to blow onto the glass to help the defroster.

Then we'd turn around. When we'd made the shelter of the bay again, it took two of us forty-five minutes or more to break the ice off the anchor winch just so we could drop anchor.

"See this, Puale Bay?" Johnny leaned into the circle of light around the chart table, pointing at a narrow bay on the mainland side of Shelikof Strait, across from where we lay. "We laid in there one February about four years ago, crabbing in an old eighty-six-foot power scow. She wasn't tough enough for the Bering Sea, but there were enough crabs in some of those bays to keep us busy and we were delivering into Kodiak. It was starting to blow pretty good out in the strait, so we scooched up close to the beach and dropped the hook. It seemed pretty sheltered in there, so we didn't figure we needed an anchor watch, and we just had a nice supper and went to sleep.

"I got up in the middle of the night, and noticed we seemed to be laying over to one side just a little bit. Curious, I went up to the pilothouse to have a look around. The windows were all iced over, totally opaque white—pretty weird. I thought only a freezing rain could have done it, that and it'd been way too cold for rain. So I thought I'd open one of the side doors to have a look around, and the goddamned door wouldn't even budge. Then it struck me what was happening. We were icing up at anchor. I tried the back door, the one away from the wind, and that was frozen over too! So I got the guys up, and finally we forced the door open.

"I hope to Christ I never have to look out on something like that again. The whole front of the boat was solid ice with just here and there something sticking out like the edge of a crab block, or the handle of a winch, or the corner of a crab pot. It wasn't that the wind was blowing hard, it was that it kicked up kind of an icy mist off the water. You could almost see the ice actually getting thicker! She had wire for the standing rigging, and those wires were about as big around as your thigh with ice. She was laying over even more with the weight of it; another boat that wasn't as wide and as stable as a scow would have already rolled over.

"We had to get the hell out of there if we were going to survive. You could hardly see where the anchor winch was! The whole bow area—there were some tanks and other gear up there—was one smooth hill of ice. I mean, it was several feet thick. Luckily, we had a portable acetylene cutting torch set in the engine room, and we cut off the anchor cable with it and got the hell out of there. But when we turned and the wind caught us off the other side, the old scow lay on the other side maybe fifteen degrees and wouldn't come back. That's how unstable she was. ·

"It was lucky the wind out in the strait had stopped. We just idled out of the bay and around the corner so we got out of that ice mist and just drifted, chopping ice for three solid hours until she seemed to come up on an even keel and stabilize. We knew we were safe enough at least to go in and get a mug up.

"But, man, if I hadn't gotten up, another hour or two and we'd have rolled over right there at anchor. And we went in there for shelter, for crissake."

Occasionally, when it was daylight and there was a break in the snow squalls, I thought I could make out the faint shape of buildings in the head of a cove on the other side of the bay. "Cannery" was the one-word notation on the chart, and once at night I thought I got a glimpse of a dim light in a window.

"Winter man," Russell said, when I asked him about it. "It's like a watch-man, except it's for nine months. "Sometimes a couple, usually older with maybe kids grown and gone. There's a lot of spots like this up and down the coast—canneries, little places where maybe they smoke or process fish for a few months in the summer." He waved back at the night and somewhere out there, the cannery. "No roads to any of these places, usually the company might send out a floatplane once a month with groceries and mail. You gotta like your own company for a job like that."

OUR CHANCE CAME at mid-morning on the fifth day. The dawn had come late and windy, with a weird cold light over the mountains to the east. Then, for the first time since we'd been there, the wind dropped out entirely, and the relentless motion of the boat, the continuous moan from beyond the steel walls, was replaced by stillness and the hum of the generators.

We'd been playing cribbage again in the galley, while Missouri Bob worked on another big brunch from his ample supplies and walk-in freezer, when the intercom spoke: "OK, guys, time for our daily stick-our-nose-around-the-corner-and-see-if-it-gets-knocked-off routine. But this one might be different. Peggy said there's a break between fronts that might actually last for a couple of days." Peggy Dyson was the wife of a Kodiak fisher-man who had taken it upon herself to put out a daily weather commentary on the single sideband shortwave radio. She'd gather her material from various sources and put together a detailed area forecast that had become a tradition of immense value to the trawl and crab fishermen of Western Alaska.

Russell and I suited up in insulated coveralls, bib-style rain gear bot-toms, and heavy hooded rain gear jacket, boots, wool hat, and gloves. When we stepped outside, I realized we should have brought sunglasses. The sun had broken through the clouds and shone on a stunningly bright scene. Even the water seemed white, since it was covered with sea smoke, or white water vapor that rises from the surface in bitter weather. The land around the bay, the mountains, and the low scrub brush and trees were all snow-

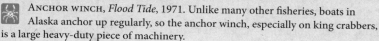
Anchor winch, *Flood Tide*, 1971. Unlike many other fisheries, boats in Alaska anchor up regularly, so the anchor winch, especially on king crabbers, is a large heavy-duty piece of machinery.

blasted, disfigured, and white, the only contrast a line along the shore where the water had receded from the high tide line.

Our ice-breaking tools again were the baseball bat and a small hammer, the hammer for working in tight places. That morning the ice buildup was less than what we had been used to. After a mere twenty minutes of beating, hammering, and kicking the ice off the bow deck into the sea, we got the big winch drum rotating, winding the thick steel anchor cable neatly onto it.

On most East Coast and Gulf Coast fishing boats, even the big draggers, anchoring is such a minor part of the fishing routine that most boats don't even have anchor winches. Anchors are small enough to be hauled by hand, or in the case of larger boats, the line is led aft and hand-pulled over a rotating gypsy drum of a winch primarily used for another purpose. But in the Alaska fisheries, where the boats are often gone from their homeports for months, anchoring is a regular part of their schedules, often daily for smaller boats. The result is that husky anchor gear and winches are a distinctive feature of all but the smallest fishing boats operating in Alaska.

Our anchor gear was a measure of its importance to us and our opera-tions. The winch itself was just slightly smaller than a Volkswagen beetle, and winding onto its drum as we operated it that bitter morning was the cable with a breaking strength of over a hundred tons. The last hundred feet before the anchor was heavy chain, each link made of one-inch-diameter forged steel, and the anchor itself was a navy-style two-fluked steel 500 pounder. To some, it would seem way more than we needed. But when you're holed up in some bay with the wind howling over a hundred miles per hour, and the boat surging back and forth and coming up tight with a jerk against the cable, you don't want to be worrying about whether the cable and anchor will hold you.

With all of us in the wheelhouse, we anxiously crept out and around the point and into the wide strait, anticipating that at any moment the heave of the sea and the slap of spray against our windows would begin the dreaded buildup of ice. But Peggy had been correct: even mighty Shelikof Strait was still. The arctic high in the Interior had drifted off to the east over distant Hudson Bay. The huge pressure differentials between this high and the Pacific lows which had been marching in off the Gulf of Alaska, creating the powerful northerly storm that had flogged us for almost a week, had finally diminished. This afforded us a short window of good traveling weather. Yet the bitter cold lingered. Outside, the temperature was still close to zero. In such conditions, the warmer water smokes, releasing water vapor that looks like fog, and we traveled through clouds of it. Struck by the morning sun, the vapor was a brilliant blinding white. Only occasionally through it peeked the forbidding majesty of the high peaks and volcanoes of the Alaska Peninsula to our north.

These lonely waters had been the range of the mail boat *Expansion* during the 1950s. The sturdy 110 footer had the mail contract and delivered freight to the Aleut and Eskimo villages of remote Western Alaska, mak-ing monthly roundtrips out of Seward. Alaska has always been a breeding ground for entrepreneurs, and the skipper and owner of the *Expansion*, Captain Niels Thomsen, was a prime example.

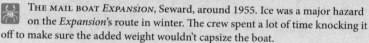 The mail boat *Expansion*, Seward, around 1955. Ice was a major hazard on the *Expansion*'s route in winter. The crew spent a lot of time knocking it off to make sure the added weight wouldn't capsize the boat.

Many of the villages serviced by the *Expansion* had no radio contact with the outside world or even nearby Native villages. Cap'n T, as Thomsen became known, had a sharp eye for an opportunity, and noticed that many villages had an overabundance of single gals, while other villages, perhaps no farther than 60 miles away as the crow flies, had too many single males. But because the waters were too rough for traveling by small craft, these villagers were unaware of the demographics of other regional villages.

So Cap'n T purchased a Polaroid camera, just then becoming available, and at each village he took pictures of young men and women, writing their names and villages on the white margins of the photos—"Nina Popalook, Gambrel Bay"—and posted them on a singles bulletin board in his boat's lounge area which he had converted into a small traveling store.

Soon, whenever the *Expansion* poked its nose around the point into a bay with a little village on its shores, he'd see excited Natives running down to the shore and rowing their skiffs, and occasionally umiaks, or traditional boats made out of walrus hides stretched over a driftwood frame, rapidly out to his boat, eager to come aboard and check out the latest snapshots on the singles bulletin board, even before he had stopped the engine and anchored. In those days, to get legally married, Natives had to travel to Cold Bay, on the western end of the Alaska Peninsula. With only small, human-powered craft for travel and without the resources to hire a floatplane, this was a burden. So Cap'n T got certified as a justice of the peace, and in addition to his skippering, freighting, and shopkeeping duties, he also began performing marriages in the villages.

In the 1950s, many of the more distant Native villages of Western Alaska, especially along the Bering Sea coast, were just starting to make the transition from the barter-subsistence lifestyle to a cash economy. Ever since the Americans bought Alaska from Russia in 1867, trading vessels had traveled each summer to remote Western Alaska, loaded with five-gallon cans of gas, flour, and sugar, as well as canned foods, rifles, ammunition, bolts of cloth, sewing supplies, tools, and the like. These ships would anchor off the villages, and the Natives, often dressed in traditional skin clothing, would come aboard with carved ivory art for trading.

Cap'n T noticed that, on occasion, his customers would bring their money in jars to purchase their needs in his little store. A little inquiry revealed that there were few banking services available to the villagers, so Cap'n T established a branch of the Bank of Alaska aboard his vessel and brought banking to Western Alaska as well.

In the late spring and summer, these shores, especially along the bays of the Alaska Peninsula, were part of the great northern flyway—the route taken by millions of migrating birds that flew thousands of miles to the vast marshes and flats near the Yukon River Delta to begin summer breeding and nesting. Cap'n T was always impressed by this dramatic migration and, hoping to attract a few tourists, he made up a little brochure: "Experience the

Captain Niels Thomsen, Seward, around 1955. "Cap'n T," as he was known, operated the Aleutian mail boat *Expansion*, between Seward and remote Western Alaska ports summer and winter in the 1950s. Note the ice-coated gear behind him.

Captain Thomsen's marketing brochure to get tourists to accompany him on his mail boat route, around 1955.

He might have added, "Help the captain work on his floating crab processor in scenic Dutch Harbor," because on each trip, he usually tried to put in a few days there scraping and painting what became his next venture.

beauty and drama of the Aleutian Islands on board the mail boat *Expansion*," and he wrote up the opportunities for bird-watching and sightseeing.

He might have added, "Help the captain paint his crab processor in historic Dutch Harbor" to his brochure, since Cap'n T had a small down-at-the-heels ship, the *Bethel I*, at Dutch Harbor and was in the process of converting it to a crab processor. Dutch was the biggest town on his mail route and the longest stop for the *Expansion*. As time allowed, Cap'n T would try to get a little more paint onto the aging craft each time he was in town. In those days, when the small king crab fishery was primarily taking place out of Kodiak, the crab processors on the island pretty much had the market and the fleet sewed up. But Cap'n T hoped to lure some of the Kodiak crab boats out to Dutch Harbor to fish for him when his processor was completed.

To that end, he carried a small crab pot aboard the *Expansion* and would set it in little bays along his route, then haul it on his next trip through, noting the catch. He would cook up a feed for his crew or passengers, but let the rest go, since he didn't have tanks for keeping the crab alive until he got to town. Over the years he accrued a body of information about the crab abundance in the many bays and coves along this rugged coast. So when his crab processor was ready to go, a key marketing point to the Kodiak fishermen he recruited to fish for him was that not only would he provide a market for their crab if they fished out of Dutch Harbor, but he would also share his detailed crab survey data.

His timing was perfect. He was able to put together a profitable little crab-processing operation with a dedicated fleet of boats delivering to him just at a time when the fishery was expanding. A few years after our trip in the *Flood Tide*, Cap'n T sold his operation to a larger seafood company and retired to the Caribbean to build a small luxury hotel and enjoy a little time in the sun after many years in the North.

FOR A DAY AND A HALF, we paralleled the south coast of the Alaska Peninsula, crossing our fingers that the break between weather fronts would last long enough for us to get through Unimak Pass and into the Bering Sea. The landscape to our north was daunting, given that the Alaska Peninsula is part of what is known as the Ring of Fire—the volcanoes, active and inactive that circle much of the North Pacific and mark the active boundary where two major continental plates rub against each other. As we made our way past, the west peninsula's volcanoes—with names like Shishaldin, Aniachak, Pavof—were sleeping lightly, with steam, ash, and lava eruptions being common events.

Indeed, in 1884, an entire island, now called Bogoslof, had emerged, raw from the depths of the Bering Sea sixty miles northwest of Dutch Harbor. The ocean floor in that vicinity, according to theory, was particularly thin and it occasionally cracked, letting salt water into the lava chambers below. Flashing to steam, the pressure was thought to push the ocean floor upward, occasionally creating islands. And so Bogoslof rose above the ocean, venting steam, lava, and ash from cracks in its surface. On occasion, after a particularly violent steam venting, the whole island would collapse into the sea, only to rise a few weeks or months later in a nearby location.

Finally, in 1910, the island was thought to be stable enough for a scientific team to visit, delivered by a Coast Guard cutter, the *Rush*. When the team arrived, Bogoslof mysteriously appeared out of the mist, with steam still wisping from a vent near its peak. The fascinated scientists were eager to go ashore, but then the captain received a radio message about an urgent mission farther to the west, so the landing had to be postponed.

The delay saved the scientists' lives. When the *Rush* approached the vicinity of Bogoslof a few weeks later, the whole area was cloaked in fog and steam and a strong sulfur smell filled the air. As the *Rush* groped through the poor visibility, looking for the island, a break in the fog revealed an erupting column of steam, smoke, and ash a quarter-mile in diameter, erupting and rising 8,000 to 10,000 feet into the air from where Bogoslof had been. The island had disappeared totally, and another six months passed before dry land again appeared in the area where the island is today.

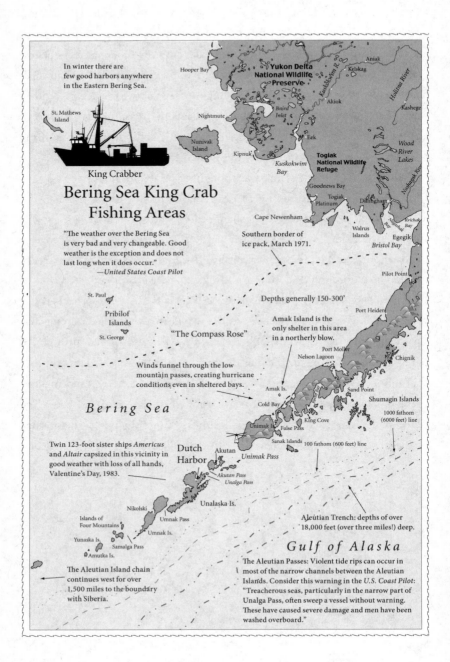

In winter there are few good harbors anywhere in the Eastern Bering Sea.

St. Mathews Island

King Crabber

Bering Sea King Crab Fishing Areas

"The weather over the Bering Sea is very bad and very changeable. Good weather is the exception and does not last long when it does occur."
—*United States Coast Pilot*

Hooper Bay

Yukon Delta National Wildlife Preserve

Aniak

Kelskag

Kuskokwim R.

Akiok

Holitna River

Kashege

Nightmute

Baird Inlet

Eek

Wood River Lakes

Nunivak Island

Kipnuk

Kuskokwim Bay

Togiak National Wildlife Refuge

Nushagak River

Goodnews Bay

Togiak Platinum

Dillingham

Cape Newenham

Walrus Islands

Kvichak Bay

Egegik

Southern border of ice pack, March 1971.

Bristol Bay

Pilot Point

St. Paul

Depths generally 150-300'

Port Heiden

Pribilof Islands

St. George

Amak Island is the only shelter in this area in a northerly blow.

"The Compass Rose"

Port Moller

Nelson Lagoon

Chignik

Winds funnel through the low mountain passes, creating hurricane conditions even in sheltered bays.

Amak Is.

Sand Point

Cold Bay

Shumagin Islands

Bering Sea

Unimak Is.

False Pass

King Cove

1000 fathom (6000 feet) line

Twin 123-foot sister ships *Americus* and *Altair* capsized in this vicinity in good weather with loss of all hands, Valentine's Day, 1983.

Dutch Harbor

Akutan

Sanak Islands

Unimak Pass

100 fathom (600 feet) line

Akutan Pass
Unalga Pass

Nikolski

Unalaska Is.

Islands of Four Mountains

Umnak Pass

Aleutian Trench: depths of over 18,000 feet (over three miles!) deep.

Yunaska Is.

Umnak Is.

Gulf of Alaska

Samalga Pass

Amutka Is.

The Aleutian Island chain continues west for over 1,500 miles to the boundary with Siberia.

The Aleutian Passes: Violent tide rips can occur in most of the narrow channels between the Aleutian Islands. Consider this warning in the *U.S. Coast Pilot*: "Treacherous seas, particularly in the narrow part of Unalga Pass, often sweep a vessel without warning. These have caused severe damage and men have been washed overboard."

5. A Bering Sea Welcome

ON MARCH 9, at nine in the morning, we entered the restless waters of Unimak Pass. Unimak is the widest and most traveled of the passes through the Aleutian Islands between the North Pacific and the Bering Sea. It sits on the great circle route of shipping between Asia and the U.S. West Coast. Earlier that winter, photographs had appeared twice on the front page of the *Seattle Post-Intelligencer* showing 500- and 600-foot freighters battered by seas in the pass, one losing a dozen or so of her big containers over the side when solid water swept her decks. So it was a huge relief when we found the winds calm and the tidal currents slack—rare conditions—when we entered the pass.

The Aleutian Islands stretch from Unimak Pass west 1,500 miles almost to Siberia. We studied the first of the Aleutians, Akutan and Akun, just west of the pass. It wasn't a reassuring sight. The shores were primarily steep bluffs rising from narrow, rocky beaches. There were no trees. The Aleutians are north of the tree line in latitude and vegetation consists mostly of ground cover and low bushes. In the almost constant daylight of the arctic summer, vegetation flourishes and the slopes are sometimes covered with wildflowers. But that March, the islands were still snow-blasted and grim-looking, with their rocky peaks disappearing into the clouds which now appeared to be on the move again. Fortunately Dutch Harbor was just fifty miles west of Unimak Pass.

At three we passed Priest Rock, the dramatic promontory that marks the entrance to Captain's Bay and Dutch Harbor. We were greatly relieved to

THE "FLOATER" (seafood processing ship) *Akutan*, Aleutian Islands, 1968. In places like Dutch Harbor in the remote Aleutian Islands, it was often much easier to install crab-processing equipment and crew's quarters aboard a small ship that could be self contained and move from place to place as it was needed. Many workers on a ship like this would also be trying to get a job on the crab boats that delivered to them.

see the sheltering arms of the land encircling the bay ahead of us. And as if to tell us that our window of good traveling weather was over, a tide rip off the entrance threw up enough spray to quickly ice over our windows, and a biting, snow-filled wind, racing down from the pack ice just over the horizon to the north, swirled violently around the boat, heeling us over with its intensity.

We suited up once again and went out on deck to drag out the frozen dock lines, looking out for the shifting shapes in the snow ahead to coalesce and reveal the port that was to be our base of operations for the next six months. First, we could see the rust-scarred shape of a crab processing ship, water streaming off its side from multiple hoses. Then the shape of a small church topped by the Russian Orthodox cross. Finally the dock of our market, Pan Alaska Seafoods, and another crab boat, apparently just in from a trip. A dock crane hovered over the crab boat's midship hold. As we watched, a wire basket of squirming live crab rose from the hold and then disappeared into the steam pouring out of the end of the cannery building. But what really caught our attention was the ancient crab boat, and as we slid slowly past to tie up ahead of it, we just gaped.

The *King and Winge* was wood, built in 1914, we later learned. She was of the so-called schooner style, meaning that her pilothouse was aft with the working deck forward. She was a few feet longer than the *Flood Tide* and ice still clung to the dark wooden sides of her hull. The railing that ran around her deck was graceful wood, supported by carved and turned columns, to which were lashed a few mongrel king crab pots of different sizes. The windows of the pilothouse were flanked by well-worn, paint chipped, but still elegant wooden trim. She must have arrived just before we came around the corner, because when we looked into her crab hold as we passed, it was full of crab almost to the top so they must have just started unloading.

We were humbled by the sight. Here we were with our new, steel, top of the line, pride of the fleet, state-of-the-art Marco 104 footer. Battling our way north and west through the ice and the wind. Turned back off Cape St. Elias, and again and again in Shelikof Strait. Only to tie up next to a fifty-five-year-old wooden boat, heavily iced in places, her crew oblivious to the ice as they unloaded, apparently just in from another successful Bering Sea crab trip.

As soon as we tied up, eager to go ashore, we encountered the first trap for the unwary sailor in those parts—the dock ladder. The tide was way down, and the bottom twenty feet of the steel ladder, already slippery from seaweed, crab entrails, and the other mysterious things that float in the water around an Alaska crab-processing plant, was also fatly coated with frozen salt water. Even wearing gloves, we found it difficult to grab hold of the swollen, icy rungs. Going up was a challenge, but at least the wind was pushing our boat against the dock so it was close. It wasn't hard to imagine coming down that icy ladder after a little too much good cheer, and not noticing the usual large gap between our boat and the bottom of the ladder. More than one fisherman had been found floating or frozen on the deck after a tumble off icy rungs.

Up on the dock, spits of snow and a bitter wind awaited us. The short day already over, we made our way along a dark, rutted road with our heads down. Here and there, dim rectangles of light from windows curtained against the cold glowed from what must have been homes.

We pushed through the outer doors and into the Elbow Room, Dutch Harbor's signature bar that was soon to become legend when the crab and bottom-fish industry boomed in twenty years. But that night there was no sign of the boisterous camaraderie that often would fill the dimly lit room as Dutch went from isolated Aleutian fishing settlement to the biggest U.S. fishing port in terms of value of catch landed. That night, no elated fisherman was ringing the big bell over the bar to buy a round for the house after a particularly big crab trip, nor was the room shoulder to shoulder with immigrant processing workers off one of the immense factory trawlers that would dominate the harbor, celebrating a rare day in port as their floating sweatshop stopped briefly in Dutch to offload frozen fish to an Asia-bound freighter.

That evening it was just the four of us from the *Flood Tide*—George had gone up to the Pan Alaska Seafood office—and three locals slumped at the bar. There was no widescreen TV showing golf or baseball on ESPN; 1971 was before cable. The only decorative touch in the place was the backlit Rainier Beer sign showing a salmon troller fishing off the Alaska coast with the dramatic Fairweather Range peaks behind it backlit by the morning sun.

I was immensely curious about the fishing news, and was pretty sure the locals at the bar would know the scoop. "Hey," I said to the man nearest me, my young voice full of excitement and enthusiasm. "How are the guys doing out there, how's the crab fishing?"

He looked up suddenly at the sound of my voice, pulled back a bit and sort of studied me up and down, and mumbled something I couldn't get, like "ice . . . fucking . . . Pribs . . . "

ABOARD A "FLOATER," or floating processor, unloading a crab boat (out of sight to right), Dutch Harbor, 1968. When the crab weight was recorded on the scale, the crewman pulled a lever on the bin and the crab were dumped into the tank, which was full of circulating seawater to keep the crab alive until they were processed. COURTESY *FISHERMEN'S NEWS*

"What's that?" I asked again. "How's the crab fishing?" We were finally in Dutch, ready to start our season, ready to get in on that bonanza we'd been hearing about.

He elbowed his buddy, who came awake with a start. They both sort of staggered to their feet. I asked the other man, certain that the first man hadn't understood me. "Hey, we just got up here. So how's it going out there, I mean how are the boats doing? It looked like the *King and Winge* put in a good trip."

A pair of heavily lidded, very bloodshot eyes tried to focus on me from a bearded and cold-reddened face. "How . . . the . . . fuck . . . do you think it is? The pack's south . . . of the Pribs."

The Pribs, I guessed, were the Pribilof Islands, just 150 miles north of Dutch, and the pack was probably the edge of the pack ice that stretched for thousands of miles over the pole to Greenland, Norway, Finland, and Siberia. The first guy turned and gave me a look like I was something that he'd scrape off his shoe. Then they both stumbled, shaking their heads, through the door and out into the night.

"I don't think that old boy liked you, Joe," Missouri Bob said, with his amiable drawl. Looking around and shaking his head he said, "And this sure ain't like Alabama."

"Aw, you can't blame these locals," engineer Johnny said. "Chrissake, look at it from their point of view—they've had this fishery pretty much to themselves in their wooden boats for years. To them, we're the Seattle guys with the big steel boats come to catch their crab."

Russell already had a couple of shot glasses lined up in front of him and was getting right down to business. "Boys," he said, waving at the dreary room, "welcome to the asshole of Alaska."

Our bartender, by the look of him, with long dark hair and a slightly Asian face with a wispy mustache, was an Aleut—a Native of the Aleutians— and responded to our queries about the happenings in town with little more than grunts. Now and again, as we nursed our drinks, feeling a good buzz getting started, we could feel the whole building shake as a gust of wind slammed into it.

Outside, when we left, the weather had worsened, blasting us with flying ice particles that slashed at our faces. We tucked our heads into our parkas and made our way toward the dock. The house lights we'd seen earlier were lost in the storm or turned off for the night, and we guided ourselves by the familiar sound of the *Flood Tide*'s generator and the dock light of the crab plant. We climbed ever so carefully down the long icy ladder and into the welcoming cheeriness of our galley.

Just as we were ready to turn in, we heard the sound of a big engine outside, and then felt the nudge of another boat coming alongside. We jumped up, pulled on our parkas, boots, and gloves, and stepped outside to take their tie-up lines. The sight that awaited us was sobering. It was a halibut boat but totally sheathed in ice. This style of boat, with a small pilothouse aft, mostly built before 1920, was specifically designed to fish for halibut in the Bering Sea and North Pacific in all kinds of weather, year-round. Halibut boats were legendary for their seaworthiness, but this one had obviously just had a close call with the storm that was now battering the buildings around the harbor. The wire stays that held up the foremast were half a foot thick with ice, and what must have been an anchor winch was a white mound. On the front of the small wooden pilothouse, the windows were all iced over except for a small circle of dark glass. Then we saw the stern. The bait shack, a small structure on one side of the stern that sheltered the crew while they baited up (halibut are caught on long-lines, miles of line set along the bottom with thousands of baited hooks), had been smashed. Just bits of splintered wood and bent steel protruded from the ice.

A grim-faced man with a bloody bandage around his forehead thrust a frozen stern line at me, while behind him another crewman was using a heavy hammer to beat the ice off a bow cleat so that he could make the line fast. I passed the line through one of the oval openings in our steel bulwarks and tried to tie it around the big cleat welded to the deck at our stern. But the line was so stiff I had to work it back and forth a few times before I could get it to bend.

THE SARDINE SEINER–style wooden crabber *Ocean Castle*, around 1965. This style of vessel was commonly available in the 1960s, and many were converted to king crabbers. It was a vessel similar to this that tied up to us the night we arrived at Dutch Harbor in March 1971. However the power of the seas that she had encountered had sheared off her port bridge wing. LLOYD WHALEY PHOTO.

Then, another shape appeared in the circle of light given off by the big lights on the crab plant dock. It was another halibut boat, Canadian by the look of it. It was what we fishermen called a sardine seiner–style boat, a vintage wooden eighty footer, with its deckhouse forward and much bigger than that of the schooner, whose galley and accommodations were below in the forecastle, the very forward part of the hull, also known as the fo'c'sle. This style of boat had two bridge wings. These were open deck portions that extended out from both sides of the wheelhouse, allowing the skipper to step out and get an unobstructed view of where the fishing gear was being worked, whether it was a sardine seine, which it was built to use, or halibut long-line gear, which the boat had been converted to. The sardiner was all iced up too. Even the sides of her hull were so coated with ice that we couldn't see her name or the color of her paint.

But what caught our attention was the bridge wing, or rather what was left of it, on her port side, as she approached to tie up beside the iced-up schooner.

Half the structure was completely gone, and the steel support stanchions were twisted. What was left looked like a strange modern art sculpture, ghostly with thick ice. As she came closer, we could see that beneath the ice on the front of her wheelhouse, plywood replaced two windows that had obviously been broken by the seas.

Finished with the tie-up lines on our side, the men on the schooner crossed their deck to take the lines of the sardiner. They had been traveling together. I wanted to ask someone aboard what it had been like out there. It was clear that they had been in a life-and-death struggle with the bitter wind and the seas that instantly froze whenever they touched the boat or rigging, whether wood or steel. But my opportunity never came. When the crews finished tying up, four of them crossed our decks with hardly a glance in our direction, while we stood, still a bit awed by their boats. They climbed up the ladder and quickly disappeared into the dark and the storm, headed, I was sure, to the Elbow Room.

We went up into our pilothouse to be out of the weather and to look again at the sobering condition of the boats beside us. We hadn't been there but a few minutes when the men returned, carrying bags of something. As we watched, they climbed across our deck, over the icy deck of the halibut schooner, and onto the other boat. A light went on in the galley, and the way the boats were lined up, we could look right into the window. The men sat down and pulled bottles out of the bags—whiskey and vodka, from the look of it. There were eight men: two crews of four, and eight bottles. After unscrewing the caps, they raised the bottles, touched them together in a toast, and started drinking. It didn't look like they'd be needing the caps again.

EARLY KING CRAB POTS during test fishing, 1950s. The big circular pots in the background are a scaled-up version of Dungeness crab pots, used off the Oregon and Washington coasts. They caught crab but wasted deck space when stacked because they were round, and eventually they were replaced by the rectangular crab pot. COURTESY BUREAU OF COMMERCIAL FISHERIES

6. The Boys Get Ready

THE NEXT MORNING came gray and ugly. The storm-battered halibut boats had moved over to the fuel dock, so we drew in the frozen lines again and moved across the harbor to a much-repaired dock, which was left over from World War II, when Dutch was a frenzy of military activity after the Japanese invaded and occupied Attu Island, 500 miles to the west.

The rest of our 150 crab pots were stored there, lined up in four ragged rows among the frozen low bushes, or puckerbrush, along with hundreds of others, waiting for their owners to take them out to sea again. Each crab pot had to be checked and repaired as necessary, and then carried by a wheezing forklift to the dock, where it could be hoisted aboard.

First, we had to hoist the pots in the crab tanks out onto the back deck. We dreaded opening the hatches, knowing that the miles of line that we had so carefully cut, measured, spliced eyes into, coiled, and then stacked into the dry holds back in Seattle, would be in a huge tangle. We had hoped that we could travel to Dutch Harbor without having to flood our crab tanks. So when we did flood them on that challenging afternoon in Hecate Strait, we'd created a washing machine. It was worse than we imagined. Under the hatches was a jumbled mass of crab pots, big crab buoys, and miles and miles of thick buoy line. Each pot that we hoisted out came up festooned with line, which had to be tediously sorted out and recoiled once both ends could be found. Then, when the pots were finally out, what remained below was a true Medusa's coil—miles of line and hundreds of buoys all intertwined as tightly as one big rat's nest. All we could do was lower the hook, lift as much as came easily, and try to sort it out. It was two days of cold and discouraging work before we got the lines and buoys sorted and coiled. All the while, the wind and snow came and went, revealing stark rocky heights, whitecaps driving across an almost empty harbor, and the stark landscape of crab pots and low, wind-stunted tundra bushes.

On today's crabbers there would have been a video player in the galley, a big-screen monitor, and shelves with movies. The skipper and crewmen's wives would send up boxes of movies they had copied or TV shows they had recorded. But in 1971 our galley was austere, the only window a porthole on the rear wall, at countertop level, with a view of the back deck. Ocean-going vessels that plied the North Pacific and Bering Sea with freight containers and supplies bound for Asia, Dutch Harbor, or remote villages of the Bering Sea and arctic coasts, typically had floor-to-ceiling bookshelves on one wall of the galley, the volumes a way to deal with the numbing monotony of long ocean passages. Our galley had none of these.

The side of the harbor where we worked was an island with no access to the Elbow Room. After working outside in the wind and snow all day, we had little inclination to go through the drill with the frozen tie-up lines and move over to the other side of the harbor, climb the ice-covered ladder up to the shore, and walk to the bar. So on those long evenings, the entertainment was most likely a game or two of cribbage, pegged on that carved ivory scene of man and ice, and then early to bed, to read whatever we'd brought. Our group was congenial and the stories flowed.

Before turning in, there was a ritual: go up to the wheelhouse and look out and around. Like most king crab vessels, we kept our rack of brilliant quartz-iodine lights, mounted high on the mast, lit day and night, since it helped to keep a load on our big diesel generators (diesel generators last longer when they are operating at least at twenty-five percent of capacity). The sight was hardly cheerful. Outside the windows was a grim world of wind-whipped harbor, gust-flattened tundra bushes, rotten pilings, and snow-blasted crab pots. The quick visit to the wheelhouse had the effect of making us mightily appreciative of the mechanical systems that maintained our cozy world inside our boat.

SINCE KING CRAB were large, the pots had to be substantially larger than the circular Dungeness crab pots used along the Northwest Coast. The "dungie" pot was a substantial affair—a rubber-wrapped steel frame enclosed with stainless steel netting, and at just forty pounds, it was easily moved around deck or stacked. But dungies were relatively small: a big crab was a pound and a half and measured a foot across. Because mature male king crab were ten to fourteen pounds, and from leg tip to leg tip measured six feet across, the massive pots that evolved for the Alaska fishery were more like cages than pots, typically made out of one- and one and a quarter-inch diameter steel bar (the larger diameter and heavier bar was on the bottom so that the pots would land on the ocean floor right side up) and covered with strong nylon netting. Pots came in several sizes, but they were all giant compared to other crab pots anywhere else in the world. Many crabbers preferred a "six by"—a rectangle six feet on a side and about thirty inches high, or the slightly larger "seven by"—seven feet by seven feet by thirty inches. Such pots weighed around 700 pounds empty. The advantage of a larger pot size was offset by the increased difficulty of moving the pot around on deck and a reduced number of pots that could be carried onboard at once. A few fishermen had giant pots built: eight feet by eight feet by three feet, but they were so awkward to handle, most of them ended up on the bottom of the Bering Sea or shoved into the bushes near a dock somewhere.

The main reason for the large pots was simple: there were a lot of crab. In many other pot fisheries, a full pot was something to be remarked on; the catch was certainly not limited by the size of the pot. The king crab fishery was very different, at least in the early 1970s. The crab were big, and at certain times there were a lot of them, so a pot size evolved that was a balance between something that was small enough to handle on deck and was large enough to accommodate the volume of crab that might be caught when fishing was good.

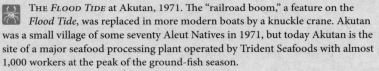
THE *FLOOD TIDE* at Akutan, 1971. The "railroad boom," a feature on the *Flood Tide*, was replaced in more modern boats by a knuckle crane. Akutan was a small village of some seventy Aleut Natives in 1971, but today Akutan is the site of a major seafood processing plant operated by Trident Seafoods with almost 1,000 workers at the peak of the ground-fish season.

The large pots meant that as a crewman, you had to be a mix of human bulldozer and human forklift in order to move the pots around deck. In later years, the distinctive mark of a king crabber would be the knuckle crane—a two-piece hydraulically articulated boom with a winch that could move pots around the deck with ease. But in 1971, no crabber yet had installed them, and the *Flood Tide*, like most early crab boats, used a railroad boom to move pots. In this arrangement, a track was welded along the bottom of our boom, along which a pulley or block moved, from which hung the cable from a winch. Another winch moved the pulley in and out along the boom. By operating the winches in unison, the operator would be able to move pots fore and aft along the deck. But it was far from ideal. The weight of the boom, up high as it was, created stability problems for the boat in some situations, and it could only move pots forward and aft along the deck but not side to side, or at least not easily. Also, the winch control station on the *Flood Tide* was located in such a way that in order to see the deck, the boom, and the pots, the operator had to stand with the winch handles behind him, which required a lot of dexterity. As the pulley was moved up the boom, it also lifted whatever it was hooked to, so both winches had to be carefully operated in unison if they were used together.

Fortunately George Fulton was an extremely innovative skipper and had worked closely with the Marco shipyard, which not only built the boat but also designed and manufactured our king crab fishing equipment and machinery. Together they came up with an arrangement of three small winches mounted on a framework across the stern that worked with a detachable hook that would pull the pots back along the deck and then upright to be stacked.

The prototype of another Marco product that was to gain wide popularity among the fleet also stood on our back deck by the base of the mast—a

COILER ABOARD THE *Flood Tide*, 1971. This buoy line coiler was a Marco prototype. The rotating chute coils the line neatly into the tall receptacle, with a wide slot so you can lift out the coils. When we were fishing in deep water with 1,000 to 1,200 feet of buoy line, the coil would fill the receptacle. The netting stapled to the wooden decking gave us better footing. The coiler proved to be a dependable, labor-saving piece of equipment that found wide acceptance in the king crab fleet.

FULL CRAB BAG, summer fishing, with the "cod end" style of bag we attached to our pots as an experiment in 1971. In heavy fishing, it would allow more crab to enter a pot. No other crabber adopted this method, and we eventually abandoned it.

hydraulically powered coiler for the heavy line that connected each pot to its buoys. For boats fishing smaller pots in shallower water, like lobster boats and Dungeness crab boats, the incoming buoy line spilling out of the pot-hauler, another hydraulically powered device, would just lie on the deck until the pot was reset again. A hundred feet or so of relatively small diameter line wasn't a problem, and could be quickly fed overboard when the pot was reset.

But like many king crabbers, we used buoy line $^{13}/_{16}$ inch in diameter—thicker than most garden hoses—and fished occasionally in deep water, sometimes in 100 fathoms. That's 600 feet, using 750 feet of line, which when coiled would make a pile about chest high. Coiling so much heavy line pot after pot is hard, demanding work, on top of the brutal work of moving the pots around deck, chopping bait, sorting crab, etc. Our new prototype coiler pulled the line out of the big pot-hauler, another Marco product, and fed it through a rotating chute into a tall steel receptacle looking like an upside-down cone with the narrow end cut off. We were hoping that it would work as well as it was supposed to.

George had developed another innovation that we, the crew, were less sure about: the "bag." The nylon netting on one end of the box of steel and nylon netting of the crab pot was cut out and a long bag of net stitched on, whose open end was kept closed by a loop of line stitched through the meshes. The idea was that when you pulled the pot up through the water from the bottom, the crab would be forced into the bag, making it much easier to empty the pot.

But, in order to empty the bag, the heavy pot had to be pulled up into a steel framework until it was suspended over our heads somewhat like a guillotine. A quick-release device, allowing it to be reset, or dumped over-board on command, also suspended the pot. If the release lanyard caught on something in the process of hoisting the pot, dumping the bag, the pot would fall, probably on one or more of us. To avoid such a tragedy, I devised a simple safety strap that would hold the pot in the event it was released inadvertently.

SOMETIMES WHEN WE were anchored in Inian Islands buying fish, icebergs from Glacier Bay would drift into the harbor. Once something woke me in the night and I went on deck to find an iceberg the size of a house scraping down our side in the current, eerily lit up by the moon. It was magic.

7. Tales from the Elbow Room

FINALLY AFTER THREE long days of replacing ripped net panels and chafed bridles, or the heavy lines used for lifting the pots, and doing other maintenance, we moved over to the Unalaska side of the harbor for the mixed pleasures of a night up in the Elbow Room. For myself, a greenhorn, the Elbow Room was a place to hear sobering tales of wind and ice, boats and men competing in as tough an environment as there was anywhere. When we walked in that night, ready for pub food, stiff drinks, and hopefully a bit of conversation, we found the same depressing scene we'd left a few days earlier—a few semicoherent locals slumped over the bar making desultory conversation amid intermittent juke box music. But John Hall and his crew from the *King and Winge* came in later and we quizzed them on how their season was going.

HALL'S BOAT, THE OLDEST in the king crab fleet, was at the time the most legendary of all Alaska fishing boats. Built in 1914 as a cannery tender, rigged with two masts and sails as well as a diesel engine, she was the boat that bucked through the ice to rescue the crew when the steam barkentine *Karluk*, part of the Canadian Arctic Expedition in the summer of 1913, became trapped in the ice off the northern coast of Siberia.

A few years later, in October 1918, she was involved in another rescue, this one tragic. The steamer *Princess Sophia* had left the gold rush port of Skagway, Alaska, with a full passenger load, including the crews of the upper

Yukon River paddle-wheeler fleet, done with their season, their steamboats pulled up on the banks for the winter. The bar was busy that night as they celebrated a return to the bright lights. But in the *Sophia*'s wheelhouse, Captain Leonard Locke was anxious. In the early dusk amid a snowstorm, he'd just gotten a glimpse of the lighthouse at Eldred Rock and was running on "time and compass," groping his way south. This was the way ships navigated in thick weather before the advent of modern electronic aids that we take for granted today. By knowing your speed and steering a compass course, you could track your position on a chart. However, on this night, the wind or the current carried him off course. And at 1 a.m. on the twenty-fourth, the *Sophia* drove hard onto Vanderbilt Reef, thirty miles northwest of Juneau. The *King and Winge* was one of the first rescue boats to arrive the next morning, ready to take off passengers and crew. But the weather was nasty, and the *Sophia* seemed to be resting firmly on the reef. Her owners made the fateful decision to wait until the weather improved before trying to get the passengers off.

It was a fatal error. After dark that day, the storm came on again, blowing hard from the north, driving the rescue fleet to the shelter of Tee Harbor, six miles north. After midnight, a terrifying radio call was heard: "For God's sake come quickly. We are sinking." But the night was too wild and the rescuers were unable to leave the harbor. In the morning, when the wind and snow finally relented, only the tip of the *Sophia*'s mast could be seen. The combination of high tide and strong winds had driven her off the reef and into the deep water beyond. Of the 343 passengers and crew, there was not a single survivor. It was the worse maritime disaster in Alaska history.

From then until 1962, the *King and Winge* worked up and down the coast in various fisheries and occupations, until being purchased by the Hall family in Newport, Oregon. The Halls were well-known Oregon commercial fishermen and used her to drag—tow a net along the bottom—off Newport for six years, until rumors of the riches to be had in the Bering Sea prompted them to rerig the Alaska veteran for yet another fishery.

John Hall, the present owner, was getting a reputation for being a fair, safe, but hard-driving skipper. As was obvious from the four or five days he took between crab trips out of Dutch, he knew his crew needed to relax as well. Such a break: sleeping late, wandering up to the Elbow Room in mid-afternoon for a long boozy evening was just what was needed following the day after day mind- and body-numbing routine of a crab trip. In later years, when the fleet grew and the competition became intense, such relaxed approaches to the fishery disappeared, and vessels and crews raced to get their share of the quota before it was filled.

Unlike the *Flood Tide*, the *King and Winge's* pilothouse stood aft and her accommodations forward. Everyone but John slept in upper and lower berths that made up the forward part of the foc's'le—one big happy family. Behind the bunks were a big table, galley area, head, or marine toilet, and the stairs up to the deck. John slept in a tight little stateroom in the wheelhouse. When they made long passages in rough weather, the drill at watch change was to call on the intercom down to the foc's'le to alert the new watch-stander to get ready for a dash across the deck, and then slow the boat down, his clue to emerge from the foc's'le, close the hatch behind him, and cross the open deck, hopefully in a break between waves. Even with the boat slowed down, crossing the deck in Bering Sea conditions could be a wet experience. More than one crewman got a bath before making it to the warmth and shelter of the pilothouse.

Their biggest challenge that winter, John told us, was the ice. The pack ice had pushed much farther south than usual, filling much of the Bering Sea from Siberia to Alaska with solid saltwater ice. Fishing had been spotty that winter as well. The worst part was that on occasion, the main concentration of crab seemed to be right along the edge of the ice pack. To set their gear where it would possibly be the most productive also exposed it to the vagaries of the pack's movement. If the wind stayed southerly, they'd be able to fish. But a northerly could bring such bitter cold that overnight the sea would freeze another half mile or so south overnight, locking their buoys in its grasp. The pack was on the move, and once the buoys were frozen in, they would be dragged along. Once the ice melted, John said, you could hire a plane to try to find the buoys. But the Bering Sea was so vast and plane charters were expensive, and if the pack had dragged the pots into deeper water, the buoys would probably be sucked down and the pots lost.

I was unfamiliar with the process of setting crab pots. John patiently explained it to me: setting the baited pots into the water in a wide pattern to determine where the crab were. Then once the crabs were located, setting the pots closer together over the spot that yielded the best catch. He explained that with a boat with more deck space, like the *Flood Tide*, and room to stack sixty or seventy pots, fishing on the edge of the ice pack was easier. If the pack started to move, we could simply pick up all or most of our gear in one very long day, stack it aboard, and move it south away from the ice. But the narrower *King and Winge* could only pack thirty pots at a time, and that with considerable effort. As John explained all this, I gained an appreciation for his talent in doing so well in such a boat.

A BEARDED STRANGER with a red, hard-looking face joined our table, with nods all around, while John was talking. He introduced himself when John was done. He was working at one of the crab plants until his boat arrived up from Oregon in a month or so. Then he told us a ghostly tale:

"Three years ago, I was on a tired ex-tug turned crabber, a real rust bucket of a boat. Kenny Haines was the captain, and we'd just gotten into the crab when it came up out of the north, all right. We'd just stacked a full load, and we started to ice up so bad we knew even running before it, we'd make ice faster than we could knock it off. And blowing northerly like that, there's no place to get out of the wind this side of Unimak Pass except Amak and we were too far away. So the only thing to do was to push right up into the ice, the edge of the pack, to get out of the seas, and just move south as the sea froze.

"Only it didn't work out quite like we planned. A bad bearing shut down the main engine for ten hours, and by the time we got it up and running again, we were frozen in. The goddamned ice was half a foot thick! Then there was this weird voltage spike that fried the radios. Stuck, we were, with the season winding down, and my family was about to get evicted from our place if I didn't make some money and send it to them. We were in a hell of a mess, I'll tell you, stuck there, and sometimes the boat would lurch from pressure waves coming through the ice. I was up in the wheelhouse, pissed, just listening to the snow hissing against the glass and now and again to the creak of the pressure of the ice against the hull. Then . . . "

Jerry, his name was, paused, as if he weren't quite sure how to put what came next. "I musta' nodded off, but then something woke me, like this soft *thock*, like something hitting one of the pilothouse windows. I flipped on the crab lights—we were still having engine troubles so we were going easy on the generators. They blinded me for a moment. Then I saw this . . . guy standing out there. First I didn't believe it, thought the swirling snow was just creating ghosts or something. Then it cleared, and I saw him distinctly, a person for sure, dressed old-fashioned, and pointing ahead of the boat, about fifteen degrees off the starboard bow. So I looked where he was pointing, and you could see this lead, a narrow slit of open water in the ice pack, maybe fifteen, twenty feet wide at the most, the open water smoking in the bitter cold. The guy seemed to disappear after that. Not like he walked off, but one of those snow squalls blasted through after that, and when it was over, the guy was gone.

"So I banged on the skipper's door and showed him the lead in the ice. Kenny wasn't too excited about where it seemed to be leading, up toward where the thickest part of the ice was, but you know how those leads are, they can go anywhere. But at least it was a lead and we'd be moving. The way the ice was building and pushing against us, I'd started to get worried about propeller damage. I didn't tell the skipper about the guy on the ice.

"So we fired up the engine, and Roger, the other deckhand, and I suited up in our insulated coveralls and grabbed hand-held radios. We climbed over the side, with a safety line, and walked up ahead of the boat on this ice. Christ, with the blackness and the driving snow blinding white in the crab lights, there wasn't no visibility from the pilothouse, so we had to act like eyes. Kenny crunched her back and forth a few times, so we had a little space to get a run at the ice ahead of us. There was a pressure ridge we had to

break through before we could actually make it into the lead. He gave it to her good, but the ridge stopped us so we decided to wait until daylight so we could see a little better just what we were getting in to.

"Come daylight, that lead had opened up a bit, put a crack in the pressure ridge, so once we stuck our bow into it, we could kind of shove our way in and it opened up for us. I'd never been through a lead in the ice. I dunno if any crabber had. We were all up in the wheelhouse, watching, and going slow. Most places the lead was thirty to forty feet wide and we could slide through easy. Then other places the ice would come together and almost meet, and we'd have to shove like hell to get through. For an hour or so, it led north, and we were pretty uneasy. Then, it swung west for an hour, and twice

CRABBERS AT THE TRIDENT Seafoods plant, St. Paul, Pribilof Islands, 1998. In later years, processing plants located in "the Pribs" allowed boats fishing the central Bering Sea a closer place to deliver than Dutch Harbor. But its more northerly location meant that the harbor iced heavily in winter, making maneuvering challenging. DARYL KYRA LEE PHOTOGRAPH, ACCENTALASKA.COM

the lead got real narrow, and we had to batter our way through, like backing up to get a running start and hitting it hard—not my favorite thing to do with a hull built in 1946. But then the direction of the lead changed again, from west to south, and that was a good sign. 'Course it was still snowing like hell, and we could barely see a hundred feet in any direction.

"Then all of a sudden we broke free! We were cheering. There still wasn't any visibility, so we put it on the slow bell and headed sou'west, where we knew the rest of the fleet had been on the crab. Three, four minutes, then bam! Ice again! We turned and followed it for a few minutes, curving around to north again, and then Kenny was swearing and pointing out the window. It was the lead we'd come in on. You could tell because there were smears of copper bottom paint on either side of it. And it was closing up. As we watched, the two sides came silently together, until all that was left was a dark line of copper paint, wandering off toward the north until it was lost in the swirling white. We were trapped in this little pool of open water, maybe twenty or thirty acres.

"Hell, no radios, no lorans, pack ice all around us, it was ugly in the pilothouse after that. Snowing and blowing, you couldn't see shit. We could'a been two-hundred yards from open water or two miles, but whatever it was, that ice around us was solid. It would have taken an icebreaker to get us out of there, and we didn't even know where the hell we were even if we could have called somebody. When the wind came, I got out and drove an iron rod into the ice. We tied a line onto it and just shut off the main, laying out in the middle of that little lake moored to the ice.

"I saw the guy again that night. I was on anchor watch, around 3 a.m. We had all the lights off and I was looking for a plane, figuring I'd send up a parachute flare if I saw one. A half-moon was sitting low in the east when something on the ice caught my eye. It was the same guy, I was sure of it. The snow had stopped but the breeze was picking up the loose snow on the ice and it sort of flowed around the guy, giving him this ethereal look, but it was definitely the guy.

"He was right on the edge of the ice and pointing down into the water. It was unmistakable—he was lifting his hand up and then pointing it down insistently to the dark water at his feet. His lips were moving too—he definitely was saying something, so finally I went outside—way up to the bow, and leaned out over the railing to try and hear what it was.

" 'Set 'em!' I was positive that's what he said, very distinctly. And it was in that Norwegian accent that I'd heard over the years from the boat decks of half a dozen boats with Norwegian squarehead skippers. 'Set 'em!' It came again, the guy pointing down into the water to make sure I understood what he meant. Then he was gone, moving away and disappearing in the swirling snow.

"Kenny thought I was crazy when I woke him up and told him I thought we should set the gear. I didn't tell him about the guy.

" 'Set 'em?' he said. 'Jesus Christ, man. First you get this wild hair up your ass and we follow this lead to Jesus knows where, probably miles from open water, and now, at three a.m. you want to set the gear through some little hole in the goddamned ice?'

" 'Kenny,' I said, 'you heard what those guys said before the radios got fried, the hottest fishing was right along the edge of the ice, and the ice was moving south.'

" 'Yeah, but that was days ago and this goddamned ice front stretches for hundreds of miles. And how the hell many pots could you set in a place like this? Fifty, sixty? What the hell would that do?'

" 'Kenny, for Christ's sake, think about it,' I told him. 'The clock's running, the season's winding down, we've got gear stacked on deck, and there's water around us. I sure as hell know one goddamned thing: those pots won't catch any crab sitting on deck. And I'll tell you something else. I was on the *Seven Seas* when we got into crab so thick we loaded up with just 55 pots, set in some little sweet spot, and loaded up 60,000 pounds in a day and half.'

"That got his attention. Hell, I thought everyone'd heard those stories of how thick the crab could be. Sure we were stuck in the ice, but what the hell was wrong with setting a few pots, just to see what the hell was down there."

"Did you tell him about the guy?" I asked.

"Naw, I didn't dare. It was just one of those things I felt I'd better keep to myself. Besides, I was already on the crew's shit list for following that lead like we did."

" 'Jerry,' Kenny finally said, 'the ice might be moving. We could set the gear and this spot's so small, five or six hours and the whole shooting match might get sucked under the ice. Sayonara fifty or sixty thousand bucks.' "

" 'OK,' I told him, 'let's just set one, fer crissake. You won't even have to get out of your bunk, we'll just dump it over the side, and leave the buoys tied to the boat. Then, in the morning, if the ice has sawed them off, at least we tried. And it's a hell of a lot better than just sitting here, waiting for the season to end and doing nothing.' He went for it, and it took us exactly an hour to free one pot from the ice, knock the ice off the buoy line coils, get a couple of bait jars loaded up and hooked on, and finally launch that seven-by.

"I couldn't sleep. Finally at eight, still black, moon down, I got Kenny and the guys up. Man, I want to tell you, I felt like I was really on the spot, setting a pot in the middle of the night. If it was a blank, I was going to look pretty foolish.

"We stood there in a little circle, looking down into the dark water as the hauler strained with the load and the pot line came up from the blackness, looking like this shining column of liquid. Surprised us how deep it was there. That whole part of the Bering Sea is pretty much one flat plain, fifty to sixty fathoms deep, but there was a deep hole there, almost down to seventy.

"Finally the bridle broke water and you could see down into the pot. Christ, man, it was so totally, I mean totally, full the meshes were bulging, full of crab, and from what we could see, they appeared to be big males—keepers. I mean we just gaped. I think I was the only guy who'd ever seen a pot like that. Finally we hoisted it aboard onto the launcher, and Kenny was down on the back deck with us with the crab measure. He opened the door on the pot and measured and threw crab into our tank for a good thirty seconds before he turned around to face us.

" 'Jesus,' he said, in this awe-struck voice, 'them's all keepers. Let's empty this sucker and get the rest of the pots in the water.' Then he turned to me, 'I thought you were nuts, you know that, but you might just save our ass.' "

(To be legal, a king crab has to be six and a half inches wide, measured across the widest part of its back. We used a stainless steel measure, a device you held in one hand that had two prongs with exactly six and a half inches between them. If it fit over the widest part of the back of the shell, the crab was too small to keep. Females, which were illegal, were much smaller and obviously different. Generally you could eyeball the size of males pretty easily, and only have to measure those that appeared close to the minimum size.)

"It was almost dark again—those days are so short up there—before we got sixty-two pots into the water. We had another twenty on deck, but there wasn't any place to put them without tangling the buoy lines and making it impossible to maneuver. Then, when we were in the galley eating, all of us excited for the first time since the season started, Kenny came downstairs and said he'd gotten one of the radios working—not transmitting, but at least he could listen. He said Fish and Game had announced the closing of the season, in just forty-eight hours. 'So get a good sleep, guys, we're going to start hauling at 4 a.m., and if there's any crab in those pots, we'll just haul around the clock until they close it.'

"It was snowing when we started. We were so excited that I don't think any of us had slept. The first pot came up like the one the day before—totally full of crab, jammed full, the meshes bulging. There were no females, rarely a male small enough that you had to use the measure. After the first dozen pots, we would go over to the rail and peer down into that black water and just wonder what lay on that cold and black bottom almost 600 feet under us. *Every pot was like that! Totally full!*

"Cookie had made coffee cakes, and every four or five hours we'd take fifteen, shovel down a quick sandwich, a coffee, a big piece of coffee cake, grunt in pure animal satisfaction, and stumble out again to keep hauling.

"With twenty hours to go, the after hold was filled: 45,000 pounds. My back was hurting bad from all the bending over with the crab, but when I thought of my family and that they wouldn't be evicted from our home, that pain just went totally away. Finally, with just three pots to go, and forty-five minutes before the season ended, Kenny came out of the pilothouse and called down to us. We could barely look up we were so tired. Kenny was pointing at the last three buoys that were sitting oddly against the very edge of the ice. As we swung around to try and go in and grab them, they sank lower and lower in the water, and then they popped under the ice just like that. You could see a little color on the ice, and then the buoys were gone. The ice had started to move! Dunno why it wasn't moving before, but hell, three pots was a cheap price to pay for the load we got.

"And just like it was meant to be, the wind started to blow from the south that night when I was on anchor watch—we were laying to that iron rod in the ice again. I'd turn on the crab lights now and again, trying to see if that guy was out there, but if he was, I couldn't see him. By morning, we could start to feel the swell again, which meant that we weren't too far from the edge of the pack. We were all aching from working forty-eight hours straight on deck, but that was sweet pain for what we got out of it. By dark, things started to happen. Instead of just a white plain in all directions, the ice to the south became laced with dark leads that were getting larger as we watched. Finally, we picked the widest one that seemed to lead the farthest south, and pushed into it, just taking it easy. Half an hour later we were in open water!

"We only had a rough idea where we were, but there's no rocks in the Bering Sea except close to the islands, so we just steamed sou'west and pretty soon picked up the land, just east of Unimak, and seven hours later we pulled into Dutch.

"Turned out we were high boat—that trip put us over the top. After that Kenny offered me skipper's job for the tanner crab season. After twenty years on deck, I finally got my break. And all because of some guy on the ice that I thought I saw." He shook his head. The story seemed to be over.

At the table, no one said anything. But after a while, I had to ask: "Did you ever tell anyone about seeing that guy? Did you ever see him again?"

"Ahh," he said. "I tell crabbers sometimes—they know what it's like out there in the ice. And a year later, I told Kenny. But you know the funny thing? By Christmas that year, I'd pretty much convinced myself that I'd been imagining things. I live in Ballard, the Norwegian section of Seattle, where all the squarehead fishermen live. I was out shopping with my wife and the kids. We were eating lunch at some restaurant where the walls were decorated with pictures of old fishing boats. I always like those old pictures. There was one of the *Lindy*, the *Northern*, and the *Tordenskjold*, all boats I'd fished on, all tied up at the dock at False Pass, before I was born, with the bay all feather-white behind them, and the snow right down to the hills in the distance. Then, I saw this picture of the *Zapora*, the first 'smoke boat'—the first boat with an engine built especially for the halibut fishery, in 1904. The picture was taken in Ketchikan, and the boat was tied to the halibut buyer's dock there. She was iced up real heavy, hull and rigging covered thick. The caption said they'd just come in with a full load, 150,000 pounds, and her crew, grim with fatigue but triumphant at the same time, was standing on deck for the photographer.

"Then I saw him. It was the guy. He was the skipper, with the same full beard, wool pants, and sealskin jacket as the guy on the ice. He was the guy. I was sure of it. But it couldn't be.

"So, did I see him? Who the hell knows. But we were in deep shit, our family was losing our house. Was it my imagination—was it something that I wanted so bad, that somehow I made happen? I don't know. But this I know: the ice takes away. But the ice can give too. That's what we learned out there."

After a long while, John and his crew stood up. They were off in the morning for another battle with the ice and the wind and the crabs. We wished them luck and had another round before we headed out into the cold and blackness that awaited us just outside the double doors.

"You believe it?" I asked Russell, when we'd made it down the dark path, across the slippery dock and down the frozen ladder to our boat.

"Hell," he said, "you stay around the Elbow Room long enough, and you can hear just about anything."

"So you think it was bullshit? Not about the guy he saw, but about the lead and the ice and all the crabs?"

Russell scratched his chin for a bit before answering. "Well, I don't know the guy from Adam. But seems like I did hear something once. About some crabber that got stuck in the ice, found a little hole to set in, and made it big. Was he the guy? I dunno. I never fished around the pack. But I heard stories. The ice is a strange, strange place. Maybe things do happen there that no one can explain."

The CRABBER *NORTHWESTERN*, Puget Sound, around 1980. This crabber, a Marco 108 footer, is traveling in good weather in the inland waters of Washington State. This is a triple-stacked load of crab pots, a very risky load if there was a possibility of ice forming. The designer of the *Northwestern*, Bruce Whittemore, considers that in conditions where a crabber might encounter temperatures cold enough to cause ice to form on a vessels superstructure or crab pots, more than a single layer of pots is dangerous. Note the hydraulic crane by the men standing on the pots. This style of crane replaced the so called railroad boom that we had on the *Flood Tide*. In 1987, after ten years of crabbing, the *Northwestern* went through a major refit at Marco, adding ten feet to her length to allow her to carry more king crab pots, and remodeling her pilothouse, in addition to other upgrades. This boat is featured in the popular Discovery Channel series, *Deadliest Catch*. COURTESY MARCO.

8. The Ring of Fire

IN THE MORNING we began loading the last of our pots. We filled the deck, with row after row of six-bys, four abreast. Then we started stacking a second layer on top. And immediately we encountered an unintended consequence of our new pots-with-bags: moving around on top of the row of pots was very difficult. If we'd had traditional pots, footing on top of the stacked, placed pots would have been awkward; you tried to stay on the steel bars, but if your foot missed, the heavy nylon netting that made up the walls of the pots was stretched tight enough to give you pretty good footing. But with the bags, one end of the pot was cut away and in its place the bag was attached; to make it easier to move the pots around the deck, we stacked them with the cutaway end on top. This meant for very treacherous footing; you had to stay on the steel bars, and a misstep could mean that you'd tumble into the pot. Not only that but when we stacked a second layer of gear—they went flat— each pot had to be tied to the one below it in several places with short pieces of line, requiring us to get down on our hands and knees on that uncertain footing.

Where we wanted to fish was 200 miles east of Dutch—twenty hours steaming and we had a lot of gear to move, 150 pots in all. We were anxious to get the gear out there and fishing. If we triple stacked—just fifteen pots on the very top row—we'd be able to move all our gear in two trips. By triple stacking the gear, however, we definitely were getting outside of our comfort zone, regarding stability.

IN 1971, MAINTAINING stability was an inexact science, especially in heavy icing conditions such as we experienced on the way up. As the fishery grew in later years, vessels less well designed than ours came to get in on the boom. Some skippers with less than a full understanding of vessel stability issues would load their boats with four and five, even six layers of pots. One brand-new, heavily loaded crabber capsized and sank just a few miles north of the locks near Seattle's Fishermen's Terminal in flat calm weather when the automatic pilot malfunctioned and put the rudder hard over. Other vessels capsized when they iced up with pots stacked high on board. Fine vessels were lost, sometimes with their whole crews.

Faced with these tragic and costly losses, the insurance industry and the Coast Guard worked together to develop a stability test. Called an inclining test, a series of weights were hung from a boom a fixed distance off the vessel's side, and the degree of heeling, or inclination of the vessel, was measured. The test measured the vessel's resistance to capsizing and its overall stability. The data would be worked up for crab boats into a table to be posted in the wheelhouse showing how many pots could be carried in summer, winter, and winter icing. In theory, skippers would not load their vessels beyond these limits. Yet, it was common knowledge that as the crab fishery grew and skippers and owners faced increasing financial pressures of huge boat payments, greater competition, and smaller quotas, skippers would load their vessels beyond the stability table limits on occasion, hoping that the weather gods would smile on them.

FOR US, IN THAT STORMY, cold March of 1971, stability tables did not exist, and we loaded a full second layer and another twelve or fifteen pots for a third layer. Yet, still fresh in our memories was how the *Flood Tide* felt that night off Cape St. Elias, how quickly we had iced up, and how close we probably had come to capsizing. That night, none of our pots had been rigged with buoy line and buoys. To jettison them would have meant losing them. But now, all our pots were rigged, so if we started icing up and the water were shallow enough, we

The crabber *Shelikof* unloading salmon to the processing ship *All American*, Bristol Bay, 1991. This load of crab pots was the highest stack I had ever seen. The crabber is working as a salmon tender after the crabbing season had closed, and probably didn't have time to offload the crab pots somewhere before she started the charter. To travel in the winter with a load of pots like this would be extremely risky. This is a so-called mud boat, built to service oil rigs in the Gulf of Mexico, delivering both drilling mud, sections of drill pipe (hence the long aft deck), and other supplies. Wide (and therefore more stable than a narrower boat) and long, a number were converted to successful king crabbers.

would have another choice: set the pots over the side. By staying within a couple of miles of land until we got to Unimak Pass, we'd be in less than seventy-five fathoms of water—we'd rigged our pots with 100 fathoms of buoy line—so in a pinch, we could set the gear, probably without even time to bait the pots. It was chilling to think of working on top of that stack of crab pots, trying to keep our footing on the icy bars, with the pots trying to slide back and forth as soon as we loosened the lines. But at least it was a workable survival plan if we encountered dangerous icing conditions that threatened the boat.

Finally, on March 15, we were about as ready as we were ever going to be. George had a weather fax in the wheelhouse, and each night as our departure came closer, we'd download the latest map and study it. The typical Bering Sea weather pattern in the late winter is a constant battle between low-pressure systems moving up from the Gulf of Alaska—basically the North Pacific Ocean—and high-pressure systems moving east from Siberia. When the pressure was high, the wind was northwest and bitterly cold. When the pressure was low, it meant southeasterly winds and snow. In other words, good weather in the Bering Sea was a relative thing. When we topped off our water tanks at the cannery dock, it was 26°F and blowing twenty. We knew that once we got a few miles from the land, the temperature would go up slightly in a southerly, but the winds would probably pick up as well. Possibly we would experience light icing, but probably nothing to worry about.

Immediately after leaving the dock for an extended trip offshore, we all had our jobs. Russell and I squared away the back deck. We double-checked all the lashings on the pots. The ones on top had to be especially tight, because if they could slide back and forth at all, even a couple of inches, they eventually would work their lashings loose. The extra coils of buoy line on the boat or upper deck behind the pilothouse had to be tied tightly, the claw on the anchor chain had to be bar tight, and lastly, on this particular trip, I took out three fifty-pound boxes of frozen herring from the bait freezer, and set them on the back deck to thaw underneath the shelter of the upper deck.

In the engine room, Johnny checked all his pressures and temperatures, made sure all tools were put away securely, the bilge pumped, and the aluminum diamond plating around all the engines was dry and clean. In an engine room, with lots of sharp edges and spinning belts and pulleys, rough weather and slippery deck plates were a dangerous combination.

Missouri Bob put down the rubberized antislip matting on the galley table that would keep our plates and mugs from sliding around, returned the magazines to the holders, made a fresh pot of coffee, and baked a pineapple upside-down cake. Coffee and snacks would be always available.

When each of our jobs was done, we took a coffee and ascended the stairs into the pilothouse. It is almost a tradition—after the going-away jobs were done, to go up, look out and around, study the chart, and muse with each other about the trip ahead. It was almost dusk; ahead of us were fifteen hours of steaming to reach the area where we would start fishing. To the south, in the failing light, was a sobering scene. Behind Priest Rock, the 200-foot spire that marks the entrance to Dutch Harbor, the snow-blasted land rose without a tree to 6,700-foot Makushin Volcano astern of us. As we passed the rock, we suddenly became exposed to the wind and the seas flowing through Unalga Pass to the southeast. We passed through the uneven chop of a tide rip, and, as if to warn us of what lay ahead, the first solid spray came over the bow, ran down the pilothouse windows, and turned to slush.

We were headed to an area of the eastern Bering Sea roughly 100 by 200 miles—larger than some small states. Fishermen call it the Compass Rose, because on the most commonly used chart, the compass is printed right on that area. Somewhere on that undulating undersea plain were the crab to fill our holds.

We were the newcomers in town, fishing a big, fancy, expensive boat. Except for George and Johnny, who'd fished a few trips to get to know the fishery, none of us had ever fished crab before. John Hall and the crew of the *King and Winge* had been courteous, but there had been no information offered about the where and when of the crab. They'd paid their dues. We hadn't.

We studied the chart. The eastern Bering Sea was bounded by the Alaska Peninsula to the south, Bristol Bay to the east, and the low, marshy mouths of the Yukon and Kuskokwim Rivers to the northeast. For the most part, the area was relatively shallow, 400 feet or less, compared to the western Bering Sea and its depths of more than two miles. There were only a few scattered Alaska Native settlements along the shores, and no roads that connected them. The landscape near the shore was generally marshy tundra dotted by countless ponds.

In the summer, the inshore waters and river mouths of the North Peninsula, particularly Bristol Bay, would be full of salmon fishing vessels, fish buyers, floating processors, and the like. In Bristol Bay alone, 1,800 thirty-two-foot salmon gillnetters fished each summer, when, in a good year, 30 million valuable red salmon would arrive to make their way up the rivers to spawn in the lakes where they were born. When the fish were running, the river mouths would become floating cities—men and boats working day and night to harvest and process the fish. On shore, the canneries were little towns unto themselves, with bunkhouses, mess halls, stores, shops, and their

own airstrips—everything needed to support the fishermen and the processing workers in an isolated location.

Now, the fishing boats were all ashore, stored for the winter, the canneries deserted except for a caretaker. The fish-buying boats and floating processors were tied up in Seattle for the winter. The *King and Winge* and *Flood
Tide* would probably be the only vessels in the whole area.

When we started to fish, we would be prospecting—baiting our pots with
herring and setting them at long intervals, perhaps a mile or more apart, in
long lines crisscrossing the ocean floor beneath us. Leaving them overnight,
then hauling them back up, and sampling what was crawling on the bottom.
A lobster fisherman along the rocky coast of Maine might watch his depth
sounder carefully, setting his pots in little holes on the bottom where lobsters
might seek a bit of protection, venturing out only to feed. A cod fisherman on
Georges Bank off Cape Cod might tow his net along a specific route, a "tow"
from one specific loran coordinate to another. To stray off the tow would mean
ripping the net on rocks or wrecks. (Before GPS, or global positioning system, became the standard form of electronic navigation in the 1990s, the less
accurate loran system was used. The position-finding electronics of the day,
loran C, was a land-based system, transmitting signals from towers placed
along the coasts of the United States and many other countries. In 1971, the
transmitters were far from the all solid-state, dependable electronic units that
were the heart of the satellite-based system that would be common twenty
years later.) But the bottom of the eastern Bering Sea was almost featureless
without sharp humps or little deep holes that might provide a place for food
and crabs to gather. Only by prospecting would we be able to find the crab.

As we steamed along, Russell asked George what he'd found out in town
about where the crab were. George didn't answer for a bit, transferring positions from two columns of numbers on a scrap of paper to a wavering line he
was drawing on the chart.

"Here's the edge of the ice," he said finally, tracing his finger along a line
that ran from the shore of the Alaska Peninsula in a westerly direction to a
point south of the Pribilof Islands. "And here's Amak." His finger stopped on

a little dot of an island, about the only island in the southeast Bering Sea. "All I could find out was that John was fishing somewhere north of Amak."

"I could have told you that," Russell said, snorting. "South of Amak it shallows up to ten or twenty fathoms. Crabs are way deeper than that this time of year."

Just before midnight, I got my coffee and went up the pilothouse stairs to relieve Russell on watch. I closed the door behind me and just stood for a moment. The wind had eased, the sky was cloudy, and the stars hidden. The only lights were from the compass, the engine gauges, the radio, radar, and loran displays—all dimmed down.

"OK, kid, here's where we are." Russell snapped a switch and a cone of dim red light fell on the chart. He'd marked our course track lightly in pencil, with little cross ticks and hour notations. "Steering fifty-five degrees. The wind has let go, so we're not making any ice. There's the occasional ice pan out there, but nothing to worry about, we just slice right through it. If we start making ice again to any degree, try slowing down a bit. Any other issues, wake George. Big day tomorrow, and . . . oh," he said, nodding his head off to the right, "keep your eyes peeled. Pavlof's been puffing every now and then." And he was gone.

I looked off to the south through the side windows, but there was only blackness. Then I studied the chart for a bit, and then the radar, but the screen was showing only the occasional snow from sea clutter, our radar waves reflected back by the tops of seas around us. No land was to be seen anywhere, except for at the very bottom right of the screen, where there were a few faint targets. It was a bit of a surprise, and I got out the dividers and checked the chart to make sure. We were about forty-four miles away from the nearest land, Unimak Island, and all that our forty-eight-mile range radar could pick up was Mount Pavlof and her sisters.

It was an odd feeling, being without the comforting shape of the land just a few miles away like it had been always on the trip up North. Over the chart table, the loran display was flickering numbers—filaments in little glass tubes. This was before the advent of the ubiquitous LCD displays used in marine electronics today. I double-checked the numbers against our penciled position on the chart to make sure they matched, and finally sat in the big comfortable skipper's chair with my coffee.

On the *Flood Tide*, the routine for the guy on watch was pretty much the same as on the old *Sidney*, except there were no fish temperatures or big refrigeration system to monitor. Every hour, I'd don the big ear protectors at the top of the engine room stairs and go down, for a walk-around. We had some engine room instrumentation up in the pilothouse—rpm's, temperatures, and pressures—but it was best to go down every hour into the engine room and stand by the big General Motors 12V-149 main engine and 6-71N generator (we had two, but used just one at time) to watch, listen, and feel for anything out of the ordinary. That way, you could find a leak or another problem before it showed up on the gauges up in the pilothouse.

Then at 3:40 a.m., twenty minutes before the end of my watch, something caught my eye out the starboard windows of the pilothouse, way off to the south. At first it was a small, dim, reddish-pink patch of sky, low on the horizon. I remembered what Russell had said about Mount Pavlof and realized it must be some sort of volcanic activity reflected on the clouds. It faded away and then was gone, and there was nothing but black again. Then it reappeared: a bright and sharply defined streak of red on the horizon, lighting up the clouds before fading away to black again. There was no sound. I had seen an eruption.

It wasn't huge, and it was strangely silent but stunning nonetheless. Yet there was something otherworldly about it as well. It was as if as we traveled in a black, lightless world, guided only by flickering electronic numbers. As if something had happened to the rest of the world, and what was out there was an earlier, prehistoric world, with volcanoes throwing out hot lava.

In the morning, while we were still an hour away from where we would begin our prospecting, my first job was to bait up. I chopped the fifty-pound blocks of frozen herring into bite-sized pieces for the crab and then stuffed the pieces into the plastic screw-top bait jars, with the little holes punched in them to let the herring juice out, which we had made on the trip from Seattle.

If I'd been on a crew a few years later, chopping bait would be very different: feeding the fifty-pound blocks into the bait chopper, whose hydraulically powered steel blades made short work of the frozen herring. But in 1971, on the *Flood Tide*, we did it the old-fashioned way. The tool was an axe head welded to the end of a piece of heavy walled, two-inch-diameter steel pipe. The whole unit probably weighed fifteen pounds and I supplied the power. And taking the frozen herring out "to thaw" was a huge exaggeration; overnight the freezer actually might have been warmer for the herring than the back deck. By the time I'd driven the chopper into the herring enough times to break it up into small enough pieces to put in the quart bait jars, I felt like I was ready for shoulder surgery—and the hard work on deck with the crab pots hadn't even started.

The day was angry, the wind was cold with spits of driving snow, and the sea was rough. We were traveling at full speed and on occasion solid water would land on the boat deck above me and sluice down into the tight space I was working in, so I had to keep my hood up as well. Once in a while a big one would smack into us and we'd lurch sideways. Welcome to the Bering Sea.

With fifteen minutes to go, Russell, Johnny, and Missouri Bob came out on deck to get the gear ready to set. My bait jars were ready. As the youngest and most agile person, it fell to me to go up on the top of the pot stack to hook the winch line onto the first of the row of tripled-stacked pots.

"Wait." Russell put his hand on my shoulder as I stared to climb up. He had to speak loudly to be heard over the bark of the engine exhaust above our heads. "You got a knife?"

I nodded, but not really understanding.

"Where?" he said.

I patted my pocket.

"Not good enough," Russell said, opening his rain gear jacket and revealing a strong nylon cord tied to the left suspender of his bib-style rain gear pants. As I watched, his right hand went up, pulled on the cord, and a small black knife appeared at the end of the string. His gloved fingers grasped the blade, and in an instant, the knife opened.

"A loop of buoy line carries you over the side, and your knife's in your pocket, it's not going to do you much good." Russell's voice trailed off. I got the message, and took a moment to fix a similar lanyard to my knife and rain gear, and to adjust the length so that I could open it one-handed as Russell had done. "You gotta' think things through before they happen," Russell explained. "Your reactions need to be automatic. If you ever hit that water, everything in your body starts to shut down. After two minutes, your hands begin to stop working. Every second counts."

Sobered by his advice, I put my gloves back on and climbed carefully up the side of a pot and onto the top of the stack, making my way to the first triple-stacked pot. Once on top I could occasionally glimpse out over the tops of the seas closest to us—a grim scene of dark, steep, twelve- and fifteen-foot rollers, their tops blown forward by the wind, with here and there a bit of floating ice. It had begun to snow, and the visibility was shutting in. It was a grim sight, and I pulled my hood down, resolved to concentrate only on the job at hand.

ONE NOVEMBER NIGHT a few years later, a young crab fisherman named Mike Jackson from Poulsbo, Washington, was thrown overboard some-where south of the Pribilofs. "I was very lucky," he told me. "The skipper just happened to be looking out his back window and saw me. He threw the boat in reverse, knowing that it was the only way to get me aboard quickly but hoping that I wouldn't get sucked into the propeller. Then he ran down on deck and threw me a line just as I slid by, and skipper and crew horsed me aboard." They stripped Mike's clothes off and got him in a hot shower. An hour later, Mike was back out on deck. The work had to go on.

The next time they all sat down for a meal, Mike's crew talked about what would happen the next time and how they could be better prepared, how they could work together better to get a man back aboard. In the critical moments after Mike had gone overboard, the crew's reaction had been unco-ordinated and ineffective. Only by a fortuitous coincidence did the skipper happen to be looking out the back window of the pilothouse, wondering when they'd be ready to drop the pot, and realize what had happened. One of the critical issues, they realized once they started talking about it, was simply being able to see a guy in the water in the typically rough conditions and determining who it would be that would have the sole job of pointing where the man overboard was last seen.

Mike began wearing the flotation device his wife had given him—a device that had been under his bunk the night he went overboard, not worn because it required extra time to put on, was bulky and hot, and restricted movement. One night two weeks later, while they were stacking pots at the end of the season, he went overboard again. But this time he jumped. Mike had been working on the top of the stacked pots when another crewman, working to chain down the load of pots, had his arm crushed between pots when the boat rolled, and went over the side.

Mike, knowing the other man had been injured and wasn't wearing any floatation, instantly jumped in after his crewmate. This time, because the crew and skipper had talked about what to do, and because Mike, with his floatation, was high enough in the water to be seen, both men were rescued before the cold water killed them. But not before living the terror of looking up and back and seeing the scimitar-like propeller slashing through the water right above them as the crabber backed through the seas and finally stopped right next to them.

After that, Mike decided to try and make a flotation device that would be less bulky. He and his wife, Kathy, built a prototype at home: a vest with a bladder that you could inflate with a CO_2 cartridge. The first unit was a little rough, but Mike wore it, and most everyone who noticed it wanted one. The next winter, they went into modest production, making the pieces at home after they got back from their day jobs. They improved the design so that the vest would inflate simply by grabbing the pocket and pulling until the Velcro detached, and pulling a lanyard to puncture the CO_2 cartridge. They began taking the device around to regional marine stores. Eventually the business they called Stormy Seas grew enough for Mike to stop crab fishing, as their jackets and vests became the favored attire for Northwest fishermen.

 "TOSSING THE COIL" aboard the *Flood Tide*, 1971. Tossing the coil aboard a crabber is a job that requires a quick touch and a lot of caution.

9. We Become Crabbers

O N MARCH 21, 1971, somewhere between Amak Island and the edge of the pack ice, our first pot went into the water and our king crab season began.

On the *Flood Tide* we had added the long trailing bags to our pots, requiring a very different routine for launching. After the railroad boom and the crew-as-human-tractors brought the pots forward, we'd open the door, pull out the buoys and line, bait up, then hook the quick-release hook onto the bridle. Then while one of us stood with the buoy line ready, the pot was hoisted so that it hung over the side, with the bag trailing in the water. When George blew the whistle, Johnny pulled the quick-release lanyard, the pot dropped into the black water, Russell threw the first coils of buoy line quickly after it, watching carefully to make sure the line paid out smoothly, and finally threw the buoys over the side. Once the first few pots were launched, making room around the launching area, everything went a little easier and faster.

The tricky part is the buoy line. The 700-pound crab pot sinks quickly while the boat is accelerating, and unless watched closely, the buoy line can tangle or snag. The man at the rail must be ready to clear any tangles quickly, and then be ready to throw over the large, heavy buoys at the end. It's the tangles that you have to worry about. Sometimes the line whips around as it goes overboard. A careless crewman, who without knowing it has his foot over a loop on the line, can get whipped over the side before he even has time to shout. This scenario has been the end of more than one Bering Sea crabber.

In addition, the buoys are substantial. On the *Flood Tide*, we used a thirty-inch-diameter orange Polyform buoy (inflated heavy-walled poly-ethylene), a smaller twenty-four-inch-diameter white Polyform buoy, and an eighteen-inch-diameter solid foam buoy with a hard plastic skin called a seal buoy. Occasionally a seal will puncture a Polyform or other inflated buoy, but the solid foam seal buoy is unsinkable. The buoys must be lifted and thrown overboard, another risky task, with the line paying out rapidly and the deck moving at times violently.

THE WEATHER THAT first day soon deteriorated into a cold, sleety wind and an increasingly rough sea that made footing very difficult. With our hoods pulled snugly around our faces and the pucker strings pulled tight, our world was that small circle of vision directly in front of us. So it was difficult to see or hear what the others were doing and, against the constant bark of the main engine and the generator, to hear shouted commands.

The worst task was working on top of the pile of pots, to untie the ones that had been double and triple stacked. By the time I got down to the last three pots in the second layer, the steel bars that I had to crawl over were all black ice and the boat was lurching violently. I had to hook the line from the railroad boom onto the bridle and have the winch operator put a light strain on the line so that when I loosed the ties, the pot would move away from me. Otherwise I faced a 700-pound pot sliding back and forth along the icy steel bars, threatening to mangle me or push me over the side. By the time we got the last pot in the water, my long underwear was soaked with sweat and I was exhausted.

George headed for the shelter of Amak Island, and the rest of the crew left me to clean the back deck. Missouri Bob started supper, Johnny worked on his engine-room chores, Russell went forward to beat the ice off the anchor winch, and I gathered up the several hundred pieces of short line or ties used to lash the pots to the rails on the tops of the bulwarks, got out another couple of cases of frozen herring, and generally got everything ready for the next morning's fishing.

I was working around the stern, with a dozen or so ties in each hand, when the boat lurched, and I saw something out of the corner of my eye. I turned to see a particularly steep sea, one of those queer ones, rising over the starboard rail as we dipped sharply. Then the rail was underwater and the top of the big sea was almost on me. It happened so quickly I barely had time to react. I dropped the straps, moved quickly over to the steel framework that supported the stacking winches, and wrapped my arms around it while the cold Bering Sea swirled waist high and pulled at me. A moment later it was gone, over the port railing and draining out the wide ports along the bottom of the bulwarks. I stood there for a long moment, slowly relaxing my grip on the steel, and trying to drive a terrifying vision from my head: What if I hadn't turned around? The sea would have caught me by surprise, and before I could react or cry out, I would have been swept overboard. I saw myself alone, terrified, freezing, sinking as the *Flood Tide* disappeared into the mists and seas. How long before anyone noticed? Not until Amak? It wouldn't have mattered.

I suppose if commercial fishing had been governed by OSHA workplace rules, crabbers would be wearing harnesses while they worked deck, with safety lines attached to the boat. But in reality, such an arrangement would have been too restrictive.

I regathered the ties—about a third of them had washed through the scuppers and were gone. But I kept a thoughtful eye on the heaving, icy seas around the boat as I worked. I knew about queer ones, or rogue waves as some folks called them. Seas run in cycles, and are often caused by far distant storm systems. On occasion seas from two or even three separate storms, all with different sizes and distances between them, will arrive at the same time. In certain situations, the peaks of the waves in different cycles would coincide, creating a wave larger than either storm system would produce on its own.

On the forward end of our deck, on the port side, was an area protected by the overhang of the boat deck on top and the hull to port. The two huge

BEFORE THE U.S. declared a 200-mile fishing limit in 1977, fleets of very large foreign fishing vessels operated year round in the Bering Sea. Aboard this Japanese factory trawler, anchored in Dutch Harbor in 1971, fish are processed and frozen.

space heaters hung there that helped to keep a load on our diesel generators. The heaters were on just then, so it was reasonably comfortable as I put the straps away and got the bait out. But the scene astern was unsettling, even threatening. "Don't ever turn your back on the Bering Sea," someone down on the docks in Seattle had told me, I assumed in jest, as we were preparing

to get under way a month and a lifetime earlier. Now I knew that speaker had been deadly serious.

The door from the back deck into the living quarters would do justice to a submarine—heavy aluminum, gasketed, waterproof, with eight pressure-tight latches around the perimeter, and a porthole. Inside a vestibule, there were hooks for rain gear, bins for boots, stairs up to the pilothouse, and doors leading to the engine room stairs and galley. And, eat your heart out, *King and Winge*—a washer and dryer. They were also a bit of a reality check. It was easy, out on deck, to think we were tough, facing the Bering Sea in winter. But, to step inside when your hands were cold, and pluck another pair of gloves, toasty warm out of the dryer, brought us back to the fact that no matter how tough we thought we were, there were a lot of boats and crews out there that had it way rougher.

I sat on the wheelhouse stairs, pulling off the heavy rubber bands that we used to keep our boots and feet dry when seas came aboard. Then off came my jacket, bib-overall rain pants, which were hung on hooks on the wall. My boots went into a bin.

Stepping into the galley was as different from the grim world on deck as day was from night. Music played on the cassette player, the smell of baking bread and beef stroganoff was thick in the air, and Bob and Johnny chattered in conversation.

"Hey, mister Joe," said Bob cheerily, "nice evening out there?"

"Ahh," I said expansively, "ain't the Bering Sea grand on a night like this?" I poured myself a coffee, doctored it up, took a piece of the ever-present coffee cake, and let myself sink onto the upholstered U-shaped bench around the table, wondering if I could stay awake until supper.

The engine slowed just then and Russell got up. It was his signal that we were entering the anchorage and that he needed to put on his parka and gloves and go operate the anchor winch when George found the right spot.

I wanted to step outside and have a look at Amak, if there was anything to see, but exhaustion filled my limbs and all I could do was shovel down some hot food and hit my bunk.

Between the jog stick and the compass, in front of George's usual station in the wheelhouse when we were fishing, was a little mahogany holder for his Marlboro cigarettes. Essentially a dispenser, it held three packs, arranged so that when pack one was pulled out, the other two would drop down, ready for action. When I first noticed it, I thought it odd. But the next morning, when we started to haul the gear that we had set, to begin the tedious process of prospecting to find the crab, I understood. For George was a bit anxious, as anyone in his shoes would be, and so for each pot hauled up he would light a fresh smoke, come out on the boat deck behind the pilothouse, inhaling deeply, and look down onto the main deck below where we were working, watching the dark water and listening to the twanging of the buoy line as it sang under tension in the big Marco pot hauler. When the pot broke water, he'd take a big drag and wait for us to attach the hook and the safety line to the bridle so that it could be hauled up into the rack, revealing what was inside. That first day we barely caught a keeper. As each pot cleared the water, revealing only a handful of small crab too small to keep, George would jerk his head angrily toward the stern, his shorthand for "stack it," flip his half-smoked butt over the side, and throttle up for the next pot, often lighting yet another cigarette as he studied the chart laid out on the table.

For us, "stack it" meant the reverse of the tedious process we'd just finished the day before: we'd pull out the bait jars, tie off the coils of buoy line, hook up the stacking winch hook to the pot, and then keeping the pot facing the right direction as the winch pulled it to the stern, making sure the winch erected it in the right spot, and when the pot was in position, tie it off to its neighbors or to the side railing. As the youngest, I would accompany each pot to the stern and tie it off.

By 1 p.m. the temperature had dropped and the spray started freezing to the stacked pots on the stern. By 2 p.m., the motion of the boat made it increasingly difficult and dangerous to haul the incoming pots up into the heavily built rack above the sorting bin. Leaving the stored pots on the back deck would be foolish when they could be in the water prospecting for us, so after an abruptly shouted "I'm steaming for a few minutes and then we'll dump those," the three of us took shelter under the overhang of the boat deck as the boat accelerated and swung to the north. Forty-five long minutes passed. The sweat under my garments turned chilly and I began to shiver. Finally the *Flood Tide* slowed, and George appeared, cigarette in hand, on the deck above us: "We'll start dumping them."

Once again we started the cycle, but now there was heavy ice on all the pots. I pounded the ties with gloved fist to loosen the ice, then untied each pot, reached up to grab the top steel bar, and then with all the energy I had, tipped the pot forward, being extremely careful to stay to the side as the 700-pound monster tilted from vertical to fall flat onto the deck. I hooked the line from the railroad boom, accompanied the pot as it was pulled forward, then switched hooks to the line from the picking boom winch, worked with the roll of the boat to swing the pot so that it was hanging over the side, opened the door, clipped in the bait jars, closed the door, and then headed back for another pot, while at the hauler controls Russell got ready to pull the quick release when George tooted the horn.

In a traditionally rigged boat, you'd simply let the boom winch pull the pot forward. However, because our pots were rigged with the bags, the bridle end of the pot was down, so we had to drop the pots on deck before hooking them up. And all the while the boat lurched from side to side, with the seas slopping up across the decks.

Finally it was done, and George appeared briefly above us and yelled down into the gathering gloom, "Hey Joe, go get those ties," waving toward the stern, "but as soon as you've got them all, I'm going to run up to the north to have a look before going back to Amak, so stay sharp." The others disappeared through the steel watertight door into the coziness of the house. But I'd learned my lesson the day before. In this case, "stay sharp" meant to stay under the shelter of the overhanging boat deck, filling bait jars, until we'd turned downwind for the easier ride back to Amak. It was then and only then that conditions would be safe enough back there for me to finish cleaning up.

We slowed down to an idle after a long half-hour, and I moved over to the winch-control station, by the pot hauler, where I could look out but still be protected by the angle of the hull going up to the boat deck, in case a queer one tried to get me.

I didn't know what George was looking for out there in that limitless expanse of sea and wind and flying spray. *King and Winge*'s buoys? I knew that it would be truly remarkable if we found one in that vast plain of the eastern Bering Sea where you can run for hours and hours with the bottom so flat that the line of your fathometer barely moves. Was he listening for something? Sensing? I couldn't guess, but only after a long while did I feel the boat surge ahead as if the throttle had been pushed angrily forward, and we swung around downwind for an easier ride back to Amak.

By the time we got to the island, visibility was almost zero in driving snow. Head down, hood up, pucker strings pulled tight, I crept up to the bow to drop the anchor when George tooted the horn. I let the chain and heavy wire run out, set the brake at George's dimly seen nod though the pilothouse windows, and finally, when I'd felt the boat lurch as the anchor grabbed and set itself securely on the bottom, set the dog, a short steel bar that locked and kept the winch drum from moving. And all that time, the driving snow was so thick that I never even saw the dark water's surface just twelve feet below our bow.

In that early part of the season, when the days were still short and I was still genuinely excited at what each day would bring, I'd get up before the others, make myself a coffee, walk quietly up into the pilothouse, and just sit, or walk slowly back and forth, looking out at the austere scene of Amak beyond the bank of windows, studying the chart, reading up on where we were in the *United States Coast Pilot, Volume 9: Pacific and Arctic Coasts of Alaska from Cape Spencer to Beaufort Sea*.

From the rugged shore bulging with what must have been huge snow-covered boulders, the land rose in steep bluffs to a dead volcanic cone, glimpsed, then lost in the swirling snow. We lay at the only anchorage, about a half-mile off the east side. The *Coast Pilot* said there had been a World War II airstrip in the island's only flat area, on the south side, but any sign of man was obliterated by the wind and the snow.

IN THE MORNING, outside all was dark and cold, but at least the snow had stopped. Now it was just sleet. The five of us sat at the table, shoveling in eggs and bacon and toast—lots of carbohydrates and fat—fuel for what lay ahead. The guys had a relaxing smoke while I was on anchor duty again, the bitter wind driving the sleet into my face, waking me up far more than the coffee had.

"What's the weather like out there, Joe?" came the question from the smoke-filled galley when I came in. I just pointed at the salty spray and sleet still frozen to my oilskin pants as I slumped onto the nice soft bench.

Then came more muscle-stretching and the mind-numbing monotony of pick and stack, George looking down, the pots coming up with slim pickings, the cigarette blown to windward, the thumb jerked toward the stern. Tie off the buoy line coils, throw them inside, pull and stack and tie, and hustle back just in time as the next pot clanks up into that awkward, dangerous rack over our heads.

In the breaks, when George was running between pots and chain-smoking and studying the chart, and he told us to take a coffee break, there would be time for stories. Russell and Johnny had been fishing off the Alaska and British Columbia coasts for years. Bob had put in his time in the Gulf of Mexico as well. That morning's tale was from Johnny, about a skipper who took his poodle to sea and about the crew that didn't care for it.

"Shitty little dog had no place on the boat, but he was skipper's pet and that was that. But one day we were prospecting—just like we're doing now, no damned crab, pick and stack, pick and stack, run and set, pick and stack, all the goddamned day, shitty weather, everyone in a pissy mood. Just as we were about to set the last pot in the last string of the day, the goddamned poodle runs out on the back deck and takes a big dump, right by where you stand for the winch controls. The mate didn't even think, just grabbed that dog by the scruff of his neck, opened the door of the pot, and threw him in. We were just so taken aback that we stood there gawking, and then the skipper hit the horn to launch the pot, and away she went . . .

"We started cleaning up the deck and the skipper started jogging for Amak—just like we were—and then the skipper came out on the back of the boat deck, hollers "Anyone seen little Fifi?" or whatever the hell she was called.

"Of course, we all played dumb—it had been rough all morning, with green water across the deck a couple of times, so we told him the last time we'd seen little dipshit was earlier when we were setting gear in that rough patch about two hours back.

"So, we stop and search the boat, bow to stern and wheelhouse to engine room, and no Fifi. Now the skipper was in a really bad mood, and we're all getting a bit pissed at the mate, even though anyone would have done what he did if given the chance.

"But finally skipper just accepted it and we turn back for the night at Amak again. We ran for a half hour, got the back deck cleaned up, and moved down into the galley for a mug up, when down the stairs the skipper comes and says, 'Suit up again, boys, I want to move that last string before we head in for the night.

"Oh, shit, are we toast, we figured, because on a string like that, you know he's gonna be right above you on the boat deck looking down into the pot, and when she comes up, he'll see little drowned Fifi.

"We suit up in our rain gear, and hook onto that last buoy, and we're standing there with the buoy line a'singing in the block, and the mate looks around at us and says, 'Well boys, sorry. We ain't got jobs no more.'

"Then the pot broke water and it was solid crab, three-quarters full in just an hour and no evidence of the little fur ball either."

"We left the string setting where it was, and when we came back to haul them the next morning, it was still just that one pot that had any crab in it, and when we'd got them all out, there still wasn't any sign of little Fifi."

George tooted the horn to alert us that he was about to come up on a set of pot buoys, and we settled back into the routine again: pick and stack, run and set, one pot blurring onto the next, a few crabs but no real volume. About 2 p.m. a norther' slammed into us. That first gust must have been sixty knots, picking up the tops of the seas around us and filling the air with them. In five minutes, the temperature had dropped twenty degrees and everything started icing up bad. George appeared above us and in one word stated the obvious: "Amak."

By the time we made it into the shelter of the south side of Amak, ice had encased the entire back deck area—rails, pot hauler, pot winches, even the wooden decking that received regular flooding. And that was running with the wind. If we'd had to buck into it, it would have been much worse. The anchorage at Amak, while providing shelter from the seas, was still exposed to a wind from the north that drove into the anchorage over the shoulder of the mountain. It was my turn to drop the anchor again. Even with my hood pulled tight around my face, exposing just a circle of flesh, I was totally chilled and my cheek burned with frostbite in the few minutes I had to stand on the bow waiting while George maneuvered the boat into the spot where he wanted to anchor.

When we lay in our bunks that night, over the sound of the generator I could hear the howl of the wind, clawing around the boat. It was Uyak Bay all over again. The wind was so insistent that I pulled on my clothes and ascended the stairs into the wheelhouse to peer out. Outside, our big quartz iodine crab lights turned night into day, revealing the bleak sight of Amak rising from the smoking sea a quarter-mile away. As I watched, snow would erupt from the steep mountain flank and spin across the water before slamming into us, and the steel anchor cable would groan as it moved across the anchor roller, becoming taut as a steel bar as the boat surged with the push of the wind.

In another situation, in such weather, we might have had someone on anchor watch to start the main engine instantly and wake the rest of the crew if the anchor might drag. But where we were that night—in the lee of Amak, with ten miles of Bering Sea between us and the next land on the Alaska Peninsula—the wind was steady from the northwest, blowing fifty to seventy with occasionally higher gusts. If our anchor did drag, we would move southward and eventually out into open water, where the motion of the boat would instantly signal us awake.

Still, the wind played on me, and in my mind's eye: I was asleep, the anchor had dragged, and no one had awakened. We'd been pushed across the ten miles of sea to the south of us, and were suddenly in the surf off the

Kudiakof Islands, with Izembek Lagoon beyond, the spray turning to ice, and no one for many miles to help us. It was a frightening vision, and it was a while before I convinced myself that all was well and I went back to sleep.

"There was this guy on the radio yesterday," George told us at breakfast. "Norwegian, squarehead, thick accent. He kept calling me, but his accent was so thick that I didn't understand even who he was trying to call. Finally I realized he was calling *Flood Tide*. '*Flood Tide, Flood Tide*, ve ar two, ve ar two, how many are you? Ve ar two, how many are you?'

"Finally I got it, he was asking how many we had on board, so I asked what boat they were in, told him we had five. He was calling from one of those Martinolich eighty-six footers, nice steel rig, just the skipper and one other guy, his brother, he said. No emergency, he just wanted to chat. But Jesus, just think of it—two guys alone on an eighty-six footer. The skipper's got to come out onto the back deck to help with each pot. Those Norwegians . . . if there's an easy way and a hard way to do something, they always take the hard way."

"Ahhhh, yes," Johnny said, "but think of the crew share."

Cribbage, a book, up into the pilothouse to stare out at the wild scene beyond the windows. So the day passed. To have struggled up the coast as we did, hustled into Dutch Harbor to get all our pots rigged and aboard, seen *King and Winge* unloading a good trip, not finding any volume of crab, and then to get blown in to Amak was immensely frustrating.

Two days of fishing, a day at Amak. Two days at Amak, a day of fishing. A week passed without finding a significant bunch of crab. Each day we fished, we'd stack and move, set again and wait overnight, pick and stack, and move again. This didn't seem to be the crab fishery that we'd heard about, with the big scores we were eager to share.

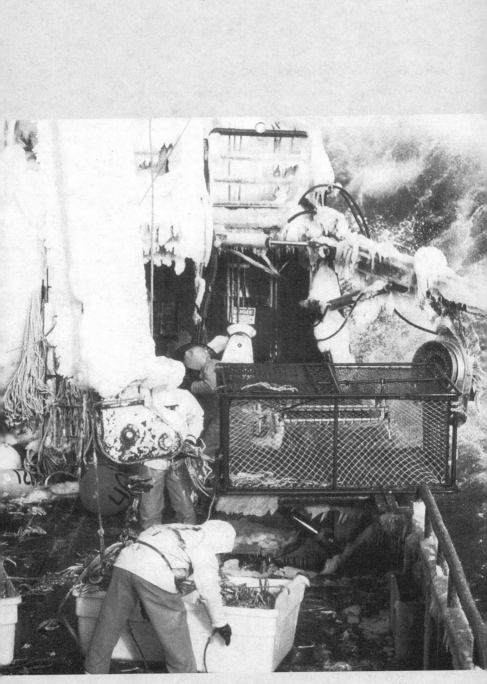

 CRABBER WORKING IN ICING CONDITIONS, Bering Sea, circa 1980. Note how badly iced the boom of the knuckle crane is. BART EATON PHOTO

10. Into the Ice

W E'RE TAKING A FLYER," George announced at the end of one particularly discouraging day, when we were back on the anchor at Amak. "The weather is supposed to ease for a day or two, so tomorrow we've gonna stack a load and take it up to the edge of the ice."

"And hope the wind doesn't catch us," Johnny said.

We all knew what he meant—stacking a load of pots that time of year was risky. If there was one thing we had learned on the way up to Dutch was that icing conditions can come up incredibly fast, and getting caught in a bitter wind and building sea with a big load of pots wasn't a situation any of us wanted to see ever again.

Yet we stacked, crossed our fingers, and ran north. The wind was twenty-five knots, but from the south, with moderate temperatures in the upper twenties, which were good Bering Sea winter conditions if there is such a thing. All we knew about the ice was what we'd heard in the Elbow Room, that it was south of the Pribilof Islands.

Twelve hours later, we found the ice. It had been on Russell's watch, but when he pulled the throttle slowly back we all woke instantly, pulled on our clothes, and stumbled up into the pilothouse. The wind had come around from the north, but was light, and the sea had gone down. We jogged along at an idle, the crab lights clearly showing the edge of the ice a couple of boat lengths to the north. It was stark and austere but somehow captivating: white and pretty much featureless, with the snow being blown to leeward by the wind. The area right on the edge of the pack seemed to be moving up and down a bit with the waves, but ten or twenty yards in, it seemed solid.

"How far does it go?" I asked foolishly.

"Go?" George snorted. "Joe, whaddya think, there's just a few miles of this? This is the edge of the pack! It covers the whole top of the planet. If you had a snowmobile and enough gas, you could drive to Norway."

With that sobering thought, we had a big breakfast and suited up in our rain gear. While we ate, George had stuck our bow into the ice so the boat remained in the same place for five or ten minutes, and he watched the loran closely to determine whether the ice front was moving. He'd told us that depending on the wind and the currents, the pack could actually move a quarter-mile a day in some conditions. He wanted to set the gear reasonably close to the pack, but not so close as to risk losing it if the pack was on the move south.

George came down just as we were suiting up. "Pack's moving slowly to the north, so we'll start the first string parallel but slanting away to the south a bit in case she changes her mind."

IT WAS ALWAYS STARTLING to leave the cozy, inviting galley (well, as inviting as white Formica walls can be) and step out into the grim, cold world of the back deck. Daylight was still a few hours away. Beyond the circle of brilliant deck lights, the Bering Sea heaved and surged restlessly. The wind had picked up a bit. Even though we were in the lee of the pack, there was enough of an interval for whitecaps to form, splashing up the sides of the hull and freezing instantly. The white surface of the pack ice was covered with a low sheet of blowing snow that stretched away to where it faded into black.

I was haunted by what George had said about driving to Norway. As we worked the deck, getting the big pots ready to launch, I kept an eye peeled to the north when it was safe to look away from the job at hand, and whenever I looked, there it was, the edge of that vast ice pack.

We started before daylight, and set all day. The hard part was when the wind came on cold in the early afternoon. After the first dozen pots were set,

CRABBER *AMATULI*, at the edge of the ice pack, Bering Sea, 1970. In cold winters like 1970–71, much of the Bering Sea froze, becoming part of the arctic ice pack, and covering much of the popular Bristol Bay crab fishing grounds. Often good fishing would be right on the edge of the pack, but crabbers had to be cautious. A strong northerly wind would make the ice pack move south, freezing the pot buoys into the ice, often never to be found again. BART EATON PHOTO

we'd moved far enough away from the pack for the sea to build up a bit, and it got even colder. With ice starting to form on the deck and the pots, getting the gear into the water was a challenge, so it was with great relief that we launched the last pot over the side. George told us later that there were a few shallow depressions along the bottom that he wanted to set into, and was trying to figure the wind and the current so the pot would land just where he wanted it.

What George's strategy meant for us was that we'd all be there standing in the "ready to launch" position for five or sometimes even ten minutes while George jogged the boat around trying to get exactly where he wanted.

We became chilled during the inactivity, the sweat we'd put out getting the previous pot into the water causing us to shiver inside our rain gear.

The day fled away to the west, sooner than it should have as the snow started to fly again, blotting out the already wan sun. As we worked, getting the gear over the side, I'd wondered idly what we'd do that night. The previous nights we'd run into Amak, but that was now twelve hours to the south.

The question was answered while I cleaned up the back deck. The boat lurched slowly to a stop and I whirled around, realizing that George had shoved the *Flood Tide* up into the ice, close enough that the ice would hold us in its grip against the push of the wind from the north. I walked over to the bulwark and looked down. It was so strange. Our deck lights illuminated a circle around the boat. The snow had stopped, so the visibility was pretty good, yet when you looked down, you couldn't see the actual surface of the ice because of a layer of blowing snow undulating across the ice.

"This is what the big boys do," George said at dinner, all of us sitting back after a big beef roast, instant mashed potatoes, frozen brussels sprouts, plump Bisquick rolls, and fruit cocktail for dessert. Even after a long day on deck with only a quick snack every now and then, it's surprising how much you can put away at supper.

"The trick is to get far enough in so that the wind doesn't blow you back out, but not in so far that you can't get out," the skipper continued.

On the tricky issue of just how far is just far enough, we decided to stand anchor watches that night. With 310 feet of water beneath us, anchoring wasn't an option, but we figured someone should stand watch to make sure we weren't getting frozen in. Mine was the eight to midnight—an easy one. About every half-hour, when I made my engine room tour, I'd put on my thick winter coat, boots, and gloves and push open the thick watertight door out to the back deck and walk all the way to the stern and look out and around. If I could see open water behind us, within the circle of our big lights, we were okay, but if ice started to close around us and the water began to recede, then I was to start up the big main engine and reverse until we could see open water again. On my watch, though, the ice around our

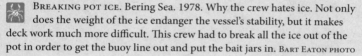 **BREAKING POT ICE.** Bering Sea. 1978. Why the crew hates ice. Not only does the weight of the ice endanger the vessel's stability, but it makes deck work much more difficult. This crew had to break all the ice out of the pot in order to get the buoy line out and put the bait jars in. BART EATON PHOTO

stern remained visibly broken up into chunks that moved up and down, and around the bow the ice was solid and unmoving.

Sitting in the pilothouse with everyone else asleep and looking out at that expanse of pack ice and the blowing snow, I thought about the story that fisherman had told us back at the Elbow Room. About being frozen in and then seeing the ghost and taking that journey through the ice and fishing in such an unlikely place. At the time, I didn't think he was telling the truth. But that night, looking out at that strange sight, his tale seemed more believable.

The pack ice must have started to close around us later in the night because I once woke to the sudden whoop of the air starter on the big main engine and the low throb of our massive six-foot-diameter propeller idling in reverse. You could feel the scrunch of the ice around the hull as we slid back ten or twenty yards, then the main engine died, and I went back to sleep.

In the morning I was the first one out on the back deck to fill bait jars while the rest of the guys took a few more minutes in the warm galley. I hadn't even glanced out the single porthole looking out onto the back deck.

I don't think anyone had. I opened the watertight door and stepped out into a surreal scene. The snow had stuck and accumulated. The deck, bulwarks, rails, pot hauler, coiler, and the dumping bin were all covered with light white snow. Everything on the boat and the frozen sea beyond was shades of white. If there was water beyond our stern, it too was hidden by blowing snow. It was a totally stunning sight.

"Hey, guys," I called into the galley, "step out here a minute and check this out. You gotta see it.

Four of us stepped out onto where the boat deck overhung the main deck. The snow wasn't as deep there so they could all stand in their low deck slippers, or "Romeos," popular with Northwest fishermen.

"Whoa!" Bob was the first to speak. "Now that's not something we shrimpers see much of."

Five minutes later, George started up the boat, and we backed out of the pack ice and into the Bering Sea again. A few minutes later, the sloshing seawater had cleaned the snow off the back deck and what had been white became black.

We went into the ice a few more times after that, but we never had that kind of snowy morning again. I had a camera in my cabin. I wished I'd asked one of the guys to get it for me. I'm not sure it could have captured the totality of what was out there—it would have needed a much wider angle lens. But that amazing sight was fixed in my mind forever—it was as if we had reached the edge of the known world in our quest for king crab.

There were enough crab that day to keep working the edge—nothing big, maybe ten to fifteen crabs to a pot, twenty five max. But the crab averaged fourteen pounds each—really big by today's standards—so we reset the pots instead of going through the tedious and discouraging pick and stack of the previous days.

FOR THE FIRST TIME since we left Seattle, for three or four days in a row we got into a rhythm that was oddly satisfying. We'd come up to the buoys, Johnny would throw out the grapple—a multipronged anchor—over the line, haul in the buoys, and then the buoy line would sing in the hauler as Russell or I fed the end of the line into the automatic coiler and watched to make sure the line coiled properly. When the pot broke the surface, I'd attach the quick-release hook and the safety strap to the bridle, and then we'd all step back as the pot emerged from the water and clanked and rattled up into the big rack over our heads. I'd pull the knot on the bag, and the crab would tumble out into the sorting bin. Then I'd retie the knot, throw in a couple of fresh bait jars, close the door, and help shove the pot over the side, unfastening the safety strap so it was ready to be dumped when George tooted the horn.

The crab were strange. I'd grown up around Chesapeake Bay with its quick-moving, sharp-clawed blue crabs, and I'd been to Maine and seen the slower, but powerfully clawed lobster. King crab were very different. They were more like underwater spiders, and they had short spines all over their bodies and thick legs. Their claws were small, and they moved slowly on deck. And they were big! Occasionally we'd get one weighing sixteen or seventeen pounds with the spread of their claws reaching almost seven feet. It was good they had small claws and were slow moving. If they'd had the claws of a Maine lobster and the speed of a Chesapeake blue crab, there'd have been a lot of fingers left on the decks of the crab fleet.

Crab seemed to travel or live in homogenous groups, so when you finally found where the big males were, you could have amazingly consistent catches. We might fish in one place where a half-mile to the east would be all small females, or a mile to the south, small males. But if we found the jackpot, we'd haul in pots filled with males so large you wouldn't even have to measure.

As we fished and the pots came up, each sampling the population on the bottom of the Bering Sea 300 feet or so below, we'd look down into the dark water and begin to sense that unlike any other crustacean population we were familiar with, king crabs seemed to travel in herds. The key to success lay in being able to find where the concentration of big males was greatest, and keeping your pots in that concentration as the herd moved.

And move they did. We'd get a day or two of steady fishing—ten to fifteen a pot—nothing big, but steady. The next morning we'd haul the gear and get only little three- and four-pound or smaller females without a single large male, the big crab having disappeared, just like that. We tried to spread out the pots in enough of a pattern, so that by the time you'd picked and stacked the pots that weren't producing, somewhere in our string we'd detect a sign as to where the big males had moved to and we'd set our gear among them.

We had four days of okay fishing south of the ice, nosing up into the pack each night. It wasn't great fishing by any means, but after all we'd been through to get to the fishing grounds, it was a relief simply to be putting crab into the hold every day. Crabs can live in a holding tank for ten days or more. But when a crab dies, it releases a toxin that can kill other crabs, so it was pretty important that no injured or dead crab went into the tank.

WE FELL INTO A PATTERN of working on deck that we kept pretty much through the season. In the morning, before Missouri Bob came out on deck, he'd make a couple of big coffee cakes or chocolate cakes full of high-energy sugar, and set them out on the galley counter, on the green rubber antiskid netting. Then once we'd started fishing, if one of us was hungry, we'd reach in through the open porthole and grab a piece of cake, sometimes even without taking our gloves off, and shove it into our mouths: fuel! It was okay to have the galley porthole open, except in the worst weather, in which case, we weren't really thinking about food.

Occasionally, George would call down to us that he was going to run for a few minutes to the next string, or to some new place to dump the pots we had stacked on the stern if a string was not producing. That was the signal to attend to our specific jobs. Usually this meant that Missouri Bob would head into the galley to clean up, start work on the evening meal, or whip up a bunch of brownies or another coffee cake. Engineer Johnny would head down into the engine room. Any mechanical failure had the potential of lost fishing time and money, and possibly moving up the scale to a life-threatening situation. If Johnny wasn't back by the time George tooted that he was ready to launch a pot, we knew that whatever he was doing in the engine room was important.

During the breaks, I'd usually fill more bait jars, gather up loose lines around the deck, and generally keep the back deck and general storage area underneath the boat deck overhang clean and organized. Russell would grab a coffee and go up into the pilothouse with George and they would have a smoke together and talk about strategy. George had skill and experience as skipper and entrepreneur. Russell was a guy who'd been skipper, crew, and deck boss on many boats up and down the Alaska and Canada coasts, and knew the tricks to keep a back deck running smoothly.

It was Russell who adjusted the height and angle of the picking boom so that the pots would slide smoothly into the odd metal frame that held the pots securely above our heads despite the rolling of the boat. Russell had made the little tweaks in the positioning and the settings for the hydraulic system that fine tuned our prototype coiler into a smoothly functioning, critically important part of our equipment. And it was Russell, who in a gravelly voice, shared with all of us one captivating tale after another from his many years as skipper and crew on boats working up and down the coast.

ONCE, ON A SHORT BREAK, with all of us under the shelter of the boat deck and more or less warm in the heat given out by the space heaters, he told us of his winters dragging (trawling, or towing a net along the bottom for flounder and the like). They were fishing the rough and rugged waters of Hecate Strait, where we'd so nearly come to grief that snowy afternoon on the trip up. Of three days at anchor for one day of fishing, before another storm system slammed them and they'd run for shelter, with the gear freezing on deck behind them, and all that for ten-cents-a-pound fish.

"One winter we were towing up the middle of the strait, in heavy snow. Two, three hours of towing, for a couple thousand pounds of fish at ten cents, hardly worth the effort. I was steering and there were these targets on the radar, like a line of ships slowly coming down the strait from north to south. Never seen anything like it—I didn't know what the hell it was, skipper didn't know, was it some weird radar glitch? So we just slowed down when the targets got closer, and what the hell do you supposed emerged from the gloom but Russian freezer trawlers. This was before the 200-mile limit, so the middle of Hecate Strait, being more than three miles from any land, was technically in international waters. Nine big Russian freezer trawlers, towing right down the middle of the strait, down to one end, then turning around, jigging over a hundred yards and towing up the other way. Never throwing nothing back over the side—when they were done, they'd cleaned out the place!"

Russell had spent a month on another crabber, getting the lay of the land, before joining George and the *Flood Tide*, so he had a clear sense of working the gear. And he gave us an appreciation of what might lie ahead if we ever got into the thick of it.

"We got into 'em on the south side [south of the Aleutian Islands, in the North Pacific]. Twenty hours on deck without a break, bunch of candy bars in a jar for snacks. Thirty hours sometimes, never a break, skipper sure didn't know how to keep a crew—we all quit after two trips. The guy'd first drink all the coffee he could stand, then start on the pills, and then when the coffee and the pills wouldn't do it any more, he had this little toothpick on a string that hung from the top of the pilothouse. He'd put it in his mouth, and if he started to nod off, it'd come tight and stab him in the cheek and wake him up. But give the crew a break? No way. I heard the sonofabitch drove 'er ashore on Akutan once, but it was just a sand beach so the tide floated him off. Lucky that time, but two trips was enough for me."

AFTER THOSE FOUR DAYS of fishing, the crab seemed to disappear, and we were back to pick and stack again, as George set the pots in patterns with the pots farther and farther apart, trying to find where the crab had gone. Occasionally we'd get into a little bunch, but whenever we did, we'd look up to windward and see the edge of the pack again.

Finally George came out onto the boat deck and shouted down to us over the sound of the wind and the engine. "It's like John Hall said, the crab are moving in under the edge of the pack, and I'm uneasy about setting so close with the wind out of the north. We've got ten days on these first crabs, so we ought to be thinking about delivering them. So we'll stack these, move them south, and head back to Dutch."

By the time we got moved to where George wanted to set and got the last of the gear into the water, it was long after dark, the wind was out of the north at twenty knots, the temperature was fifteen degrees, and it was snowing. But that only meant moderate icing, plus with no pots on deck, we didn't have to worry about stability. So we could change into clean clothes, enjoy a big dinner, and savor the feeling of heading in to town, such as it was.

Sleeping in: wow! It was such an exquisite treat to wake up knowing that we didn't have to go out there and face the rigors of the back deck. To just lie there a while, day dreaming, thinking of my other life: my girlfriend, my family, future plans. To get up slowly, take a long hot shower, get a big mug of coffee, and just amble up the stairs to the pilothouse, and sit and visit with Russell, the boat rolling slowly from the northerly swell, and Dutch still five hours away.

IT WAS HARDLY the sort of trip that crab dreams are made of: 40,000 plus pounds at a half a buck a pound. Take away the expenses like fuel and bait, and my share would be less than $1,100. But even so, this was 1971, so it was a considerable piece of change for a couple of weeks work for a single guy with no mortgage and no car or credit card payments.

In the 1990s, however, crews would salivate over those 40,000 pounds, but at five dollars a pound. And my 7 percent share would be $14,000. Now that was a good crab trip! Remember, however, that in the 1990s the rising prices almost always meant large fleets, and the whole king crab fishery might just be a single eight- or ten-day opening, so that trip would basically be the whole crab season.

The important things for us that March 1971 were that we'd gotten out there, worked out the wrinkles of fishing with our slightly different gear, gotten to work together as a crew, and faced without flinching the rigors of the Bering Sea in winter. Also we'd learned, in talking around Dutch Harbor between trips, that what we were experiencing was some of the worst winter weather in many a year.

RUSSIAN ORTHODOX cemetery, Dutch Harbor, 1971. The faded and worn inscription on this wooden grave marker reads: "Albert Nutbeem. Age 28 yrs. Born in England. Died at Unalaska, Sept. 17, 1901." Judging by the date, Albert probably died during the Yukon gold rush, when many steamers bound for the Yukon River would stop at Dutch Harbor going and coming.

11. In Dutch

IN LATER YEARS, when king crabbing was pretty much a derby fishery where there was a set quota, the fleet fished around the clock until the quota was taken. There was no such thing as a mellow turnaround in Dutch. You went in to unload, take on fuel, bait, and water, and got the hell back out to the fishing grounds to get your share of the quota until it was filled. Usually the crab plant sent down a crew to unload your crab.

If you were really organized with your other jobs to be done in port, you might get to the Elbow Room to hoist a few and catch up on the scuttlebutt. But more likely, your time in Dutch would be filled with critical repairs and errands. Everyone would be full of the latest gossip about who had delivered what and there would be guesses as to where they had been fishing, all of which only served to make you more anxious about getting out there and getting on the crab.

But that boom was still almost a decade away, so when we slid into the dock at Pan Alaska Seafoods and struggled to break the ice on our frozen tie-up lines, we were the only crab boat in the harbor and the scene was unrelentingly grim: decrepit houses, stark mountains, constant bitter wind, and snow squalls.

"We'll get unloaded and cleaned up today, and stay here for a couple of days," George told us. "We got some parts coming in once the weather breaks and planes can get in. There's another dozen pots or so we got to drag out of the puckerbrush and get rigged, but that's about it, so you guys can sleep in tomorrow and have the day off."

By the time we got unloaded and the boat cleaned, it was dark, cold, and windy again. But the Elbow Room beckoned and so up the icy ladder we went.

THE SAME ROUGH characters, the same stale air. But the drinks were strong, the food was hot, and it was a chance for the three of us to talk about things we didn't really want to discuss around our skipper.

"What do you think of those bags?" I got the ball rolling. I was a new-comer, but so far I hadn't been impressed with George's idea of the bags that we had sewn to all the pots. I'd gotten a look at the way other crabbers were set up. They all had what they called a launcher—a big steel rack that the pots sat on while they were emptied and rebaited. It held the pots securely, and then when it was ready to go over the side you pushed a lever and over it went. I liked the idea that the pot was sitting on the deck and not over our heads. Basically that seven hundred-pound pot was hanging over our heads while we were untying the bag and emptying the crab out. I had developed the safety line that would catch the pot if the quick-release line snagged on something, but still, it made me nervous.

"Ah, it's pretty early to really decide on those," Russell pointed out. "The idea is that when you get into really heavy fishing, you can fit more crab into them than you could get into a pot. Now I haven't seen fishing like that, we certainly didn't see it this trip. But you talk to any crab veterans, and they all talk about what it's like when you get into them thick. Pots coming up so full the meshes are bulging. I know they're a fucking pain in the ass, but they might pan out. Old George does get some good ideas sometime, and I'm not yet sure that this isn't one of them. That coiler is his idea, and that works pretty good."

He was right. I'd tried hand-coiling a time or two, and that in the rel-atively shallow water of the eastern Bering Sea. My shoulders were aching after coiling just two or three pots. And that was just coiling seventy-five fathoms—450 feet—of buoy line. I knew that when you fished the Pacific side

WOODEN CRABBER *North Beach*, around 1960. Compare this boat to the state-of-the-art *Katie K* (page 160). Eventually many single-deck pilothouse-style boats with a flying bridge like this one, if they continued in the king crab fishery, were fitted with a small pilothouse on the upper deck (instead of the flying bridge) to give the skipper better visibility. In the Bering Sea, the weather was seldom good enough for the skipper to make use of the flying bridge. COURTESY *NATIONAL FISHERMAN*

of the Aleutians, as we would do in the late summer and early fall, we might be in 150 fathoms of water (900 feet) and using over 1,000 feet of buoy line, a pile that easily would be chest high. I couldn't imagine coiling such a big pile of line, pot after pot, day after day.

"There's more crab out there, right?" I asked. I wasn't privy to what George had learned from the superintendent of the crab plant about who had delivered what and from where. But from all the talk around the docks in Seattle, I had expected a lot more crab.

"The crab are there," Russell answered. "*King and Winge* delivered seventy-five thousand pounds two days ago. They're out there all right. The Bering Sea's a big place. We'll find 'em."

The bartender came around again, and after he took our order, filled us in on the big news around Dutch. When we'd nosed up into the pack ice while the northerly had howled, it had struck Dutch with a fury. A couple of boats dragged anchor, but got started up and reanchored okay. But the buzz was about a trailer just below a ridge about a hundred feet up near the head of the harbor. Four guys in the trailer had it all buttoned up tight against the wind and the bitter cold, and this powerful gust came along and the whole trailer disintegrated around them. One moment they were drinking, listening to music, playing cards, and the next . . . poof! They were out in the snow. They finally figured out that wind was blowing so powerfully over the top of that ridge that it created a partial vacuum in the lee and just popped the trailer open!

A few more boats docked while we'd been out fishing. They had fueled and baited up, and headed out into the vastness of the Bering Sea to try and find the wily king crab. The new arrivals included the *St. Mark* and the *Pacific Fisher*, wooden boats both built in the 1940s as sardine seiners for the warmer waters off California. I'd seen them down in Seattle, gearing up when we were getting ready to leave, and I saw their crews: big serious professionals, not greenhorn kids like me.

Even for the most prosperous and well-connected fishermen, building a new boat for the king crab fishery was a huge, expensive, and risky endeavor. Few people were connected with the owner of a major shipyard like George was. The first really modern steel boats were just starting to appear, but for most fishermen wanting to start fishing crab, it meant simply doing the best with what you had. For most, it made a lot more sense to invest $100,000 or $150,000 in their existing and probably already paid-off boat for a new engine, steel crab tanks and pumps, perhaps new decks and steel bulwarks than spending the $400,000 plus on a boat like the *Flood Tide*. And on top of the cost of a new boat, there was the cost of the crab pots, buoy lines, and buoys; a fully rigged pot would be around $700, and most folks figured you had to have 80 to 100 pots to be really competitive. And those were 1971 dollars; a similar boat today would be probably three times that.

It was apparent to us after a single trip, fishing for Bering Sea king crab in the wintertime was hardly a get-rich bonanza. For all the buzz along the waterfront in Seattle about the crab fishing to be had in the Bering Sea, the reality of it once you got up there could be starkly different. George was a good fisherman; we had the best equipment. But for us, at least in the beginning, the crab were elusive. Only knowing of big deliveries like John Hall was making with the *King and Winge* gave us confidence that the crab were out there.

THE NEXT AFTERNOON was above freezing and the sun was struggling to get through the clouds, so I put on my leather boots, climbed up the dock ladder, and headed out for the first real walk I'd had since we'd left Seattle more than a month before. I wanted to get away from the ever-present thrum of diesel engines, and work my legs for a few hours. The wind had scoured the snow away from the few roads, pushing the drifts aside and allowing for reasonable walking.

What we called Dutch was actually the village of Unalaska, home to perhaps 1,500 mostly Aleut residents, on the island of the same name that was perhaps forty miles by ten miles. Hidden in the clouds four miles west of town was 5,900-foot Makushin Volcano, dormant now, its top covered by a big glacier. Once it had been active enough to have blown out the many cubic miles of magma that eventually solidified and eroded away over time, to create Unalaska's deeply indented coastline with many winding inlets, protected harbors, and bays.

Unalaska was an adaptation of the word *Ounalashka*, meaning "near the peninsula," used by the original settlers, Aleut Natives, to name their home. But the inference of "Unalaska" is pretty accurate, since the place is about the opposite of the image that Alaska typically brings to mind. Even if the Aleutians had had trees, it's so windy they would have been uprooted or stunted long ago. The ceiling, or cloud cover, is often so low that Reeve Aleutian, the regional airline, maintains a bunkhouse and mess hall at Cold Bay, on the mainland 150 miles east, to house Dutch Harbor–bound passengers when they're stuck waiting for weather. The most polite word that comes to mind to describe the winter landscape is bleak.

Yet, as I walked along what must have been a road, passing frozen Unalaska Lake and following the Ilialiak River up toward Pyramid Peak, I encountered a whole other world. Large, old buildings missing windows, the paint faded and chipped, were deep in snow with no sign of recent activity. I pushed open a door and went inside. Surprisingly, the roof hadn't failed yet, and apart from snow that had drifted in broken windows and open doors, the interior was reasonably intact. There was no sheetrock, and the studs, beams, and rafters were all revealed. They were cut from arrow-straight, clear-grained Douglas fir, wood that today is so valuable as to be used only for trim in high-end houses. The wood was fine enough that it should be salvaged and reused, if it weren't in such an inaccessible location.

"Military," the old clerk in the only store, the Alaska Commercial Company, told me later when I stopped in. "During the war, the Japs invaded Kiska and Attu, out to the west. It was a big deal. Folks figured Seattle and San Francisco were next, so they threw money at it—sent lots of ships, thousands of troops, built a big airstrip, lots of houses. Japs even bombed Dutch once. Our boys got ready to invade those two little islands, everyone figured it was going to be a big blood-letting. But when we finally got there, they were empty. The Japs had moved out."

Before World War II and the Japanese invasion, I learned, the Aleutians had pretty much slept, the Aleut Natives slowly recovering from their brutal treatment at the hands of the Russians, who came for the valuable pelts of the fur seals and sea otters. Before the arrival of the Russians, the Aleuts had been a hardy people, living in earthen lodges and hunting marine mammals in their remarkably seaworthy baidarkas, kayak-like boats made of skins stretched over a driftwood or whalebone frame.

Then came Vitus Bering, exploring the Alaska coast in 1741. On his return, he shipwrecked on a Siberian island and died of scurvy. But twenty of his sailors were strong enough to build another boat out of the wreck, and sail back to Kamchatka. The sea otter pelts that they brought home ignited the immensely profitable fur trade that was the catalyst for the Russian settlement of Alaska. By the late 1700s, the Russians had established settlements as far east as Sitka, and essentially used the Aleuts and other Native peoples as slaves to harvest sea otters.

The Aleuts were proud and independent, but were no match for the brutality of their new Russian masters who threatened to kill entire villages unless the men agreed to hunt sea otters for them. The Russians forced the Natives to build larger three-seat baidarkas, so a Russian with a rifle could sit in the back, ready to shoot Natives who didn't hunt the sea otters effectively or quickly. The Russians and their enslaved Aleut hunters traveled as far south as Baja California in their relentless quest for sea otter pelts.

By the 1850s, the once-abundant sea otter was, for commercial purposes, extinct. Meanwhile, the Russians, defeated by France in the Crimean War, were looking for ways to consolidate and streamline their empire, and Alaska was deemed expendable. Russia sold Alaska to the United States in 1867 for seven million dollars or two cents an acre. What remains of the Russians are the Russian Orthodox churches, including the one in Unalaska, the many landscape features with Russian names, and descendents who continue to follow Russian cultural ways.

American commercial fishing entrepreneurs, pushing up the coast and through Unimak Pass into the Bering Sea at the end of the nineteenth century, created the beginnings of a cash economy in this distant land. About the same time, merchants such as the Alaska Commercial Company were moving into the larger remote settlements including Unalaska, giving the mostly Native residents a place to trade and to spend their newly acquired cash.

THE MARCO 108-foot *Katie K* in Wrangell Narrows, near Petersburg, Alaska, October 1973. Crab pots are stacked about six high on deck, way too many if there was any chance of icing. The 108 footers were Marco's most popular crabber model, followed by the much bigger and more expensive 123 footers.

When the first king crab buyer came to Unalaska, the Aleuts mostly had forty- and fifty-foot salmon boats. But like the Kodiak boats, they managed to do fine by just making day trips to the bays around the island, keeping the crab alive in their dry holds by dousing them with a saltwater hose occasionally and delivering their catch every evening. It was a low-tech fishery, but Unalaska had enough bays that whatever way the wind blew, there were sheltered areas to fish.

THAT NIGHT, up in the pilothouse, George waved out at the lights of Dutch Harbor. "This place is going to boom," he said. "Guys will make a lot of money here. You talk to anyone who knows about the crab markets, and all they can see is the price going up. Already guys are talking to Pete [Peter Schmidt, owner of Marco] about building a bigger crabber."

"Whoa," I thought. "Bigger?" To me, the *Flood Tide* at 104 feet seemed plenty big, although I hadn't spent a full season to get a sense of how well our boat would work in the worst weather or the best fishing.

"I know you'd like to go back to Southeast," George said, "but you ought to keep an open mind about staying on up here."

It wasn't a secret that I'd enjoyed my summer of fish-buying among the thickly wooded islands of Southeast Alaska a few years earlier. I'd talked about fishing salmon in protected channels and bays with places to anchor up and get out of the weather when the wind blew, and the quiet communities where a guy might be able to get a piece of land and build a cabin on the water. It was my dream to build a place where I could look out the front window and see my boat moored peacefully in the harbor below the house.

"A lot of my Bellingham buddies seine for salmon there," George said. Seining required a good-sized boat, fifty feet plus, which was a big investment and needed a crew of four or five. What interested me was salmon gillnetting or trolling with a thirty to forty footer, a less expensive boat that could be handled alone or with just another person, maybe a wife or girlfriend.

"The Bellingham guys are doing good, really good," George continued. "But remember, most of those guys already have their boats paid off. Starting up without a big wad of cash to get you going is hard."

I told George what I was thinking about: a smaller boat, building a cabin on the water somewhere.

"Well," he said, "I don't know much about those small-boat fisheries. But this can be really big here. I know this first trip has been a bit of a struggle, but I've talked to a lot of guys before I built the *Flood Tide*, and they pretty much all say the same thing: if this fishery keeps going like it's been going, it could be the biggest thing to hit fishing in a long time."

"I'm not making any decisions, George." I said. " I just want to put in a good strong season here and then see what the next step might be."

The wintertime, for most Alaska fishermen, was when their boats were laid up, even hauled out of the water in many places where the harbors froze. It was a time to spend with family, a time for visiting with friends and neighbors, a time for boat projects. After my summer buying fish and the summer gillnetting with the *Denise*, I felt I had tasted what I wanted. This business of stepping out onto an icy heaving deck long before dawn and working until long after dusk, pushing your body to its outer limits was a good way to make money, I hoped, to finance the next step in my fishing career. But I was pretty sure I wasn't going to want a steady diet of it.

Dutch was also a chance to hear the faraway voices of my parents and girlfriend. The unspoken worries about my safety with my parents, and the unspoken, "How can we have a relationship if you're in the Bering Sea?" from my girlfriend in Boston.

THE TWO DAYS at Dutch flew by. We took on bait and fuel, and soon were on that long ride toward the Compass Rose, rising and falling in the swells with the spray turning to slush on the pilothouse windows.

We hoped for a good pick when we got back to the fishing grounds. We'd left the gear in a good productive location and felt that a four-night soak would yield plenty of crabs. We would soon find out. At 3 a.m. George rolled us out. We had a quick-energy breakfast—lots of pancakes and lots of bacon—suited up, and took our places out on deck in the slushy cold. And waited. And waited. Ten, twenty minutes.

"Fucking George," Russell grunted, turning his head toward the shelter of the pilothouse to light a cigarette. "A skipper with half a brain would wait until he was up on the first buoy before getting the guys out on deck, and maybe slow down a bit to give the guys a few more hours sleep. It's not like we're in the thick of it and have a delivery date."

George came out on the boat deck and yelled down to us. "Hey guys, go get a mug up. The loran's screwed up. We might have to wait until daylight."

In the galley, with our jackets off and our rain-gear pants pulled down to our knees, we all took the familiar fishermen's rest position: slumped, heads down on our forearms on the table.

On occasion, weather or mechanical glitches would degrade the accuracy of the loran signals. For coastal mariners, loran was a convenience, but a vessel's position could easily be found by observing landmarks. Offshore fishermen who worked irregular bottoms could navigate using landmarks on the bottom of the ocean. But for us, fishing out of sight of land, and on a bottom that was essentially a featureless underwater plain, the loran was critical.

When the signal was bad, the station automatically transmitted an "undependable signal" alert that displayed on the receivers, but there was no information on how long the system would be down. If it stayed down, we'd have to get within radar range of the coast, get a fix from landmarks like Pavlof Volcano and Amak Island and then head out to where we had set our gear. This was a tedious and time-consuming process, especially when the visibility was down to a few hundred yards. With our pots set in lines sometimes a half-mile apart, finding them by that method when the visibility was limited would be a challenge.

GPS, a satellite-based system would have stunning accuracy when it came into widespread use in the 1990s. A friend who made trawl nets for the big factory trawlers that came to Alaska in the 1980s occasionally would go aboard the ships to test new products or fine-tune nets and rigging. He told me that the big rigs would have a GPS on either side of the big bridges, and the readings would be slightly different, to reflect the thirty- or forty-foot distance between the two sets. For pot fishermen, such accuracy was truly wonderful—you could punch in the coordinates of your pots into your auto-pilot, even if they were a hundred miles away, and if you weren't careful, you would run over the buoy!

We had a nice two-hour break before we heard the engine start. The loran was up again. A quick mug up, and we went back to work.

The modest herd of crab that we had counted on were gone and hadn't left a forwarding address. The first pots came up with just two or three lonely keepers in each. The cigarette flung to leeward, the thumb jerked toward the stern, the unspoken words from the skipper, "Stack 'em." As we went through the strings, we hoped as the pot warp hummed through the hauler for each new pot, that it would be the one with a good show of crab, that we could reset it, reset the rest of the string, and start setting some of the idle gear that was starting to accumulate on the back deck.

TYPICAL BERING SEA crabbing weather, *Flood Tide*, 1971. photos always seem
to make the sea look flatter than they are. That's probably a twenty-five-foot sea
out there and moving around is difficult.

12. A Bering Sea Breeze

THE WIND AND SEA picked up, the temperature started to drop, and the spray began to freeze again. Before the deck was two thirds full of pots, we could feel the difference in the motion of the boat as the flying spray froze on the nylon netting and the steel frames, as well as on the steel pipe frame rigging over our heads. As the pots kept coming up containing two or three crabs, with an occasional disgusting empty one, and we stacked them on deck to catch ice, the boat sank a little deeper in the water and rolled a little slower.

On the upper deck, George's words were carried off by the wind, but we got the drift of it. We needed to get rid of our load before the icing got any worse. We'd have to prospect again: set strings over a wide enough area to find the crab.

We huddled in the lee of the boat deck, and we all were thoroughly chilled before the boat slowed and we started dumping the gear. The freezing spray had frozen the ties between the pots into the solid layer of ice that coated the steel frame, so I had to run forward and get the hammer to break the ice so we could untie each pot. The deck had become very icy, and the car on the railroad boom started to jam in the ice building up twenty feet over our heads.

Hoods up, heads down, we each did our job. Occasionally a pot would be iced so badly with its neighbors that the winch line from the railroad boom couldn't break it free. Then I'd have to hustle forward across the icy deck, grab a crowbar, and lever it out of the ice.

When the wan light of day came, it brought driving snow. I was working the back deck, hooking pots to the winch, and I was the one who had to face into the wind for the return to the forward part of the deck where the rest of the crew worked, sheltered from the wind and the waves. The sea had risen with the wind, and it was difficult to move around on the open deck. Around the hauler and the coiler, the area where much of the work was done, we had sections of nylon netting nailed to the deck for traction. But it was impossible to do this on the rest of the deck because any netting would be scraped off by the heavy pots being dragged back and forth. Our decking was heavy fir planks, fastened to steel cross-members so that the deck was raised about ten inches over the steel deck. The theory was that in cold weather the wood would hold less ice, but in reality, on a bitter cold day with the snow and freezing spray flying, the deck was extremely slippery. When it got rough, I would make my way forward along the side, with a steadying hand on the rail. Another problem was that the angle of the pull from the winch was slightly upward, so as the boat rolled and the pot was pulled forward, the pot would yaw back and forth. I quickly learned to follow behind the pot, in case the boat took a violent roll and the lurching 700-pound pot got ready to crush me against the steel bulwarks.

The state-of-the-art *Flood Tide* wasn't intended to huddle out of the weather but rather to face into it boldly. But huddle we did. It was coming on dark when we dropped the last pot and swung south for Amak. Usually, in a situation like that, Missouri Bob would have begun to rustle up another one of his great dinners, the highlight of our days. But as I stood for a moment by the watertight door, watching our wake, I had a pretty strong feeling that dinner would be later than usual, that we would take a heavy beating before we got into shelter. Fortunately, the wind and the seas were from the northwest, so we had a downhill and quartering ride to shelter.

The sight was spellbinding. The storm was building rapidly, and the swells were traveling faster than we were. Looking back into the circle of light from our little ship, hills of dark water would appear, tops all blown forward into spray and tumbling foam. As they approached, the stern would lift and the *Flood Tide* would accelerate forward slightly and the tone of the engine would change. As the great sea came closer, you could see our wake, clearly, against the darker shoulder of water, running dramatically uphill behind us and over the crest. We'd surge forward a little faster, and then when the sea passed beneath us, we would yaw dramatically to port—a roll that would have cleaned off the galley counters had Bob been cooking. I was mighty glad that the storm was behind us and that Amak was only thirty miles away, for even traveling with the wind with flying spray at a minimum, the seas were flinging their tops into the air, to freeze instantly on whatever they struck.

In some areas of the globe, storms such as we experienced that evening, overnight, and the next day are given names. Even if they aren't given proper names like for hurricanes and typhoons, they still make their way into legend as "the storm of '76" or such. Yet in the Bering Sea there are many winter storms, and on the water and on the land, there are few people to experience them. Towns are well sheltered from the reach of the wind and the seas. The Aleuts and the Eskimos come from a tradition of dirt and snow dwellings, designed to huddle down away from the great storms that regularly blow in from the Siberian steppe or the vast reaches of the North Pacific. Today, many houses are prefabricated, often brought up by barge in the good weather, but almost all, low and one level, are designed to hunker down when the wind comes to clutch at eaves and roofs and relentlessly batter the landscape around them.

Thus a great storm might pass, battering the shore, but barely disturbing the residents. In summer, many Natives move to fish camp at locations where they have modest tents on wood platforms or simple cabins, and set gillnets to catch migrating salmon. They might take a walk along the shore that they had visited regularly over the years and notice that there was fresh driftwood high on the shore, way above its usual line. Only by such observations would the passing of a great storm even be noticed.

Occasionally a big freighter, container ship, or log carrier would be caught on the Great Circle Route between Asia and the U.S. West Coast.

Perhaps it would arrive in Seattle or Long Beach with containers askew on deck and some missing. Perhaps an alert observer might ask questions, although the shipping lines preferred to keep such events quiet. And a picture might hit the paper with a short piece about the great storm that had battered the ship somewhere in the North Pacific or among the bleak Aleutian Islands.

Inside, the galley was quiet. I carefully poured myself a half-cup of coffee—any more would have spilled out—and made my way to the pilothouse. The air was thick with cigarette smoke. Russell was steering with the jog stick, tweaking it back and forth and looking out the back windows. When one of the seas overtook us, he had to be ready for rapid response if it caught our stern and threw us sideways. Called a broach, it can damage even a sturdy boat such as ours.

They grunted when I came in, and I sensed they weren't in a chatty mood. George was pacing and chain-smoking. I guessed it wasn't so much the weather he was chafing at but rather the crab herd that seemed to have disappeared. Although I had no way of knowing what his payments were for the *Flood Tide* or what his financial arrangement was with Marco, I guessed they were substantial. From what I had learned around the waterfront, the *Flood Tide* was the first boat that George was a partner in. Skippering someone else's boat was one thing, but shouldering the bills and startup costs for an expensive boat in a new fishery was another.

There was something else, too, that I had sensed in our interactions with John Hall and other skippers back in the Elbow Room. These were men who had worked on deck for years, finally made enough money to buy older wooden boats, and had gone on from there. John Hall appeared to be a hugely talented fisherman, yet he was fishing a sixty-year-old boat. The new line of Marco steel crabbers cost substantially more. Not only that but the *Flood Tide* wasn't just another Marco crabber. She was the first of a new class. And here was George, who, as far as I could tell, never had his own boat before, or at least not a big one with the latest and greatest from Marco. I remembered something John Hall had said when he and George had been talking about the pot bags and his high hopes for them.

"George," John had said, dismissively cutting short George's detailed explanation of how the bags were going to work, "there's no substitute in the king crab fishery for long hours and hard work." It had stung George, and I knew that at some level, George felt that he had to prove himself with the *Flood Tide*. Even though it was clear that John was one of the most clever skippers in the king crab fishery, we knew it was humbling for George to see John delivering a much bigger trip than ours.

That was one aspect of commercial fishing that could be hard to come to grips with: the "you are what you catch" mentality. For an aggressive type A person, it was natural to look on your catch as the measure of your success. The more you caught, the more you made, the more your crew made, the bigger and better boat you could get, and so forth. This was particularly true in Alaska, and even more so in the Bering Sea winter crab fishery. It was so terribly expensive to rig up, travel up there, and just participate in the fishery in the first place, in conditions that were so appallingly rotten and downright dangerous. Why would you do it if not for the money? Yet, as I had seen in my season fish-buying aboard the *Sidney* and my abbreviated Puget Sound season aboard the barely seaworthy *Denise*, there are a lot of ways of looking at commercial fishing.

When the seiners came in to deliver their fish to the *Sidney*, there were always one or two skippers who wanted to know who had been the high boat so far that day. If it wasn't them, they were clearly unhappy. You also sensed in their crews that an unhappy type A skipper often makes for an unhappy crew. And then there were others, usually good steady producers, whose boats and crews just seemed to be together and happy. It was almost like the Zen of commercial fishing: you knew that it was going to be cold, shitty, and dangerous, but there was an attitude, maybe even a consciousness, that would enable you to get through it easier.

Of course, that was easy for me to say; I didn't owe $300,000 or $400,000—an enormous boat loan back in 1971—and find myself caught

between perhaps an anxious bank and the immense challenges of fishing the Bering Sea in winter. In any case, George was edgy, and those Amak days weren't fun.

We made the lee of the land, and it was my turn to suit up and go up onto the bow to operate the anchor winch. Even though we had been traveling

WET DECK, on the *Flood Tide*, 1971. Even in as seaworthy a crabber as the Marco-built *Flood Tide*, seas can come over the side unexpectedly and sweep the deck with the capacity to injure or wash men overboard.

downwind, enough freezing spray had been flung around that I had to take the heavy hammer with me to break the ice off the chain on the drum, and ever so carefully, off the winch controls.

The land was high and volcanic there, so it was a good lee, no sea at all; we would rest easy that night. My hood was up, the drawstrings tight. Yet even with my vision through that small circle and all sound muffled by the wool hat and heavy rain gear, the wildness of the night beyond the shelter of Amak's shoulder was stunning. Occasionally, as George jogged back and forth and I worked at knocking the ice off the winch, we'd swing so that our great quartz lights shone out on the seas beyond the point. They were angry, tumbling over each other, their tops flung far downwind. We came through that? It seemed hard to believe.

I waved to George when the winch was ready, and he crept up as far as he could toward the land, glancing back and forth between the fathometer and the radar, and finally signaled me with a toot on the horn when he was on the spot. I spun the brake wheel and the 500-pound anchor and heavy chain thundered over the bow and splashed into the sea. Once the cable was running out, I tightened the brake a bit to straighten the chain and move the anchor along the bottom so the flukes could dig in and get a good bite, all the while watching George, who was judging the amount of cable running out. When he gave me the fingers-across-the-throat sign, I snugged down hard on the brake wheel, stopping the drum. Ahead the cable rose from the sea, fell a couple of times, and then rose again until it was almost straight from our bow into the water a hundred or so feet ahead, and I felt the boat lurch as the anchor dug in hard and stopped us. George throttled up in reverse for a minute or so to make sure the anchor was firmly dug into the bottom and I moved forward and put my hand on the cable. If the anchor was dragging, its motion through the bottom would be transmitted through the cable and I could feel it. But it was hard as an iron bar, and George nodded at me, throttled back, took the engine out of gear, and I edged carefully around the side of the pilothouse and in the back door.

"Could we even fish out this far if Amak wasn't here to run to when it blew?" I asked the question after supper when we were all sitting around savoring our coffee and rich chocolate cake with chocolate icing, after a wonderfully filling pasta and shrimp dish Bob had created after we had anchored. All of us felt that glow we got when a very hard day on deck was followed by a great meal and time to sit down and enjoy it. Judging from the power of the

williwaws—sudden violent wind gusts that slammed down into the anchorage from the volcanic heights above—we suspected we'd be sleeping in the
following morning, not an altogether unpleasant prospect.

"Hold that thought," George said. "I'll get the chart." He went up to
the pilothouse and returned a moment later and spread the Bering Sea chart
number 9302 on the galley table before us. Amak and the area we were fishing were in the lower right section of the chart. Above that, pretty much taking the whole area between Amak and the Pribilof Islands was the Compass
Rose, where much of the Bering Sea crab fishery took place. In the upper
left part of the chart, about twenty miles west of Northwest Cape, the most
northerly point of Saint Lawrence Island, a dotted line ran diagonally across
the chart and up through the middle of the Bering Strait marked U.S.–Russia
Convention of 1867. Beyond that was Siberia with its distinctive place names:
Mys Chaplina, Anadyrskiy Zaliv, Proliv Senyavina.

"All this," George's hand swept across the 300 miles of the north side of
the Alaska Peninsula, "is a lee shore when it's blowing nor'west, and there is
no place on God's Earth to hide except Amak.

"False Pass," he continued, his finger pointing to a bay and a narrow
channel marked Isanotski Strait, which connected through to the Pacific,
"there's breakers all the way across. Nelson Lagoon," he said, tapping another
small bay eighty miles east, "breaks. Port Moller, breaks. Port Heiden, breaks.
Cinder River, breaks, Ugashik River, breaks. All shallow river mouths with
sandbars with heavy breakers in any kind of a norther'. Okay in the summer,
when the Natives might put buoys out for the salmon tenders and it's not
blowing onshore. But not in a winter northerly."

"How about Unimak?" I said, referring to the ten-mile-wide pass between
the end of the peninsula and the first of the Aleutian Islands. "You could head
through there and lay in behind Cape Ludke if it was really bad, right?"

"You could," George said, "and guys do that sometimes. But if you're that
far west'ard, you might as well just cross the pass and go into Akutan. The
harbor's sheltered and there's even a little Native village. And," he tapped the
pass, "Unimak can be a bear. The tides roar through there and the mountains

funnel the wind. You seen those pictures of log ships and freighters that get smashed up in there, and they're a hell of lot bigger than we are.

"No," he said, sitting back, "Amak is the only shelter in this whole coast when it's blowing northerly. Either Amak or up into the ice like we did."

Just then a big williwaw slammed into us, pushing us over slightly and back until we lurched suddenly and the anchor cable creaked in the chock.

"Without Amak," George went on, "you'd have to be really careful fishing this far to the east'ard in winter. It'd be one thing if you could rely on the forecasts. Peggy's a big help and all, but there's not many observation stations nor'west of us into Siberia, so you just don't have the kind of information that you get when a storm blows in from the Pacific. These northerlies come up sometimes without any warning. You could get caught with no safe place to go."

"Where do you suppose *King and Winge* is?" I asked. When the northerly had blown us into Amak, we'd half-expected to find John Hall's boat in there, assuming that he'd been fishing somewhere out where we were.

"He must be off to the west'ard farther, maybe laying in Akutan." George said.

"Or maybe he's laying up in the ice," I ventured.

"Naw," Russell spoke this time, "I talked to John about that. He says you got to be careful when you're driving around in a sixty-year-old boat. He said he'd go up and lay on the edge of the ice to get a lee if there's no other place to go, but he wouldn't dare go up into it and shut down like we do. It's just taking too much of a chance in an old wooden boat.

"But he says it's not so much the sea ice that he worries about, but the bay ice. He said last winter another wooden crabber was in some bay on the south side of Unalaska when it turned bitter cold. There wasn't any wind, imagine that. When they awoke, the bay had frozen, just a little skin, not even a half inch thick, and he thought nothing of it, just picked up the hook and started steaming. They got through it, and a bit later the engineer comes up and said they was leaking bad. They had to break their trip and go into

Dutch and haul out. It was that thin layer of ice, just like glass, he said it was, sawing through their planks."

A night like that with the wind howling and all of us sitting around—it would have been nice to have a drink. But we were a dry boat. Some boats have booze on board. I could have certainly used a drink after some of those long days. But you could see how it could be a big problem. New boat, financial pressures, bad weather, poor fishing, why not have a drink? And one more, and one more after that. I liked the attitude of the halibuters who'd tied alongside us that first night in Dutch: hold it together until you get into port and then pull out all the stops.

Later that night we had our own weather report howling around the hull, heard over the drone of the generator. We didn't have an anchor watch; the hook was dug in well. Still I woke up, restless, around 2 a.m., got a glass of powdered milk, and went up the stairs quietly into the pilothouse just to look around. It was snowing hard and the windows were iced up except for the side windows and a spot where the little electric defroster was working. Our big quartz lights were on, lighting up the bleak world of the white volcanic cone ahead of us, and the wind whipped water around us. Occasionally there would be a burst of white on the shoulder of the mountain and you could see the wind whipping the water into a frenzy as another williwaw slammed down onto the anchorage. The power of the gust would make us surge back until the anchor wire came tight and we would stop with another uncomfortable jerk.

George had the radio turned down, and you could hear a couple of faint voices. It sounded like a freighter, far out to the west by the sound of them, talking to the U.S. Coast Guard. They weren't asking for help but they just wanted to alert the Coast Guard that they were struggling in heavy seas. I never did get their position. They could have been off Hawaii, or California, but from the sound of the weather and from what was pounding Amak, I was sure it was in the Bering Sea somewhere.

Suddenly something caught my eye coming around the corner of the island to the west, something that was lighting up the snow around it. It must be another boat, I thought, and watched as it got closer. And then I could see it—it was another crabber, pilothouse forward like us. And the ice! It got closer and I could see it better through the snow, and a chill ran down my neck. It was iced up worse than the halibut boats that lay beside us in Dutch a few weeks earlier. The whole boat carried so much ice that it had a ghostly look, the sharp edges of the rigging and the bulwarks soft with the buildup. They swung around into the limited shelter of the anchorage, and two guys appeared out on the upper deck and began beating the ice off the anchor winch. Then the snow came on thicker and they were lost in swirling white.

WE ALL SLEPT in the next morning. You could tell from the way the boat reeled from the gusts that we weren't going anywhere. It had snowed steadily all night, and everything was white except for a few dark places along the sides of the back wooden deck where seawater had slopped through the free-ing ports. To me the snow was a sobering sight, emphasizing how isolated we were, and how dependent we were on the pistons, gears, wires, and pumps that filled the room below me. Yet we knew we had something to savor, a day of rest. We stayed in our bunks late, until the delightful smell of bacon and eggs and pancakes wafted in and lured us to the galley.

"I talked to those guys this morning. Wooden boat, old sardiner," George said, as we sat around, the ruins of a great breakfast on the table before us. "Sounds like they were lucky to get in here when they did. It was their first trip out—they'd been up by the edge of the pack setting gear when the north-erly set in hard. They didn't want to go up into the ice so they headed down here. They'd been farther to the east'ard, so the seas were more on the beam and they were rolling like crazy and making ice too. Luckily they'd gotten all the gear off. Then the engine died. All the rolling had stirred up all the crap in their tanks and plugged the filters. Before they could get it squared away, the generator died too. How'd you like that, rolling around in some dark engine room, trying to hold on, tools flying, and trying to change a filter? Then the engineer had to bleed the injectors to get the air out of the lines—with only a flashlight to see by! He said by the time they got the generator going and all the filters changed, they'd taken on a hell of a load of ice, and had to creep along so as not to make any more. Creeping along, changing filters every half-hour . . . ," George's voice trailed off.

"Old boats, old tanks," Johnny said. "In winter, the Bering Sea will find your weaknesses."

"I used to think steel boats would ice worse than wooden boats," I said, "but I'm not so sure anymore. I was upstairs when those guys came in last night. You should have seen them. Worse than the halibut boats that came in that first day we got to Dutch, worse than that crabber we saw in Icy Strait. If they'd had to travel another couple of hours, they'd have been toast."

"Maybe when it first starts to get cold, a steel boat would ice up worse than a wood boat," George answered. "But once it gets good and cold, they all ice up about the same. But the difference is, these new steel rigs, at least the ones like us built specifically for the crab fishery and the Bering Sea like us, have smaller houses and longer decks. Those old sardiners, they got the same size house as us. But the deck is shorter, so their center of gravity is probably higher, even before they start to ice up. We have less rigging too. These tripod masts ice up much less than those rigs with all those wires holding up the masts. We're lucky, boys, to be up here in this nice new Marco rig, and that's the long and the short of it."

A bit of reading, many hands of cribbage, visits to the pilothouse for the sober view of the world outside—so the day went. Although I didn't envy our new neighbors their wooden boat, I did envy their galley windows. Those old wooden sardine seiners all had a galley that ran the full width of the deckhouse, typically with a set of three windows on either side. For those operating only in summer, buying fish for some cannery, the windows would sometimes even open. For all the boats converted to crabbing or any other winter fishery, tough Lexan plastic sheets were screwed permanently over the windows. Even so, what a treat to be able to sit in the galley and look out. Our only view was of the back deck, through a porthole, set into the back wall over the counter.

Ex MUD BOAT turned crabber *Isafjord* working in pancake ice near the Pribilof Islands about 1994. When the sea ice is like this, ten or twelve hours of zero weather with no wind will freeze it into a compact dense mass, capturing any crab buoys and possibly dragging them many miles as the pack moves. DARYL KYRA LEE PHOTOGRAPH, ACCENTALASKA.COM

13. The Siberian High

THAT NIGHT THE wind stopped and it became very cold. I was anchor cranker in the morning, and the sea smoke was almost masthead height, hiding everything around us. The sun was still down, showing only pale yellow in the east, and the sea smoke was brilliant, almost blinding white in our lights.

Gloved hand on iced railing, I made my way forward, relieved that the winch was frosty but not iced over. I eased the brake, swung the lever to start bringing in the cable, and watched as the cable, vertical with the wind gone, slowly angled forward, but snapping little pieces of ice as it did! I stopped the winch and went forward to peer over the rail. The head of our anchorage had iced over in the night, and the snow lay on top of the ice. It was thin, no more than a half-inch thick, and a black line showed where the anchor had ripped through the ice. I couldn't remember a time when the harbor had frozen around us at anchor, even on those cold days at Uyak Bay, because the wind had always been blowing so hard, stirring up the sea.

Inside again, I looked at the thermometer: two degrees above zero.

"Cross your fingers for no wind," Russell said.

"Never seen sea smoke quite this thick," I said.

"Peggy said this is the big Siberian high she'd been watching for a while. We'll go up and shuffle the gear around for a while, but if a wind comes up with the thermometer this low, we'll head back here." We still had almost two hours running to get to the gear and Bob was just starting to fix breakfast.

It was eerie. Except for that night when we battered our way out of the ice at Seward Harbor, I couldn't remember the sea being so windless. There was still a bit of leftover swell once we got out and away from Amak, but there wasn't a breath to ripple the swells and the sea smoke was all around us.

Halfway through the gear that day there was a little showing of good-sized males, twenty to twenty-five to a pot—enough to give us a sniff of where the body of crab had gone—so we stacked and moved. We wore cotton liners under our rubber gloves, but after forty-five minutes or so, our hands would still get pretty cold. In an older boat, there was nothing to do but suffer unless your skipper would give you a warm-up break every hour or so. But on the *Flood Tide*, there was the magic dryer, full of toasty, warm gloves and liners, spinning away, just inside the watertight door, so we'd pluck out a fresh hot pair when our fingers got cold.

Working in such cold brought other problems as well. When it came time to reset the stack, the coils of buoy line would have frozen. We'd have to open the crab hatch and dump the whole coil into the circulating seawater to let it thaw so that it could pay out properly when the pot was set. The bags would freeze inside the pots and a couple of us would have to struggle to get them out before we hoisted them over the rail.

At least there wasn't a sea out there this day. The cold took a toll on us, but in a different way than the struggle to keep our footing when it was rough. We worked until around seven, shut down the main engine for the night, and just drifted. If the wind had been blowing, we'd have run for Amak, even though it was two hours away, just so we could get a good night's sleep. We didn't even keep someone on watch. There were no freighters that far north, and there was no place to go—all the harbors and towns to the east of us were frozen in for the winter. But I knew George would get up a couple of times in the night to check our position.

We spent two days struggling in the extreme cold, the temperature around zero, the wind light, the strange sea smoke enveloping us and not even disappearing when the dim sun came over the horizon. We even took lunch breaks. We needed it. After working hard all morning in that bitter weather, we'd started to shiver by the middle of the day. We needed to sit for a bit in a warm space and put down some hot food. Those mid-day breaks weren't much for talking. We saved that for the end of the day. We were just a bunch of guys with rough, cold, reddened faces sitting around eating as quickly as we could, and slumping down to rest for a few brief minutes before George gave us the signal to go back out.

On the second evening, I was intent on pulling the frozen bag out of yet another pot we were struggling to set, when Russell put a hand on my shoulder and said, "Look," pointing. Forty miles away, Mount Pavlof had just cleared her throat, blasting hot ash and lava 20,000 or 30,000 feet into the air and illuminating the horizon of snow-covered peaks with its eerie red light. Deep beneath the Alaska Peninsula, the hot cauldron of magma that the continents and the sea floor floated on bubbled a bit, and a second violent puff of red blasted out of the crater to fill the night sky. If we'd been closer or downwind, we probably would have heard the blast. Yet, seen like that, so dramatically filling the night sky to the south and yet so silent, it seemed all the more impressive. Then came a third eruption, and by then all of us except George up in the pilothouse were watching in awe, as finally the last of the red hot cinders, ash, and lava fell to earth and all was dark and still again. The residents at False Pass, Cold Bay, Port Moller, and Nelson Lagoon probably were all tucked in for the night. We may have been the only ones to see the spectacular drama that night.

George was pushing hard. We'd be out the door and on deck before six in the morning, and we didn't quit until almost ten at night. By then we were almost totally done in. No one said anything, but the next day we started at 5 a.m., and eighteen hours later there was no sign that George was ready to call it a day. Russell excused himself and went into the pilothouse. Shortly after that, we called it a night. By the time I got the back deck squared away, Johnny did his engine room chores, Bob had cooked, and George and Russell had smoked their four or five cigarettes together, chewing the day over, we just wanted to get a hot meal in our stomachs and feel that sweet bunk beneath us.

I asked Russell the next day what he had said to George.

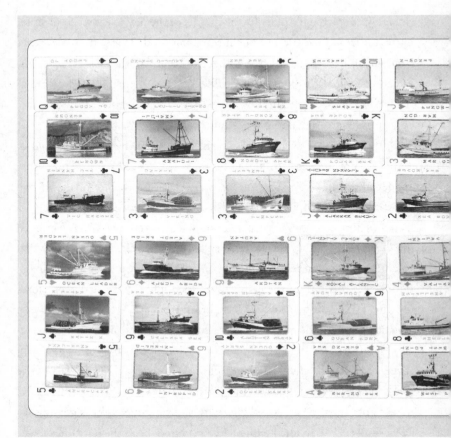

"I just said if he wore the guys out on shitty fishing, he wouldn't have much left when we really got into it. I mean, Jesus Christ, we're getting eight or ten keepers on a two- or three-night soak, and we're beating ourselves up for that. He needs to settle down. I told him this ain't like a short salmon season. He's got all year to make it."

Whatever Russell said, worked. We knocked off earlier after that.

We had our first hard southerly after that, with enough east in the wind that the anchorage at Amak was untenable. We knew it was coming. Peggy's forecasts for southerlies were usually right on. In that kind of a southerly, the shelter is right off the beach on the north side of the Alaska Peninsula. We

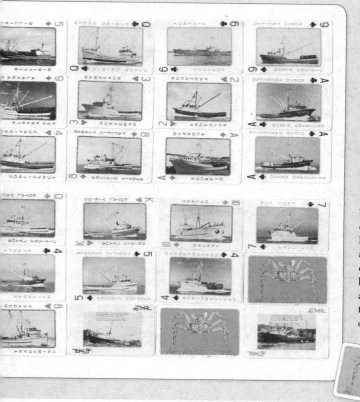

RARE KING CRABBER PLAYING CARDS. If you see a pack of these cards in a garage sale, buy them! They have become quite rare. Plus a number of the boats featured on the cards have been lost at sea, and the cards have become sort of a memorial to them. AUTHOR'S COLLECTION

knew that if the wind came up, we'd be bucking into it for five long hours to get to shelter, so we quit before noon.

Five miles north of the beach the wind came up, the first gust sixty at least, picking up the spray and freezing it all over the front of the pilot-house. Fortunately we didn't have far to go then, so we just put it on the slow bell—slowed way down—and jogged into the beach and anchored off the low tundra shore between Izembek Lagoon and the entrance to Isanotski Strait, known to fishermen as False Pass, without icing up too badly. But that first gust and blast of freezing spray made us glad we'd knocked off early.

If we'd been fishing farther west, we'd have run in under the high land on the western part of Unimak Island, and gotten out of the wind. But where we were, there wasn't any high land, so we could get out of the seas but not the wind. I looked at the chart: only three miles of marshy low tundra lay between us and Morzhovoi Bay, which was totally open to the south and the east and the big winds pouring off the North Pacific. As the *Coast Pilot* put it, "The bay forms a natural draw for the wind, which sweeps in and out with great violence."

And blow it did, seventy and eighty knots at suppertime, when we felt the boat shudder in the higher gusts and the anchor cable creak in the chock, as we sheered one way with the wind, came up tight against the anchor and sheered back the other way to start it all over again. About 2 a.m., it really came on, and we all went up into the pilothouse just to look in awe at the wind gauge: gusts in excess of 100 made the boat lurch and heel over. You couldn't see much—the windows had iced over—but at least we were far enough back from the beach so it was only sand and gravel spraying us, not small stones like we'd been hammered with in Uyak Bay.

We sat tight that next day. It was still blowing a steady seventy plus— the powerful southerly was howling through all the low passes. We turned on the defroster so we could at least look out. There was more landscape to look at than just Amak, and I spent some time in the pilothouse just study-ing the shore with the binoculars. It looked like a great beach to explore for glass balls, traditionally used by Japanese fishermen on their nets. The place might have seen years and perhaps even decades without a human footprint, but with our skiff back at Dutch and gusts lifting gravel and small stones off the beach, it wasn't much of a day for an outing.

As in the Aleutians, there were no trees on the shore. Beyond the beach, the land rose only a few feet, and in the middle distance you could see fro-zen tundra ponds similar to those that dotted tens of thousands of square miles of Northern and Western Alaska. Beyond that was the maze of inter-connected shallow lagoons at the head of Morzhovoi Bay. On the east side of the bay, the chart showed a cluster of tiny black rectangles and the notation

"Cannery (aban'd)"—one of the ubiquitous abandoned canneries that had sprung up in almost every Alaska bay with a good salmon run sixty or seventy years earlier when the Columbia River salmon magnates discovered the vast Alaska salmon resource.

This whole part of the Alaska Peninsula was part of the Izembek National Wildlife Refuge. In another few months, it would be teeming with birds, when literally millions of sea and marsh dwelling birds arrived on their annual migration up the coast to their summer breeding and nesting grounds. But on that bleak and wildly windy March morning, any life that was there was hidden and awaiting better weather.

THE NEXT MORNING it was still blowing fifty steady, but it was a bit warmer—up in the 20s. I was amazed that George wanted to go out. He said in those southerlies it always blew through the low passes much harder than it did when you got out a ways, and he was right. Two miles out it was blowing just a modest twenty-five to thirty, actually a good day for the Bering Sea in March.

That hard northerly we'd just experienced was sort of winter's last gasp. We had northerlies after that, but never with the power that froze the anchorage at Amak and brought below-zero temperatures. And the hard southerly that had us anchored off the Alaska Peninsula for two days had pushed back the ice front. We ran past our gear that next day just to see where the ice front was. It had moved north about four miles, and probably would keep moving, opening up more fishing ground as it did.

WE FISHED ANOTHER WEEK that trip, moving gear regularly. We'd find a little bunch of good-sized males, move all our gear to where it seemed they might be congregating, and then the next pick would drop way off again. Those were frustrating days, and I was glad it wasn't me standing there on the boat deck, looking down into the dark water as the buoy line came up, lighting a fresh Marlboro on each pot, and deciding whether we should stack or reset it.

On the back deck we were slowly achieving that smooth rhythm of working together that is the hallmark of a good crew. With the temperature in the mid-twenties we were barely icing. Salt water doesn't freeze until around 28°F. So working the deck and the pots was much easier than it had been earlier—with "easier" as a relative concept. At least the pots weren't frozen together, the net bag frozen to the pots, and the coils of line a single icy mass.

In Dutch it was still raw, frozen winter. We'd get in, unload our catch, clean up, and actually have a couple of days between trips. The Elbow Room became old and expensive, even for crab fishermen, so I found another hangout, a small rundown house belonging to an acquaintance where the dope was free and the music loud. People and food would come and go, night would blur into day, and I'd stumble blinking into another grim Aleutian day, and head back to the white Formica walls of our crabber's galley.

Sometimes, usually on trips into Dutch, we'd glimpse one of the big Japanese or European factory trawlers that worked the deeper waters north and west of Dutch. These immense fishing boats, 200 and 300 footers, towed nets both along the bottom and in mid-water for pollock and other species. This was in the days before the United States declared a 200-mile limit in 1977, and apparently many of these powerful foreign vessels were in the Bering Sea that spring.

Someone in the Elbow Room said that there were Japanese tangle netters, too, fishing for king crab with monofilament nets that laid flat on the bottom, though we hadn't seen a trace of them or their gear. We heard that the Japanese had tried using the big pots like we used, but that their crews, being generally much smaller than Americans, were unable to bull the heavy pots. I couldn't imagine the tedious work required to pull spiny king crab out of their thin, nylon tangle nets.

IN THE LATE SPRING, we got another crewmember, a stocky, friendly German named Walter Kuhr. His dad had been skipper of one of the big German freezer trawlers that fished the banks off of Iceland, Greenland, and

Newfoundland. They would be at sea for months at a time, and Walter had gone aboard as an apprentice when he was twelve. Short and rotund, dressed in the dark rain gear of the day, the crew called him Bomba, for he looked like the hollow steel balls used as floats on the headline of the trawl, *bombas* in German, and the nickname stuck.

Walter had an interesting story. He had worked as crew, and on a trip to fishing grounds off South America, the boat stopped in Chile to offload and give the crew some R&R. Walter met a woman, and when the trawler left, he decided to stay and make his life there with her. By then, having worked with his dad for years, he knew the intricacies of operating a trawler, from the pilothouse to the back deck to the engine room, and had enough money to get started with a small vessel. Within a few years, Walter had moved up to a larger boat, and was one of the more successful fishermen in Southern Chile.

In November 1970, Marxist President Salvador Allende took office in Chile and immediately started nationalizing many industries and establishing laws to protect the working class from poor treatment by the companies and individuals that they worked for. The reach of these new regulations extended all the way down to commercial fishing.

"When my crew get married, I haf' to give him bonus, and month off," explained Walter in his halting English. "Wife haf' baby, bonus and weeks off; in between trips, days off, holidays off, Sunday and Saturday off."

In addition to the rules came new taxes. When the government realized that the effect of the changes was encouraging fishing vessel owners to leave Chile, the government made it illegal to take boats across the border. Walter started buying gold watches with his money.

"And one day, I say to crew, 'Here, you want boat? Take boat.'"

Walter came to the United States with just his family, a few possessions, and a small case of gold watches. George had met him when he had been demonstrating trawl gear on the Chilean coast in the *Gringo*. Knowing Walter's talent and drive, our skipper was thrilled to have him aboard with us.

We were too. Walter was a bulldog on deck—quick, strong, and funny—everything you'd want in a shipmate.

RUSSELL FULTON, hand coiling aboard the *Flood Tide*, Bering Sea, summer 1971. We often hand coiled in the shallower depths (300–500 feet) in the "Compass Rose" area of the eastern Bering Sea, just to keep our skills up. But in the much deeper (1,000–1,200 feet) crab grounds of the North Pacific, south of the Aleutians, the pile would be almost up to Russell's cigarette when the pot finally came up, so we let the automatic coiler do the work.

14. Spring in the North

In the Lower 48, spring swept across the Great Plains: tractors planted, grass greened, and bulbs erupted into flowers.

And up the great flyways came the birds.

One morning in early May, I found fifteen dead birds lying on deck, just aft of the deckhouse. I picked one up, a shorebird, some sort of sandpiper, and his head flopped over, neck broken. It was odd, never finding a bird on deck before that, and then fifteen, all at once.

"It's the lights," George explained that night. "You got to kill your crab lights at night once the migrations start, unless you're fishing. It attracts the birds." So after that we shut off the big lights at night.

Then one morning, when I got up to pull the anchor, still groggy from a long day and a short night, I stood up on deck for a moment, trying to comprehend what I was seeing. We'd anchored near the Bering Sea entrance to False Pass. Even though the sky was just starting to get light, the sea was dark and had a strange moving texture. I had never seen anything like it, and went to the rail to take a closer look.

In a moment, I grasped what I was seeing, and stood there truly mesmerized. I was seeing a massive bird migration. The numbers of birds were beyond counting. They were flying maybe a foot off the water, parting as they got to our bow, and seeming to rejoin in a seamless carpet again behind the boat. It was a swiftly moving hoard of millions, maybe tens of millions, of some dark shore or marsh bird, flowing smoothly, like a broad, dark, river out of Isanotski Strait (False Pass) and spreading as they entered the Bering Sea. I walked out onto the back deck to get a better view. The flowing carpet was probably five feet below the rail. The light was still dim, and only if you looked intently could you see individual birds, flowing with the rest, driven by a powerful and mysterious force of nature.

These birds were bound for the tens of thousands of square miles of marshes and wetlands, countless tundra ponds and lakes in the deltas of the Yukon and Kuskokwim Rivers in the North. That region sees few humans and slumbers frozen and lifeless for most of the winter. Yet when the days in those high latitudes get longer and the sun rises higher in the sky, plants, animals, and birds flourish with an explosion of life unfamiliar to those of us who live in the middle latitudes. Long daylight hours nourish life in the waters and on land, creating endless food sources for many life forms, and also allowing for longer breeding and feeding times.

To this ultrarich biosystem in the Northland, birds from all over the world migrated each spring: the bar-tailed godwit from New Zealand, the golden plover from Hawaii, and the arctic tern, all the way from Cape Horn in South America, 10,000 miles over water without stopping. Even humpback whales and gray whales come from Hawaii and Mexico to feast on the krill-rich northern waters. This powerful phenomenon was unknown to me until that experience.

So numerous were the birds that only for a short distance beyond the stern was the water even visible at all. I watched for a few minutes, and then the immense flock thinned out and was gone. There were few stragglers. The arrow-like sense of direction seemed to be embedded in the birds' collective mentality.

ONBOARD THE *FLOOD TIDE,* spring mostly meant that there was less chance of icing, that we could put a full load of pots on deck, triple-stacked if we had to, and travel free of that gnawing fear of getting iced up. The ice pack receded up the Bering Strait, and more gales came from the southwest and southeast.

Down in Seattle, in preparation for breakup when ice would recede from tiny harbors as well as the great Yukon and Kuskokwim Rivers, big barges were loaded with all manner of supplies for summer delivery to the Native villages and settlements that dotted the coast. Everything that didn't come in by expensive bush plane came up from the Lower 48 by barge. And for many of the communities, frozen in for the winter, the first barge of the season after "breakup" of the shore and river ice was a big event.

We started to see them go by in mid-April, although many of the harbors to the north were still frozen in. The ice-free season was so short, especially in communities above the Arctic Circle, that the barges came and waited, to be ready to get to shore and offload as soon as they possibly could.

In many coastal settlements, the harbors were too shallow for the big tugs to get in close. The winter ice, pushed by the current, scoured the shore, making it difficult to build any sort of permanent breakwaters. A barge on the Bering Sea route could be recognized easily by having a powerful crane, lowered for traveling, and perhaps even a small thirty- to thirty-five-foot tug securely lashed on deck.

In shallow places, the big crane would be raised and used to lower the little tug into the water, where it was used to push the shallow draft barge closer to shore. Then the locals would send out their small boats with a smaller and even shallower barge, which the crane would load with the one or two containers, or in the smaller villages, just a few pallets of much-needed freight.

In a land with few trees, most of the villagers' houses were heated by oil. In the fall, the last barge of the year would top off the tanks of all the village fuel distributors. But if the winter had been especially hard, by the time the first fuel barge headed up the coast in the spring, the villages would be short on fuel for heating and cooking.

And as we were crabbing that winter and spring of 1971, another major change was coming to rural Alaska: the snowmobile. For Alaska Natives and rural residents in Western and Northern Alaska, the dogsled was the traditional form of winter transportation. The snowmobile would change all this. Firing up your snowmobile on a chilly arctic morning was a lot easier than

A CRAB POT in the "hayrack" just after the bag has been dumped into the sorting bin, *Flood Tide*, 1971. It's easy to see why this arrangement was unpopular with our crew. The 700-pound steel pot hung dangerously over our heads.

harnessing up your dog team, which had to be cared for and fed throughout the rest of the year as well. And so the dependence on the fuel barge and the demand for gasoline along with heating oil was becoming even greater.

BUT THE BARGE that made me stop and look in envy for a long, long time was the first Bristol Bay barge of the season. As I was learning from George and

Russell, one of the biggest small-boat salmon fisheries in Alaska took place each summer at the head of Bristol Bay, 300 miles east of Amak.

One day in mid-May, I was head down sorting crab, when Russell put his hand on my shoulder. I looked up in surprise: a big ocean-going tug was steaming abeam of us, just fifty yards away, towing a very large barge stacked six high with containers from one end to the other. And on the very top, lashed down, were a dozen shiny new thirty-two-foot salmon gillnetters.

I thought about the small boats . . . where you could be captain and controlling your own destiny. I looked around at the deck of the *Flood Tide*. Fishing was okay, but not great. The crab we were finding had the big keeper adult males mixed in with the sublegal males and females. Each pot might come up with a couple hundred crabs in it, but only twenty-five or thirty were keepers. The rest had to be tediously sorted. The fishing wasn't good enough to let the gear soak, so we were stacking, three layers high. Sometimes I felt crab fishing was like an extremely dangerous factory job except we couldn't go home at night.

George had a different perspective. He was getting older and probably hadn't put together much of a retirement for him and his wife. Then the king crab boom came along, and he had the connections to put together the *Flood Tide*, a first-class boat. For George, the Bering Sea represented a chance to make it big and build a nest egg for retirement.

All the skippers I met up in Dutch were self-made men. They had started with little, many emigrating from Norway or Iceland as young men with little more than the clothes on their backs. They went fishing as other emigrants to the Northwest had, starting on deck on family boats, working their way up, maybe getting their first boat with money from the community as young men, getting bigger and better boats as they became older, putting in long seasons year after year. Finally some of them got a boat big enough for the crab fishery, often wood, and often borrowing heavily to get to the Bering Sea.

IN THE NORTHWEST commercial fishing community, there were thousands of little boats, ranging in length from thirty to sixty footers, primarily salmon boats that spread out all along the vast Northwest Coast every spring. It was impossible for one person to know all the other salmon fishermen.

But the big boats, those over eighty feet, were a different story. There were far fewer of them in the early 1970s. Because of the lack of good haul-out facilities in Alaska then, almost all of them hauled out at the boatyards around Puget Sound to get worked on every year or two. The community of big-boat fishermen was much smaller, and most of the skippers knew of each other. Starting in 1971 the new steel boats would come to dominate the king crab fishery. When one of the biggest yet was built for a guy who had never owned a big boat before, my impression was that it turned a few heads in the tightly knit community. "Who was this guy with the newest and fanciest boat in the fleet?" might have been the common impression. In this sense, George probably felt additional pressure to prove himself. He wanted to show the other skippers that he was a production fisherman, trip after steady good trip, even in the worst weather in a generation.

George had made it clear after a few trips that he was looking for someone to bring into the crab fishery—just like the Norwegians were doing, helping good young fishermen get their own boats. I couldn't be sure with George what was true and what was bluster. But he had said if I wanted to stay on for another season, I could be relief skipper, taking over for the trips to and from Alaska, and during some of the off-peak summer fishing. It was an exciting thought. Talking with other crab crews, I learned that a job as relief skipper was a huge step up from what was starting to seem like backbreaking work. Relief skipper was the natural career path that could lead to big boat ownership, or at the least, if the crab fishery remained healthy, a more secure financial future than being a deck slave.

IN MID-JUNE, as we worked the flats east and north of False Pass, an area with a flat bottom about 250 feet deep, we'd see power scows—barge-like fish-buying boats—headed east to Bristol Bay for the short salmon season there. The flat-bottomed barges were built during World War II to take supplies to the Army bases in the Aleutian Islands. The Japanese were occupying two of the islands, and the Army and Navy were getting ready to launch a major effort to dislodge them. The barges were perfect for the shallow rivers and the big tides of the eastern Bering Sea. Many canneries had shallow water or mud and sandbars in front of them at low tide, and the flat-bottomed scows could just settle on the mud without tilting on their sides.

Crab fishing that early summer, we were so busy sorting crab that our lives reminded me of something Russell had said when I had asked him about scallop fishing. On scallop boats much of the crew's work was opening the scallop shells and carefully cutting the meat, or muscle, cleanly off the shell. The work went on, shell after shell after shell. "If you stop to light a cigarette," Russell had told us, "you light one for your buddy too, and he barely has the time even to smoke it."

We were a tight crew on the *Flood Tide*. After the season we'd probably go our separate ways. Would we get together socially when we weren't working on the boat together? Probably not. But we were bound together by the challenge and risks of our work. Deck work was such an interlocking series of actions that we all felt it acutely if someone wasn't pulling his share of the load. It wasn't that we'd get irritated if someone didn't seem to be sorting through the crab as quickly as his deckmates. It was more of a question of timing, of fitting as accurately as possible into that ballet of maneuvers required to make things go smoothly on deck.

Sometimes in the galley when we were relaxing, in that all too brief interval between food and the bunk, we would talk about how to make things go a little smoother, a little faster on deck. We talked about small things, such as lengthening out a few of the nylon lanyards on the bait containers so that they were all almost identical. Or burning a few ends on the poly line that we used to tie up the buoy line coils with when we had to stack pots; some of the ends had started to unravel, making the effort to tie knots difficult. Or working on the coordination to get the coils of line out of the coiler and into the pots when we had to stack gear. Just those little moves and refinements that made activities on deck go a little smoother and a little faster. Working on deck was frustrating enough with the wind and the cold, and the deck always moving beneath you. Striving together to make it all go smoother was a way of making it easier for all of us.

In fishing school, the course of commercial fishing skills at the University of Rhode Island I attended before the *Denise* fiasco, we had studied navigation, diesel engines, hydraulic systems, electronics, and more, but I felt like there should have been another course: surviving on deck. Nothing had prepared me for the unrelenting work and the grim surroundings of the Bering Sea.

The challenges were both physical and emotional. I was twenty-five in 1971, fit and healthy. But some mornings it was all I could do to get out of bed when the call came to suit up. I ached in places I didn't know I had. We wolfed down vitamins, ibuprofen, and fluids constantly. Russell was twice my age, had arthritis, and smoked more than a pack a day, yet he pulled his weight day after day without complaint. The mental challenges were there as well, especially before the weather improved in the spring. You were cold and exhausted day after day. You ached from the moment you woke up to the moment your head hit the pillow or the galley table, sixteen or eighteen hours later.

The concept of a wedding and married life seemed to be receding into the future and becoming more and more unlikely. The money was okay but wasn't big enough yet to justify what we were going through.

Almost all the guys I'd been to fishing school with were from East Coast fishing families and their fathers all worked in coastal fisheries. Their dads were draggermen, lobstermen, herring chasers, and mackerel catchers. Out the door, early to be sure, at 4 or 5 a.m. when the weather served. But home at night, supper with the family, maybe a movie and dinner out on a Saturday night. They were able to go to their children's soccer, basketball, and baseball games, piano recitals and ballet performances, all the usual comings and goings of a normal life.

A guy could get blue thinking about all those things, I finally decided. The best remedy at the moment was simply what we as a crew already were doing—focusing totally on the job at hand, taking pride in doing it as well as we possibly could.

I BROKE A RIB around the first of June on a day when things seemed to be really looking up. There was a bit of a nasty chop, but the sun broke through every now and again, and the fishing was steady enough that we weren't doing much stacking. We'd just set a pot and I had turned to jog toward the stern to hook up the next one to set when George gave a long toot on the horn, the "bad one coming" signal. Almost at the same time as the blast on the horn, we lurched down and to starboard, and a big solid green sea came over the rail, swept me off my feet, spun me around, and slammed me into a pot lashed to the stern. I was instantly soaked inside my oilskins and felt a sharp pain like the stab of a hot knife, and I knew that the impact had broken a rib. I lay there for a minute holding onto the pot with both hands while the sea pulled at me. The pain was incredibly sharp and burning. Russell was suddenly beside me, and I could vaguely hear the engine slowing to an idle.

"Just help me up," I said, wincing at the pain when I took a breath. Step by painful step, I made my way into the galley with Russell's help, and he sat me down, helped me remove my boots and rain gear, and got me a glass of water to chug down four ibuprofen tablets.

"I'm okay," I said. "Just give me a few minutes."

Giving me a long questioning look, he then went out. And in a minute I could feel George throttle up, and knew the guys were getting back to work without me.

After a while the ibuprofen dulled the pain enough for me to get my soaked clothes off and get into the shower to warm up. When I was just sitting in the galley with a coffee, George came down the steps.

"Rib?" he asked.

I nodded.

"Want me to find you a ride to town?"

I shook my head. I wasn't coughing up blood, so I knew it hadn't penetrated a lung. It was just painful as hell, but there wasn't much that could be done with a broken rib.

"Just let me sit for a bit," I said. "I'll get out there in an hour or so. Maybe I can just run the hauler and the coiler for a day or so."

So it went. I knew the drill. When you had a job on a good boat like the *Flood Tide*, unless you were bleeding bad or broken enough to need medical attention, you just kept going. I knew there were a lot of capable guys in

Dutch looking for an opportunity to get on a boat. "Too bad your man got hurt; you looking for someone?" all in the same breath. I couldn't afford to let that happen.

For four days, it hurt so much that once I finally got into my bunk each night, it was almost impossible to find a sleeping position that wasn't unbearable. The ibuprofen just took the edge off, so George gave me something stronger from the medical kit.

The guys let me run the hauler and the coiler and the stacking winches and didn't complain when I obviously wasn't doing a full share of sorting crab. They knew that if the tables were turned, I'd do the same for them.

THE CRABBER *Viking*, riding out a blow near the entrance to False Pass from the Bering Sea, Unimak Island, May 1971. When a powerful storm blows in from the North Pacific through the low passes in the hills of the Alaska Peninsula, it accelerates and intensifies the power of the wind. The wind is probably fifty or sixty miles per hour, but because we and the *Viking* are in the lee of the land, the sea hasn't had a chance to build up. It is also through these low passes that millions of birds migrate each spring and fall.

15. The Long Days

"HEY, BOYS, I guess this is summer," George yelled down to us from the pilothouse one June day about 100 miles north of Unimak Pass. At first we didn't get it. Then it hit us: we had shed our rain gear tops for the first time since arriving three months earlier. It wasn't like we were in T-shirts. We still had on long underwear, a wool shirt and sweater under our rain gear, and a sweatshirt on top of that. But shedding the heavy rain jacket and working with our sweatshirt hoods down made it feel like summer.

And the Bering Sea summer brought something else that few folks state-side experienced: those long, high-latitude days. For the month or so on either side of the summer solstice on June 21, the longest day of the year, the sun was in the sky from about four in the morning until almost midnight, and even at the end of the day it just sort of slid slowly below the horizon slightly west of north and then rose a few hours later slightly east of north. It never got dark. When the sun was down, the sea and the sky were illuminated by a lingering twilight.

Of course, being crab fishermen, we wanted to make hay while the sun shone, so this meant even longer days on deck. On most days Russell was having his first smoke of the day before 5 a.m. as we waited for the toot on the horn to announce that we were coming up on our first pot. If we were lucky, we might even get a fifteen-minute sit-down lunch, eating quickly before getting back out on deck and hitting it again for another ten hours. It would be an unusual day that we'd sit down for supper before 11 p.m. We figured it was a good day if we hit the sack before midnight, and four and a half hours of sleep was a good night.

By then we'd been collaborating as a crew for three months or so and had finally gotten into what I called "the dance"— the complex interwoven tapestry of individual actions and motions that a good crew gets after working together for enough time.

Throwing the coils was one of the arts of crabbing. We're talking about a coil about three feet high. The trick was to be standing at the rail with the first 100 feet or so held loosely in your hands, so that if the pot were released inadvertently for some reason, you wouldn't be pulled over the side tangled in line. As soon as the pot was released, you stepped to the rail and sort of laid the coil onto the surface of the water, then stepped back and carefully picked up the next section of line and tossed it overboard. The trick was to make sure that the coil hit the water right side up so it would feed out without tangling. It wasn't a job for the careless. But at least in summer, or what passed for summer in the Bering Sea, we didn't have the problem with the coils getting iced up when we stacked gear.

With an increased volume of crab that had to be sorted came something else—back pain. In the winter, we hadn't gotten into big volumes of crab. But with the good weather, sometimes we were hauling pots with several hundred pounds or more of legal males mixed in with hundreds of smaller males and females, which had to be individually sorted. When we weren't bulling the heavy pots around the deck, hoisting the heavy coils of buoy line in or out of the pot, we would be bent over sorting, and pretty soon ibuprofen became as much a part of our days as coffee and brownies.

Because king crabbing was a volume business, the trick for the skipper was to keep the pots on the biggest male crabs, those that would be big enough that we could tell at a glance that they didn't need to be measured. The fewer crabs we had to measure, the faster we could load the boat: this was the key to being a highline skipper. And it was a constant challenge, since the herds of crab were always moving on the ocean floor beneath us. And despite having a very sophisticated depth-finder, it wasn't able to discern herds of crab, much less their composition, so the skipper had to be constantly exploring with part of our string of 175 pots, so as to try to keep most of our strings where the big males were.

Some trips seemed like endless days of bending over piles of crab in the sorting bin, measure in hand, three of us heads down, sorting, throwing the keepers into the deck openings of our crab tanks, hoisting the sorting bin to dump the small males and females over the side, just in time for another buoy to appear alongside and we'd start it all over again.

Each of the *Flood Tide*'s two big crab tanks had to be filled to the top with seawater, with the big circulating pump in the engine room constantly pumping in more. The purpose was to avoid something called the free-surface effect. The weight of the water in large holds such as we had, was substantial, and in order for it not to affect the stability of the vessel by sloshing back and forth, it had to be kept full to the point that water was usually flowing up and out of the open hatch in the deck through which we tossed the keeper crabs.

Finally one trip, late that spring, when I'd sort of resigned myself to mediocre fishing until the supposedly legendary fall fishing, something unexpected happened: we got "on the crab." But, oddly, it sort of crept up on us.

We'd started off that day with the dreaded angry "stack it" jerk of the chin and Marlboro thrown over the side. Then twenty or thirty pots later, more keepers appeared in the gear, and we started setting more back than we stacked, then set what we had on deck, and kept picking and setting back.

You get on autopilot after a while on deck, especially if you're just picking and setting. The crab were mixed, and we had to do a lot of sorting—just bending over hour after hour, trying not to get thrown around, since even on a nice day, the Bering Sea is rough enough to surprise the unwary. But at least my rib had finally healed. I was down to two ibuprofen in the morning instead of six.

Then our forward hold, which can hold over 70,000 pounds, appeared full. The crab were right up to the hatch in the deck. It surprised all of us. We knew we had a good trip going, but we didn't think we had that many aboard yet. "Shut the hatch and turn on the light in the engine room," George called down to Johnny.

John hesitated, unsure what he was supposed to do. George called down to explain, raising his voice to make himself heard over the whine of the engines, "Crab are attracted to light. That's why they put a porthole in the engine room bulkhead with a light bulb in the engine room side. Shut the hatch, turn on the light, start putting crab in the afterhatch, and try it again later."

So we did. And when we opened the forward hold two hours later, we looked down into the water in amazement. It no longer looked full. The crab were all piled up against the forward bulkhead, attracted to the light beyond the engine room porthole.

Heads down, more sorting and throwing, into the forward hold again this time until later in the afternoon, it was full, full, full. We just sort of looked at each other in amazement for a moment; it was the first time we had filled the big forward hold. On our cracked and tired faces, something approaching a smile appeared briefly. But then the horn tooted: the next buoy was at the rail, and another 700 or 800 pounds of mixed crab was coming up and headed for the sorting bin. Occasionally we'd have a break of two or three minutes, while George took a radio call or took a little longer to get to the next pot. The sun was actually shining in that notoriously cloudy place, and we'd hustle over to the porthole that led into the galley, take our gloves off, stuff in a big hunk of thickly frosted cake or whatever sugar-loaded treat Bob had made that morning into our mouths, and just lean back and feel the sun warm and fine on our faces until the horn tooted and we went back to work. Such moments were rare, but we savored them.

That was our biggest trip so far, almost 90,000 pounds, by the time the first crab were ten days onboard and it was time to head in to unload. We were far from being plugged. The *Flood Tide* could hold almost 140,000 pounds of live crab. But putting in a good trip like that sure put a spring in our step when we got to Dutch. We weren't highliners by any means, but we knew through the grapevine what the other boats were doing, and that trip was right up there with the rest of them.

I'd begun to realize something about commercial fishing. That those big scores you'd hear about down on the docks in Seattle or up in the Elbow Room sometimes, the big, big crew shares, those were the top guys on the top boats, guys who'd maybe put in their time year after year to get where they were. We had a great boat, an able crew, and great gear and equipment. But finding that legendary crab bonanza on the great wide plain of the eastern Bering Sea was a lot harder than the guys on the docks down in Seattle made it sound.

WE FISHED A BIT on the northern approaches to Unimak Pass that June, always an interesting place at that time of year. Through it went all sorts of freighter traffic going from Asia to the West Coast of the United States. Bulk carriers, tankers, log carriers, trampers, and heavily laden container ships would steam northeast from Asian ports, then pass Russia's Komandorski Islands off the Kamchatka Peninsula. They'd enter the western Bering Sea and pass along the Aleutians, before ducking down through Unimak Pass to begin their long arc across the North Pacific to their destinations. Other traffic included fuel barges and their tugs, and small freighters.

Thirty or forty years earlier, the last of the world's square-riggers still in the freight trade would be making the voyage from San Francisco to the distant canneries of Bristol Bay and the remote Bering Sea coast. This was the famous Star fleet of the Alaska Packers Association—big windjammers with names like *Star of England, Star of Greenland,* and *Star of India.* Starting at the turn of the twentieth century, when the huge summer salmon runs up the Naknek, Kvichak, Egegik, and Ugashik Rivers were discovered in the roadless country of Western Alaska, it was clear to the packers that the only way to harvest the fish was to bring everything up in the spring, from cans to fishing equipment and even crews—Asian cannery workers and Norwegian and Italian fishermen. The season was amazingly short, just six or seven weeks.

In early March, the big ships would load up in San Francisco with everything that a big cannery—essentially an entire temporary town out in the

wilderness—would need for the salmon season. In April, the windjammers would get towed out of the bay and were cast free beyond the Golden
Gate Bridge to begin the 3,500-mile sail up to Unimak Pass. A big steam tug
would have been sent up ahead of them, to station itself at the entrance to
those treacherous tide-wracked Aleutian waters, ready to tow the big rigs
through so that they could continue east to Bristol Bay without delay. Once
there, they would anchor off the remote canneries. The caretaker, who may
have gone almost ten months without any company other than his wife and
family, and perhaps a few Natives if there was a village nearby, would thrill
to see the big rigs, receive mail and supplies, and welcome the activity of the
salmon season after a long, lonely winter.

Sometimes when we were working close to the high bluffs and smoking volcano that comprised the eastern shore of the pass, there were times
when we had a few minutes between pots and I was caught up on all my deck
work. I'd look out at that desolate sight and imagine that very last square-
rigger, sometime in the mid-1940s, deeply laden with thousands of cases of
canned salmon and the weary canning and fishing crews, probably taking
their first rest since they arrived nine or ten weeks earlier, tacking slowly
back and forth in front of the pass, waiting for the tide or the right wind, and
then finally gliding through to disappear into the mists of time.

Next to disappear were the cod schooners, big three- and four-masted
rigs that would leave Seattle in April or May to fish codfish from dories in
the Bering Sea, and delivering salted cod to Puget Sound ports four or five
months later. When the schooners arrived on the fishing grounds, they would
launch twenty or more big dories, each with a single fisherman aboard. The
men would row or, in later years, motor out, looking for a likely spot, and
then start fishing with hooks and lines. Codfish are big, and if it were a good
day, a fishermen would come alongside the schooner again in the evening,
his dory deep in the water with a full load of perhaps 250 big codfish. Like
any other Bering Sea fishery before or since, codfish fishing required long
hard hours in the dories, and then more hard work when the crews got back
aboard the schooners and carefully cleaned, washed, and then salted down

the fish in the schooners' cavernous fish hold. The last schooner to make a codfish trip to the Bering Sea was the *C A Thayer*, in 1950.

Then there were the several thousand sailing gillnetters of Bristol Bay. Even though small dependable gasoline-fueled marine engines were available starting in the 1920s, regulations prohibited them in the Bristol Bay salmon-fishing boats until 1958, long after the rest of the Alaska fishing fleets had switched over to power. The idea was to legislate inefficiency into the rules so that more fishermen would be able to share the harvest.

I'd met a few fishermen who remembered those sailing days. It was a short fishery, just five or six weeks. During that time, millions of red salmon passed annually from the Bering Sea into the wide river mouths, where the fishermen waited, and into the rivers and lakes beyond. The twenty-five-foot tides rushed back and forth in the shallow channels, and at the end of the day the little thirty-two-foot single-masted fishing boats with their two-man crews would sail into the rivers to unload their catches, with the swift currents pushing them on. Then as now, it was an immensely competitive fishery. As the sailing gillnetters swarmed into the rivers headed to the anchored fish-buying scows, the more aggressive fishermen would try to shove others out of the way at the barge.

"With that current pushing you on," one old fisherman told me, "all you've got is one shot at throwing your tie-up line to the crew on the barge. If you miss or the guys on the barge don't get it cleated off in time, that current just shoves you away upriver, and you've got to throw the anchor out and wait for the tide to turn." If another boat shoved you away just as you were making your approach, you missed your turn to unload. It wasn't a place to be nice to the next guy. The favors didn't get returned.

SALMON/HALIBUT BOAT, Port Protection, Southeast Alaska, 1972. The dream that kept me going through the long days of crab fishing was something like this: a smaller boat that could be operated by one or two, fishing out of some quiet small island community in the southeast part of Alaska.

16. The Job Hunters Come

EACH TIME WE WENT into Dutch to deliver our crabs, there would be at least one new boat in town, either another wooden rig some brave entrepreneurial fisherman had sunk all his money into, or one of the new steel rigs. And something else: all of a sudden we were veterans. We hadn't even had a full crab season under our belts, but we'd already been through some of the coldest and windiest months that anyone could remember. We'd be standing on deck with the tie-up lines in our hands as George slowed down when we entered the inner harbor, looking out at the new boats with their crews looking out at us, just in from another crab trip. We could sense their respect as they prepared for their first crab trip. We were veterans and after just four months!

Something else we saw was the new job hunters. In the bitter depth of winter when we first arrived, the name of the game around town was survival. The idea that someone would come up there without a job was alien. There was no place to live, there was no work, and everything was very expensive. But now with the temperature regularly climbing into the fifties, and occasionally, on a very nice day, breaking sixty, and with more boats arriving and the crab plants starting to look for workers, people actually flew in to Dutch to look for crew jobs. Some of them took work in the crab plants to enjoy the modest benefits of the bunkhouse and mess hall, or in some cases, squatting in one of the many abandoned Army buildings behind town.

The Elbow Room, home in the heart of winter only to the most hardcore drinkers and crab crews, got even more crowded, with so many boats in. You could tell which guys were looking for jobs: they'd be nursing their drinks, saving their money, as opposed to a crab boat crew like us, just in from a trip, pounding the drinks about as fast as we could get them down. They would ask us what it was like out there, trying to glean every scrap of information they could get about what the deck work was like, and if we knew of any boats that might be short a crewman.

Actually the chances of guys we bumped into in the Elbow Room and around the docks getting a job weren't bad, and probably a lot easier than getting a job back at Fishermen's Terminal in Seattle. The boats down there were all crewed up with family and friends; many were new to the fishery, and their owners had the whole construction and fitting out period to hand pick their crew.

Once the boats were up in the Bering Sea and fishing, if a hand got sick or was hurt or had to leave for some reason, it was difficult to get someone up from Seattle at the last moment. The few flights out from Anchorage were often full when the crab plants rotated work crews, and flights were canceled regularly because of weather. So the chances were that if a guy already in Dutch talked a good line of bullshit about his experience and presented himself well, he might get a job if an opportunity arose.

Working at one of the crab plants, especially on the dock, was another way to position yourself for getting a crew job. The dock workers who took your tie-up lines and operated the unloading winches and came aboard to unload the crab, often had a chance over the course of a few months to establish a bit of rapport with the skippers—a scrap of conversation here and there, helping the skipper out when he needed something from the plant, or maybe a quick run into town with the company pickup to get a last-minute item from the Alaska Commercial Company. And when the opportunity arose, you could throw in the zinger: "Hey, if you ever need a hand on short notice, I'm available."

In 1971, there were very few training programs for commercial fishermen like the one that I had attended at the University of Rhode Island, and none in the Puget Sound region, which was home to more than 1,000 boats that spent a long season in Alaska each summer, mostly fishing salmon. You pretty much got a job networking with friends and family or, as I had initially, prowling the docks and hoping some kind skipper would take you on. Once you had worked that first season, it was much easier to get a job the following season. Usually if you did a good job, the skipper would offer you the position again. If for some reason he didn't, by then you would have met enough folks around the fishery to find another job.

The salmon fisheries were growing slowly, and most of the crew jobs, especially on the seiners, were taken by men who were content with the work and returned season after season. These were great summer jobs—generations of young Northwest fishermen had put themselves through college working on salmon seiners in Alaska.

Now, looking around the waterfront at Dutch Harbor, you could tell that this was a boom fishery. The Northwest shipyards were beginning to reach capacity, and already the first of the crabbers built in the Gulf of Mexico were arriving.

Yet it was in a boom that a sharp guy, even with no money behind him, could rise quickly from deckhand to mate, to relief skipper, and eventually to full-time skipper. With the huge investment required to build and fit out a 100-foot plus crab boat, a dependable skipper was of critical importance. Initially, most of the new boats were skippered by their owners, who would try to recruit someone as a relief skipper, for the long trips back and forth between Seattle and Dutch at first, and then maybe a bit of off-peak fishing later.

As opposed to the salmon fisheries, the physical and mental strains on a crab-boat skipper were immense. A lot of the crab boats had several skippers, who rotated off and on. The owners would be there for the peak of the season, and turn it over to a relief skipper and go back home to spend time with their families during the slower months.

Owning a crab boat was a big step up from the salmon business. Most of the boats were individual corporations or limited liability companies, and often had a full-time bookkeeper or manager on the payroll back in Seattle.

But for a salmon crewman on a small troller or a gillnetter, a career might look something like this: work for a number of seasons as crewmen, learning the ropes and getting to know a wide circle of fishermen as well as making those critical contacts among the salmon canneries or freezer plants. If you wanted to step up and eventually own your own boat, you would probably have a job in the winter as well to build up your cash.

So with the bank and the cannery helping you, you would get a nice salmon boat and launch your career as skipper. As you quickly learned, however, driving the boat around and making a tricky landing at the fuel dock when the tide is running like a bullet and the wind is blowing hard from the north is far from easy. The hard part is determining where exactly do you set your net (or put your hooks into the water). It's a big ocean out there and all of a sudden it seems even larger when you have to decide which direction to turn the wheel to find the fish.

Still you probably have friends out there from your days as a crewman. You see where they are setting their nets or hooks, and drop yours in not too far away, catch a few fish without snagging on the rocks, and the whole process begins. Hopefully, if the fish gods and the weather gods and the breakdown gods show you a halfway decent face, you'll finish up the season with at least enough to feel good about yourself and your decision to be a boat owner, pay your bills, and have enough left to go fishing again the next season, probably with a winter job.

Thus your career as a boat owner-operator begins. The good side is that you have your own boat, you are your own boss, you can savor the true pleasures of sliding into some exquisite little Alaska anchorage at night, after a long day pulling fish out of the sea, have a dinner with a nice fresh salmon on the table, and put your head down for the good sleep. If you are really fortunate, you can find a woman willing to do it all with you.

The down side is the bane of many fishing boat owners—boat payments. The nicer the boat that you get, the larger your boat payment is. Payments can be a problem unless you manage to put together a large nest egg somehow, maybe from a big crab season, like I was hoping to do. Generally, banks are accommodating to fishermen; often loans might require interest only for much of the year, then a big principal payment after the season. But the bottom line is that if you have a bad season, you better get home quickly to talk to your banker and line up a winter job or even two!

When prices are high and the fish are running thick and fast, as I saw in my one season of buying fish, everyone has a pretty good smile on their face toward the end of the season. Not only is there the financial reward of a good season, but there is the much bigger reward of getting together again with your family at the end of the season (unless you are lucky enough to have them with you.)

You might leave your Puget Sound home around the end of March. If fishing was good, you might feel by mid-August or so that you were close enough to having your winter money that you could consider heading home by Labor Day or so, sparing yourself the ordeal that a cruise down the Inside Passage could become a month or six weeks later after the weather turned gnarly. Sometimes wives would fly up for a week or so in the middle of the season, maybe even with the kids if dad's boat was big enough. But many salmon fishermen wouldn't see their wives or families for months on end.

After the first few seasons when you had to work hard at a money job in the winter as well to stay solvent, you finally got in to the enviable situation of making enough money from the long fishing season so that you could kick back in the winter—spend time with your family, go to all your kids' games, maybe have time for craft projects.

It helped if your wife had a job with benefits. For a self-employed commercial fisherman, health insurance for you and your family was expensive. Also, you did not withhold income or social security taxes month by month. All your taxes were due at once on April 15, just at the time of year when you had a lot of expenses getting ready for the season and before any money was coming in.

Some of the Alaska salmon fishermen were married to teachers, whose schedules allowed them to be at home with the kids in the summer and even come up North for long visits.

Another, harder to define benefit to being a small-boat fisherman was the satisfaction of having your boat to work on. For many, their boats were their winter jobs. During the fishing season, you spent months far from the places where you could get things fixed or find parts. A breakdown that cost you a week at the peak of the season could make the difference between an okay season and a really good one. So it behooved you, over the winter, to go over all your boat's systems: electronics, hydraulics, fuel, engine, steering, refrigeration if you had it, and so forth. Make sure that everything was in the best condition that you could afford when you headed north in the spring.

Many of the small-boat fishermen lived in small waterfront communities around Alaska or in Puget Sound, and usually their boats were just a short drive, or if they were lucky, a short walk from where they lived. There was, for these men, a great satisfaction not only in having their boat close, but also in being part of the local community of fishermen from that harbor. Almost every waterfront community in Puget Sound had the men who went "up North" every summer.

The way I saw it, going down to work on your boat a couple of days a week when the weather wasn't too rotten, and maybe when you wanted a break going up to the coffee shop with your buddies and talking about fishing wasn't a bad way to spend the winter. Of course, if you got home after Halloween and left at the end of March, you had to jump right on your winter boat projects. As far as putting together some sort of a retirement, as a guy in my twenties, I wasn't looking that far ahead. But it did seem that the salmon fishermen that caught their share of fish and were prudent with their money, were able to save for the day when they couldn't fish, especially if their wives had a job.

Crabbing, on the other hand, was a key example of the boat driving you versus you driving the boat. Because of the huge investment required, many crabbers were financed by partnerships of several fishermen. Looking ahead, it was clear that as more boats entered the fishery, the crabbing season would be reduced. Yet these boats were too expensive to be allowed to sit at the dock if the seasons became shorter, so they needed to be put to work at other jobs, such as working as salmon tenders in the summertime.

It appeared as if the financial rewards of crabbing would be a lot higher than small-boat fishing, but at least from my perspective, it had to be balanced against other aspects of the operation. I had a lot to chew on as the weather improved and we began to see more and more of small boats, primarily thirty-two-foot gillnetters headed to the salmon fishery in Bristol Bay.

I DISCOVERED THAT crab fishermen get to do something that salmon fishermen might never do—take a vacation in the middle of the summer! Because we were essentially putting in an eight-month season, George had suggested we might want to take some time off in the summer. Fishing would be at low ebb before the expected heavy fall fishing began, when the Alaska Department of Fish and Game would open the so-called "south side," the zone south of the Aleutian Islands. He'd arranged for eager recruits off the docks at Dutch to fill in for us, so that the *Flood Tide* could continue fishing.

With a sense of amazement and unreality, I emptied my drawers into a couple of boxes, put them in the storage area up in the bow, put on my traveling clothes, and got a ride in the crab plant van out to the airport.

Flying out of the Aleutian Islands isn't like leaving other places, where you can go to the airport and almost always at least leave on the same day. The route from Anchorage out to Dutch, crossing several mountain ranges and traveling out along the Alaska Peninsula was probably the most challenging route of any scheduled airline in North America. The biggest problem were the giant weather systems that we knew so well. As mariners, we had seen how the winds could accelerate to hurricane velocity through the passes between the islands. For pilots there was another danger: when the big fronts pushed over the mountains, the terrain created areas of invisible boiling turbulence—powerful up- and downdrafts that could reach up 5,000 or 10,000 feet over the tops of the ranges.

On the day I flew out the weather was tolerable, but there was a different problem: a crabber was in trouble. The plane arrived and we got off the ground okay, but shortly after takeoff, the pilot announced that a boat was in trouble in Unimak Pass and the Coast Guard had requested that we circle the area to keep an eye on things until it could get an aircraft out or another fishing boat could arrive on the scene.

All eyes peered out the windows as soon as he spoke, and soon we found a grim sight as the pilot put us into a wide circle over Unimak Pass. The wind was from the northwest at thirty-five to forty knots, and somehow a crabber, a Martinolich-built eighty-six footer by the look of it, had gotten ashore on the eastern side of Unimak Pass. They were already on the beach, so they were in no danger of sinking, but they were getting a wicked beating from the high rollers booming across the shallow water and slamming into their side and throwing spray far above their mast and rigging—spray that was immediately blown away downwind, showing the force of the wind. It was a good thing it wasn't below freezing because they would have quickly been sheathed in ice so thick it would have been hard for the crew to get out of the boat when the chopper arrived. Even more sobering was the tide rip out in the channel. It was near full moon and the full force of the northwest gale was stacking up the seas into short nasty combers. There was an area of calmer water on the east side of the pass where the current must have been lighter, and an area of flatter water between the tide rip and where the rollers began on the edge of the shallow water. Maybe the crabber had been coming through the pass from the south, picking his way between the edge of the breakers and the nasty combers of the tide rip, and had engine trouble. In a situation like that, he would have had only a few minutes at the most to get the engine going again before he'd be in the breakers.

On about the third pass, someone emerged from the pilothouse and waved briefly up at us before quickly ducking inside again just as another big comber slammed into the boat.

Fortunately it looked like the beach was sloping gravel, without any big boulders that would have punctured the hull. However, they were being driven higher onto the beach by the force of the surf. We were just a day or two away from the highest tide of the month. Unless a tug or some other powerful vessel could get in there quickly, to try to pull them off within the next couple of days while the tides were still big, they might have to wait a month until the tides were big enough to try it again.

After forty-five minutes or so, we could see another crabber, rolling heavily in the seas as she approached the tide rip. The current had almost stopped, as the tide rip had lost much of its turbulence. It wasn't clear what the crabber could do other than stand by to be of moral support, but in any case, shortly afterward, our pilot reported that the Coast Guard had released him, and we swung out of our banking circle and headed east, along the south side of Unimak Island.

 DESOLATION SOUND, British Columbia, summer 1971. Getting off the *Flood Tide*, with its noisy diesel generator running day and night, and spending a couple of weeks sailing among these islands with my fiancée was just what I needed to recharge my batteries for the brutal fall king crab season that awaited me back in Alaska.

17. Southern Waters

FORTY-EIGHT HOURS after arriving in Seattle, my fiancée from Boston and I were on a little twenty-six-foot chartered sailboat, headed for an area of the British Columbia coast known as Desolation Sound. The first night we tied up at a sleepy marina at Port Townsend, the jumping off place for crossing the Strait of Juan de Fuca to the San Juan Islands and the Canadian Gulf Islands beyond.

To walk around the streets of that turn-of-the-century town in the warmth of the lingering evening light, to eat and drink looking out at Admiralty Inlet and the snow-covered North Cascades looming in the distance, to wander the docks, looking at the other boats, chatting with their owners, asking about their plans, and most, of all spending time once again with my fiancée filled me up. After the unrelenting grimness of the Bering Sea and the company of men for six months straight, it was beyond magic.

And the silence was powerful. I had lived a dozen feet away from the *Flood Tide*'s diesel engine. Even in Dutch, walking around town, it was hard to escape the noise. The town was powered by a diesel generator, the crab-processing plants had big generators, the boats in the harbor had their diesel generators on. Even walking back into the hills beyond town, which I did on the rare occasion when one of our trips to town coincided with good weather, true silence was elusive. You'd walk down into some hollow, and think you'd escaped it, and some trick of the wind and the weather would bring the noise to you again.

In the Port Townsend marina, in the harbors in the American San Juan Islands, and then in the Canadian Gulf Islands north of that, we would sit in the cockpit of our little boat after a good day of sailing and just savor the silence, broken perhaps by the fading noise of a boat passing in the distance, the clink of a dish being washed in a nearby boat, or the low murmur of a couple walking along the dock together.

Summer evenings on the West Coast, and particularly the Northwest are very different from those on the East Coast where I grew up. The East Coast is on the eastern edge of a time zone, the West Coast on the western edge. The effect is that darkness comes noticeably later in the Northwest than in the Northeast. In Boston in August, it would be dark at 8 p.m., but in British Columbia, the sun would still be up, and even after it had set, the twilight would linger.

And so we would sit with glasses of wine, talking softly and taking in the landscape around us in the softening evening light. Those were exquisite days and I did not want them to end.

The San Juans were busy with boaters, but then when we crossed into Canada and began to explore the Gulf Islands, the crowd thinned out. We lingered, savoring those sleepy island communities. Then one morning we got an early start—sails up with the first of daylight, pushing across the wide Strait of Georgia with a good following breeze, inside of Texada Island and far up Malaspina Strait before laying in remote Van Anda Cove for the night. After another long day's push and with the sun slanting away far to the west, we came around Sara Point and encountered the dramatic scenery of Desolation Sound that I had been told to expect.

Desolate it wasn't. (English explorer Captain George Vancouver had so named it in May 1792, during a particularly dreary and wet spell.) To lie anchored in those coves in the stillness of the evenings and dawns, with the dramatic mountains rising up out of the woods to snowy tops behind us, was a treat almost beyond words. A unique feature of geography makes the salt water there warm enough for a pleasant swim.

So we swam, morning and evening, and in between. Some days we never moved the boat. Instead we explored by dingy around those intricate anchorages, maybe going ashore with towels and books, walking up to a lake in the hills, to swim, lie in the sun, read, and talk the day away. Oysters grew wild and thick there as well, hanging in clumps all around the shore at low tide, and we'd pick and eat a dozen or more each day.

Our two weeks were bittersweet as well. My fiancée had grown up in a Boston suburb and now worked and lived in the city. When I was in fishing school at the University of Rhode Island, I had a nice rental a block away from the water. On weekends she would visit or I would go to Boston. We'd gotten engaged just before I came to Seattle that fall, but we hadn't set a date, wanting for me to get more settled.

Now the reality of my life lay like a stone between us. For starters, I didn't even have a home, just a rented room in a friend's house. And even if I should get a place, I'd be heading north again in another week, and probably not be back until Thanksgiving. We had explored the idea of my finding a job for her at Dutch Harbor so I could see her between trips. There was work at the Alaska Commercial Company, and the owner also had a little fourplex, with one unit available for rent. But I wasn't naive enough to think that a dingy apartment on the shore of the grim and desolate Bering Sea and a job stocking shelves in a general store would be any kind of a life for someone used to the sophistication and busy pace of Newbury Street in Boston. Also I knew that she would be fresh meat in the shark pool at Dutch Harbor, though this I did not share.

We talked about my dream: of getting a smaller boat and fishing in Southeast Alaska, and what kind of a life that would be for us. But as we talked, I could sense that what was truly exciting to me—making a living along those spectacular wilderness waterways—was less so for her. I understood that I was asking my fiancée to share my passion, but I knew it wasn't hers, and I knew that there weren't many couples who could put in the long seasons that the fishery required.

There was something else. Desolation Sound was the jumping-off place to the wild and lonely land beyond, the winding channels of the Inside

ROSCOE BAY, BRITISH COLUMBIA. In the long crabbing season of 1971, crews sometimes got to take vacations! I explored the winding coastline of British Columbia by sailboat with my fiancée. It was about as stark a contrast to the grim world of Bering Sea crabbing as you could imagine.

Passage that led to Southeast Alaska. To the south of us was Georgia Strait, surrounded on both sides by much of the population and industry of British Columbia. Desolation Sound and the Discovery Islands to our west were lightly populated indeed, with few roads. To the northwest, beyond the ferocious tidal whirlpools at Yuculta Rapids, the landscape changed to almost total wilderness. Channels and islands and sheltered bays almost beyond number: it was as different from the Bering Sea as night is from day.

And it called to me. I remember when we lay at a place called Redonda Bay after a wonderful day of sailing in Sutil Channel, whose sides were so steep that I'd sail until I could look up and sight from where I sat and line up the spreader tip on the mast with the top of the mountain. In a cove, there was an old abandoned cannery, and we wandered among the ruined buildings. That night while we ate in the cockpit, we heard this faraway rushing noise, faint, but distinctive. We talked about it; there was a remote fishing lodge or two and a Native settlement in that direction, but nothing that would account for this sound. Then I got it: it was the sound of Yuculta Rapids, seven miles away. The sound had carried through the night air to where we were.

I knew that those rapids were a gateway to the North, beyond which lay a very different landscape. Even the climate beyond Yuculta Rapids was different: cooler, cloudier, and wetter than Desolation Sound and the whole Gulf of Georgia area. But for me, as I listened that night, on the southern edge of that vast wilderness, the rush of the tide was the North, calling me.

It blew northwest the next day, a good going-home wind from Desolation Sound. Four days later, at the busy Seattle airport, we said our sad good-byes. Though unsaid, it was clear that our future together was uncertain.

WALTER "BOMBA" KUHR and me (right) aboard the *Flood Tide*, Aleutian Islands, fall 1971. Walter was a hugely talented fisherman and went on to become a successful and well known owner/captain of both crabbers and trawlers. The Bering Sea hair crab lives in the waters around the Pribilof Islands.

18. Back in the Saddle Again

WHAT PASSED FOR SUMMER in the Bering Sea was gone when I flew back in to Dutch Harbor in early September. A powerful low-pressure storm system was pouring among the islands and mountain passes between the North Pacific and the Bering Sea. Our plane got no farther than Cold Bay, ninety miles east of Unimak Pass, and Reeve Aleutian Airways' rough bunkhouse and mess hall. As I lay in my bed that night, the furious wind slammed into the low building again and again, shaking it hard enough to rattle my book off the nightstand. In the morning, even in the shelter of the bay, the sea pounded heavily on the shore and was a seething mass of gray and white as far as the eye could see.

Finally, in the afternoon the wind eased enough for us to climb anxiously into the battered looking four-engine DC-6 and, at the pilot's direction, buckle our seat belts extra tight. The flight to Dutch was short and turbulent, with the first two approaches aborted at the last moment when the gusting winds over the landing strip made the plane almost impossible to control, even for those experienced Alaska pilots. After the third approach the wheels hit the pavement so hard I thought we'd blown the tires. As we descended the steps of the plane, the woman ahead of me threw up as soon as she stepped on the ground. Welcome to Dutch Harbor.

After the warmth of those companionable weeks in the Gulf Islands and Desolation Sound, Dutch was the end of the earth but familiar: figures hunched over against the wind as they went from building to building

REGULAR CRAB POT, *Flood Tide*, 1971. A traditional crab pot with maybe fifty nice-sized king crab is being hoisted over the rail.

around the crab plant, fishermen stumbling out of the Elbow Room and lurching down to the harbor and the boats.

There were a few more boats in town, getting ready for what was expected to be the best part of the 1971 crab season: fishing the "south side," the North Pacific side of the Aleutians. There, the fleet would participate in a quota fishery, a recent development for the crab fleet.

UNTIL A FEW YEARS EARLIER, the seasons, in both the Bering Sea and the North Pacific, opened and closed on set dates, determined by best guess to allow the crab resource plenty of time to recover from the fishing effort. But as the crab fleet grew and efficiency improved, resource managers realized that if conditions were just right and the fleet happened to find the thickest concentrations of crab quickly, more could be harvested than would be healthy for the fishery. Instead of a fixed season, a quota was established, and the crab plants reported both their daily deliveries and best guesses as to what their fleets had aboard. When the Alaska Department of Fish and Game had calculated that the quota was close to being taken, they would announce over the radio a date for closing the fishery.

The effect of the quota system was to put a lot of pressure on the fleet to fish even harder. Although the best guesses were that the quota wouldn't be taken until sometime in mid-November, there was always the possibility that if some of the fleet got into heavy fishing, the quota could be taken in a considerably shorter period. Fortunately for us, we had started our 1971 crab season in March, so we already had caught a lot of crab before the fall season began. But for the new boats just arrived in Dutch with, I was sure, huge mortgages and start-up costs, the pressure to find the crab quickly and stay on them must have been enormous. In addition, whereas in the Bering Sea a boat could fish as many pots as it could manage, and many boats fished several hundred pots, on the south side, where fishing was traditionally heavier, there was a seventy-five pot limit.

I found the *Flood Tide* tied up over at the Pan Alaska plant, and the size of her load of pots stopped me in my tracks. The pots were triple stacked, from the stern almost to the back of the boat deck behind the pilothouse; I'd never seen her with so many pots aboard, and then of course, I understood: all our seventy-five pots were on board, a bigger load than we'd ever carried before when there was the danger of icing up. But the immensity of the load made me instantly nervous, for I'd seen clearly from the plane what the sea conditions were like. I knew that in such conditions, even with no ice, such a load could put even our conservatively designed and heavily built boat on the outer edge of her stability envelope. Were we even supposed to carry seventy-five pots, in any conditions?

The only thing that gave me a bit of courage was that I had gotten to know the Marco builders and designers of the *Flood Tide*, and in particular Bruce Whittemore. I knew that they were all deeply concerned about the safety of their vessels and the men who fished on them. Bruce had designed two subtle but very important features into the Marco crabbers. First, he had put a lot of sheer—the amount that the deck curves up in the stern and bow—into the design. And he had raised the level of the deck in the lazarette—the aftermost compartment—an additional ten inches to make it flush with the wooden planking on the rest of the working deck, giving it greater buoyancy. The effect of these design elements was to greatly improve vessel stability when conditions got bad.

This was the corollary of a quota system, also called the derby system. The season opened on a certain date, so you had to get all your seventy-five pots out there quickly, in one load if possible. And if, in the best of conditions, the *Flood Tide* was certified to carry seventy-five pots, as I hoped, it was clear that some of the smaller boats, especially the wooden boats, would be overloading themselves to get as much gear out there as they could.

"Well, I hope you got laid fifty times," George said when he greeted me, slapping me on the back. "You'll need something to keep you smiling when we get out there." He nodded out toward the mean-looking waters of the outer bay. "We're lucky. We were lying in here, rigging gear when that last blast hit. But a bunch of these guys," he said, jerking his chin over at some of the new arrivals that were tied three and four deep at the crab plant docks around the harbor, "got beat up bad. And it's still summer!" He barked a bitter laugh.

The team was together again: Johnny and Bob had returned from their breaks as well.

I put my gear away in the shared cabin, and joined Walter in a drafty warehouse where he was putting eye splices into one end of a twenty-five fathom (150 feet) shot of buoy line. He'd kept fishing through my summer break.

His eyes lit up when I came in. "Ah, Pepe," he said in his broken English, "is boring working alone. You have good vacation?"

I gave him the short version of those sublime weeks, and looked at his splices, impressed again with his talent. The trick with these splices was to make the eyes small, and taper the splice so that it fed smoothly through the hauler and the coiler.

In the chilly warehouse, Bomba filled me in on what I had missed. "Was gud wedder," he said. "We fish Slime Bank. George alvays sez ve gonna find crab zis trip, but is never big. Is yust spotty fishing, alvays, 'stack 'em.' " And Bomba gave a good imitation of George's dreaded wave to stack the pot we had just hauled.

"*Sea Spray* hav gud trip," he waved out the door at a Marco ninety-four footer unloading at a floating processor tied across the harbor. "But most boats is yust like us, nothing big."

Another day of hard splicing until my arms ached and I had blisters on my fingers, and it was time to load and stow the extra coils, get our bait, and have a last night in the Elbow Room. It was crowded and way too smoky for me. Most of the crews in the harbor were jammed in there. You could tell the newcomers: they were excited about getting out and getting into the crab. The guys who'd already put in part of a season were more subdued; we already knew what awaited us and it wasn't anything to get excited about. Finally, with a good buzz on, I walked back to the boat in the windy dusk, made it down the ladder ever so carefully, and found myself up in the pilothouse, tuning up the radio and listening to some conversations.

IN THOSE DAYS, with the old AM double-sideband radios, you'd never know where someone might be talking from, especially at night, when the radio waves might bounce between the electrically charged layers of the upper atmosphere for hundreds and even thousand of miles until they bounced down to your antenna. Sometimes you'd only hear one boat and not the other, half of a conversation. And sometimes a transmission would stop right in the middle of a sentence.

"Ah, Eddy," said some skipper with a gravelly voice who knows where. "I shoulda' stayed in. There's a hell of a roll going out here. The guys musta' been hung over; they didn't get the back deck tied down and it was a hell of a mess once we got out into it. If I'd known it woulda' been this ugly, I might'a stayed in one more day."

"Oh, buck up, fer crissake," a cheery voice answered. "You know you'd rather be out here, where the wind blows free, than mowing the lawn at home. Ha ha ha. It is a hell of a lump though. Someone's gonna get the shit knocked out of them somewhere. Hey, you see where it was breaking when you come across? South of the buoy, fer crissake! They gotta move that buoy again or one of those damn pukerboat's gonna get its tit in a wringer."

They went on for a while and faded out. The mention of breakers and a buoy cinched it for me—almost surely the conversation came from off the Oregon coast, out of one of those towns like Depoe Bay or Newport or even Astoria on the mighty Columbia River. These were places where the harbor was a river mouth, where there was a breakwater that tried to harness the current to keep the channel clear. But the waves, sweeping obliquely across the entrance, always moved more sand than any dredge could keep up with, and so the channel was always changing.

Fishing in Alaska had a lot of challenges, but at least, except for a few harbors on the north side of the Alaska Peninsula, and on the mainland north of Cape Spencer almost 1,500 miles to the east, the entrances were deep, and when the wind blew you could get in without worrying about shifting sand bars.

There were a few Oregon crews working the crab fishery, and I'd listened to their tales of waiting too late to try to get back into their harbor and having to face the seas at the harbor entrance, with the houses and lights of town visible just past the breakers. Sometimes, the guys said, it would be too dangerous to try to get in across the bar when it was breaking, and they'd have to jog into the weather for a day or so, even though they could actually see their houses nearby. So near and yet so far. Not for me, thanks. I switched channels and listened to a couple of voices come on, speaking in heavily accented English—probably Norwegian-descent halibut fishermen from the Seattle area.

"I nebber go Puale no more. Oscar vas in dere von time and he tell me vind vas so bad he drag and drag and drag hiss anchor and vas no wind outside."

"Dere be little vind now. Sea iss not bad. You can yust shut down and drift all night. Ve close to Shumagins, go Lost Harbor, anchor dere."

They faded out, and I breathed a bit easier. It sounded as if they were just 150 miles or so east of Dutch. One of them was going to shut down and drift for the night, so conditions couldn't be too bad out there. This was long before there was a weather channel button on most marine radios—you could just punch it and there was your weather twenty-four hours a day. In 1971, the forecast just came on a couple of times a day, and sometimes you were better off by chasing around the frequencies and trying to find someone you could listen in on. Chances were that if there was a big storm coming, a swell big enough for most fishermen to comment on would precede the storm by at least a day.

A VERY, VERY BIG LOAD, stacked six high aboard the Marco 108 footer *Viking*, at Fishermen's Terminal, Seattle, 1980. Obviously you could only carry such a load in good weather. If this vessel got into icing conditions with a load like this, her stability would quickly degrade to the point where unless pots were dumped quickly, she could capsize without warning. The *Flood Tide* was four feet shorter and two feet narrower than the *Viking*, and for us even triple stacked in the very rough conditions around the Aleutians in the fall was pushing her stability limits.

19. Triple Stacked

I WAS TIRED but sleep came hard. It seemed as if I'd hardly drifted off when there was the whoop of the air starter below me and the big GM diesel rumbled to life. I sat up and looked at my watch: 2:30 a.m., time to get under way. Pulling on my clothes, I got a coffee and went up into the pilothouse. George and Russell were having cigarettes for breakfast and looking at the chart together. There was a bit of frost on one of the windows: not an auspicious sign. Outside, I could see the running lights of a few boats already leaving the harbor for the noon opening of the season.

"What do ya' say, kid," George said in his raspy voice. "Ready for the main event?"

I nodded toward the stern and said, "I'll be glad when we get this load into the water. Triple stacking always makes me nervous, especially with this." I tapped the frost on the windows.

"Ah, we'll be okay," answered Russell, always a bit more cautious than George. "They're giving just light northerlies and forty degrees, so on the south side, where we'll be going, we'll be in the lee even if it blows."

"Why am I not reassured?" I answered.

"Relax, kid," Russell slapped me playfully on the shoulder. "This is a Marco boat, top of the line. Most crews would jump at a chance to work on a rig like this. How'd you like to be working on something like that?"

He pointed out the window to an old eighty-foot sardine boat that had been converted to a crabber and was sliding by, triple stacked like us.

But narrower, and wooden. To me, it looked like an accident waiting to happen.

It sounded now as if the weather gods would smile, at least long enough for us to get that awful triple-stacked load of pots into the water. Still, we knew how quickly the weather could change in the Aleutians and how unreliable forecasts were. I looked at the boat disappearing into the darkness and hoped he wasn't planning to go too far offshore. I still remembered vividly the terrible feel of our boat that night off Cape St. Elias when we iced up so badly, and that was with just fifty pots or so, not even double stacked.

I pulled on a couple of sweatshirts, grabbed a flashlight, and went out to the boat deck. We were stacked so high that it was easier for me to step from the boat deck onto the second tier of pots than to climb up awkwardly from the main deck. Glad there was no ice, I made my way carefully along the pile to the stern, and I climbed down over the framework holding the stacking winches to the stern cleats. I took off a turn of the heavy tie-up line, and waited for George's signal. As I waited, I was reminded of how isolated you were back on the stern. Already the days were noticeably shorter; we'd be working a lot of nights, probably all night if the fishing was thick, and I knew that it would be me as the youngest, working the stack—climbing around on the pots, untying them to send forward to launch, or tying them down to run. And I remembered: beyond the rail was death.

"Okay." A voice from the dock above me brought me out of my what-if scenarios, and I untied the heavy line from the stern cleat to give some slack. The dockworker pulled the eye off the cleat on the dock and dropped it neatly in the space at my feet. "Good luck out there," came the hail, and I could tell he was looking at our triple-stacked load.

George kicked the stern away from the dock with a shot of power, then reversed to back out into the harbor. And suddenly there it was: that awful sickening slow roll. With our top-heavy load, the boat felt so different, rolling ever so slowly and then almost seeming to hesitate at the end of the roll, as if it weren't sure whether it was going to roll back the other way or just roll all the way over. When George finished backing up, and I could feel the hydraulics swinging the heavy rudder below where I stood, and when he applied the power in forward, we took on that long easy roll again.

That was the sinister part: if you didn't know how the *Flood Tide* felt without a load of pots, you would have thought this roll was comfortable and safe. I tried to stop thinking about it, tied the line securely to the steel framework that held the stacking winches, looked around carefully to make sure there weren't any loose lines around that might wash through the freeing ports and into the propeller, and climbed up onto the pots to make my way forward. That was the thing about the Bering Sea and the North Pacific that George and Russell had taught me over and over again: they were unforgiving places. Our tie-up lines were two-inch-diameter nylon: they were strong enough and long enough that if one washed overboard in heavy going and got sucked down into the propeller, it could stop our 1,500-horsepower diesel. Boats had been lost for less, Russell had drilled into me.

Back inside the pilothouse, I stood out of the way for a bit, just watching. George and Russell were talking, and didn't seem too concerned about the trim and feel of the boat. After a while I went downstairs, and out onto the back deck to get a couple of cases of bait out of the freezer to thaw while we made the ten-hour run out to where we'd start our season.

In the galley Bob was puttering around, laying the nonskid mat on the table, putting out a freshly baked cake, humming to himself, as content and unconcerned as if he were at home in a stable little house somewhere, instead of heading out into the North Pacific with the biggest load of pots we'd had aboard all year.

"Y'all better get some shut-eye now," he said in his easy drawl. "This'll be the best chance we'll have for a while." He patted me on the back in passing and ambled off into his cabin.

I lay down, but sleep didn't come. It was that same uneasy feel in the roll of the boat that had woken me up off Cape St. Elias. I'd fall asleep, then suddenly come awake, still in the throes of that same terrifying dream: Russell and I were up on the bow chipping ice in the windy, howling black, safety lines tied from our waists to the bloated, ice-thickened pipe rails, the only

thing between us and the cold, black sea. In my dream, the bow was dropping and dropping, into the sea, the black water quickly rising up over our
ankles, our thighs, up to our waists. George's pale, staring face in the little
circle of ice-free window behind us. Time stops, Russell's voice mouthing
some words, but flung away downwind and drowned out by the wind and
the engine noise.

Then I awoke, covered with sweat, slowly realizing that I was safe and
cozy in my bunk. Then a hand on my shoulder and a voice: "Showtime,
kid. Better get some chow in you, before we get out on deck." I looked at my
watch: It was 10:30 a.m., ninety minutes before the season started. I dressed,
grabbed a coffee, and went up to the pilothouse, holding the railing against
the motion of the boat—that same uneasy roll, but also pitching at the same
time, as we worked our way through the seas.

It was nasty out there: not a big Gulf of Alaska storm, but the wind
was building twelve- to fifteen-foot seas from the northwest that seemed to
be working crossways against a low swell from the south. Their tops were
all white with a lot of spray blown downwind. In the distance I thought I
glimpsed the furry green shoulder of Cape Ludke on Unimak Island, and
above it and to the east, what looked like 9,300-foot Shishaldin Volcano,
trailing a wisp of steam or smoke: your basic unfriendly Aleutian landscape.
Once I thought I caught a glimpse of another boat way off to the west, when
we were both on the tops of big waves.

Johnny and Walter appeared with mugs of coffee. George throttled the
engine back to make it a little quieter, and spoke. "Okay, here's the drill: no
one's set any gear down on this side of the islands for almost ten months,
so where the crab are is anyone's guess. We'll be prospecting, setting long
strings, and hopefully we'll get onto 'em before too long. Our delivery date
for this first trip is nine days away. Who knows how long the quota will last.
Last year it took two months plus to catch it all, and this year the quota's the
same, but as you could see, there are a lot of other boats in town, too.

"We've got a hell of a load on deck. So take your time on the stack, Joe.
It's forty-five degrees, so there's no chance of ice, but still, we're triple-stacked

and it's rough. Work with the roll of the boat, watch your hands don't get pinched between pots. I hope this is the only time we'll triple stack. Hell, I don't even like to double stack. It's not the stability—hell, they just don't get any more stable than these Marcos—but you never know what to expect with the seas up here. We're starting off with a hundred fifty fathoms of line [nine hundred feet] on each pot. You guys made up a bunch more shots, and I hope we don't have to use them, but it's deep out here and the current runs like a bullet when you get close to the passes, so we'll add if we have to, and hope to hell the coiler keeps working. If we do get into really deep-water fishing, that's our edge—not many crews can handle hand-coiling lengths like that.

"Pan Alaska's started this thing with delivery dates. The downside is that if we get into heavy fishing, we may get plugged before our date. I hope we get that lucky, but here's the deal: If it's just for a couple of days, you can really pack the crab into the tanks before worrying about dead loss. But you'll get to a point where it will seem that you can't get any more crab into the tanks, even doing the trick with the lights. If that happens, we'll just deck-load the boat with crab, and then, when we get a chance, run up into the shelter of some bay and pump down the level of the water in the tanks a couple three feet. Then we'll throw in a half sheet of plywood for Joe to sit on, and you'll pass him the crab and he can toss them back into the corners of the tank. We end up crowding the tank pretty bad, but if we're headed in to unload after-wards, they'll be fine.

"We had eight days in town to get rested and geared up and we're gonna need it. We're gonna fish as hard and as long as we can for these next two months. We've put in a pretty fair season to date, a lot more than these guys who are just rolling into town, and if we can put in a good fall here, we'll all go home smiling. But it's only going to happen if we work together and take our time, and don't have any injuries."

We went down to breakfast and while I was eating, Russell asked to see my pocketknife. He rubbed the blade across his thumbnail and passed it back to me. "Sharpen it," he said. "Get it like a razor. If the buoy line pulls you overboard, that knife's all you got to get clear." He pulled a little sharpening stone out of his pocket and passed it to me. It was his little mantra; I had heard him explaining it to other young crewmen around the docks, and it had probably already saved lives.

"TWENTY MINUTES until showtime." The overhead speaker crackled and it was time to go to work.

The first pot already had the line from the picking boom attached, and there was barely room for the four of us to stand, so I worked my way around the coiler to chop some more bait from the thawing herring blocks and fill a few more bait jars. When we started setting gear, I'd have to climb up to the top of the pile.

I knew boats capsized in such triple-stacked conditions, and tried to visualize how we would make it to the surface and get to the life raft, if the automatic release and inflator worked. These were not pleasant thoughts, but I knew that if anything like that ever happened, it would happen quickly, maybe without warning. And like the trick with the sharp knife and the right length of lanyard, we would only survive if we had thought it out in advance.

Tucked into the little cubby under the deckhouse, filling bait jars, I reviewed all the moves: where to put the hook on the pots, how to tie the pots off when we were stacking, how to insert the stacking winch hook, and how to use the controls of the railroad boom if I needed to. That was actually one of the trickiest jobs on deck, since the only way you could use the controls and see what was happening was to stand with your hands behind your back on the control levers. Engineer Johnny was good, but there were times when I'd be up on the pile and he might have had to attend to some engine room chore and someone less familiar would be at the controls. Then I'd be on the pile, totally dependant on someone else's skill, dexterity, and, most of all, timing. With the boat corkscrewing around in the seas, the critical thing was to use the roll or pitch of the boat to help move the pots, and, as much as possible, drag the pots forward or backward along the pile, with the hook slightly elevated for easy sliding. Actually lifting the pot into the air free of the pile was a big no-no. Once free of the pile, the 700-pound free-swinging weight would be very hard to control.

With a long toot of the horn, the first pot slid into the water, Walter deftly throwing the coils of buoy line after it, with sharp-eyed Russell making sure that the line ran clear and free, and throwing the buoys over at the end. It was my moment to climb, and I made my way carefully up over the pots, holding on with both hands, and waited for the hook. I had a few minutes so I had a chance to have a good look around.

The "light northerlies" and "being in the lee of the land" that George had told us to expect were total fiction, as were most predictions of weather in that part of the world. The wind was northwest, blowing a strong thirty to forty knots—gale force winds anywhere else but just a good breeze in the Aleutians. The sea was confused—a fifteen-foot swell from the southwest, and a much shorter period ten-foot chop from the northwest. Every now and then the two wave trains would coincide and the result would be a twenty-foot wave, which, if it caught us just right, would corkscrew us violently. Whoever had tied the pots onto the pile back at the dock in Dutch had done a good job, but the whole pile began wiggle back and forth as we lurched through the seas.

For all that, it was a grand sight in a way. The northwest gale came out of a cloudless sky as they usually do there when the arctic highs flow southeast from Siberia. From my perch on top of the pile, probably twelve feet off the main deck, I could see the distant land, brilliant emerald green in the strong September sun, dramatic in its own way, even beautiful. Every now and then a fifty-knot gust would come roaring down from the northwest, blowing the tops off all the seas, which were brilliant white in the sun against the dark blue of the water in the troughs.

Once, on the top of a big one, I glimpsed a big container ship, maybe five miles away, eastbound from Unimak Pass, throwing spray far and wide. But the noise! Our exhaust stack was high, to carry the engine noise as far above the deck as possible, but up where I was it was so loud I couldn't hear voices below; just the occasional whine of the hydraulic winch on the picking boom.

When one of those gusts roared through, the combination of the engine and the wind screamed. It reminded me of the descriptions of working up the masts of the old square-riggers as they battled their way east to west against the fierce Cape Horn storms. Almost every writer who had been there talked about the thunderous roar in the rigging when the wind blew at strength—so loud that even if your shipmate was right next to you, you couldn't hear each other.

As I held on tightly to my perch, I could tell that the guys on deck were struggling to get the pots into position to set. The problem was that George wanted to set his pots spread out over a roughly northeast-southwest line, a course that put us in the trough of the still-building seas from the northwest. The motion of the boat was violent enough that even holding on with both hands was hard, and I knew it would be extremely difficult when I had to use both hands to untie the lashings.

Finally George came out the back pilothouse door, holding onto the rail all the way as he made his way back to the rear end of the boat deck and tried to talk over the noise to the guys on deck, out of sight from me. Even though he was only maybe thirty feet away, the wind snatched away all the words. But after that, when George ran to where he wanted to set the next pot, he would change course and jog directly into the northwest seas, easing the motion of the boat so the guys could maneuver the next pot into position with the picking boom winch without getting a hand or a finger smashed to jelly.

Four pots later, it was finally my turn—Russell climbed up from below and handed me the hook from the carriage on the railroad boom. I put it into the bridle of the forwardmost of the top row of pots, and held the hook until Johnny had taken up the slack on the winch. Next, I untied the short lines that held the pot to the others below it. Johnny was watching me carefully. By the time I came to the last tie, George had swung around into the wind and swell so Johnny could control the pot better. He nodded at me, and I quickly untied the last clove hitch. Then Johnny pulled the pot forward slowly and carefully, allowing it to slide over the edge of the pile and thump heavily onto the deck below. There the others quickly opened the doors, pulled out and unlashed the coils of buoy line, hooked in two bait jars full of herring, hooked on the quick-release hook from the picking winch, and lifted it over the side. George tooted the horn, the release snapped, and the pot disappeared over the side as the engine throttled up. Russell handed up the hook, and it would all start over again.

Sometimes during the run to the next spot, the motion of the boat would be so violent I would wrap both hands around a pot frame and jam both boots against another, head down as solid heavy flying spray beat heavily onto my back. I'd feel the boat slow and turn, and look around to make sure we were turning into the seas. Then I'd start untying the straps, trying hard as hell to just use one hand. Even jogging slowly into the seas, there was always the chance of getting slapped hard by a queer sea, and lurching hard enough to one side to throw me off the pile and overboard if I wasn't ready for it at all times.

The wind was getting stronger. Just in the half-hour or so since I'd climbed on the stack, the pressure was more insistent and the driven spray was hitting me harder. When the spray hit me before I could turn away, it was as if someone had slapped me hard full on. Down on the main deck, the guys were pretty much sheltered from the worst of the wind, but up on the pile it was wild. With each pot, I'd work farther back, away from what little shelter the pilothouse offered. I kept as low as possible, working slowly and carefully, pot by pot, thinking out each move in advance, keenly aware of the motion of the boat and the wind clutching at me.

Johnny had just nodded at me to start unlashing the last of the triple-stacked pots at the rear of the pile, when George gave a long warning blast and I looked up to see an odd triangular-shaped sea lurching high, ahead and just to port of us. The whole top of the sea suddenly exploded when a hurricane gust slammed into it just as we lurched violently to starboard. I had a glimpse of George's pale face staring at me through the window in the pilothouse door, and then the top of the sea, or what was left of it, slammed into me—solid water, ripping one foot clear of its hold—as we heeled even more dramatically to starboard. It was all I could do to keep my head jammed

BOW VIEW OF THE MARCO 108 VIKING with her big load, Fishermen's Terminal, Seattle, about 1980. She almost looks like she is fresh from the builder's yard and ready to head north with the big, big load. Twice during the crab boom years, boats loaded like this (but not Marco boats) capsized in the sheltered waters not far from Seattle when their autopilots malfunctioned, putting them into a hard-over turn.

flat against the nylon webbing of the nearest pot and to hold on for all I was worth.

And over we heeled, thirty degrees, forty degrees, and more. It was the dreaded "queer one." We rolled and rolled, until it seemed as if we would just

keep going. I had a glimpse of green water starting to come over the rail on the low side, and still we rolled. Finally slowing, the hurricane gust passing, the *Flood Tide* paused at the very end of the roll. And I understood in that moment the whole thing with stability and triple and quadruple stacking.

The weight of the pots in a roll like this, high up in the pile, made it difficult for boats to recover from such extreme rolls. It was like a seesaw. On one end was the weight on the bottom of the boat: the fuel, the engines, and so forth. On the other end was the weight on top of the boat: the rigging, the pilothouse, but mostly the heavy pots. At some point, if a roll was severe enough, the weight on top would simply overpower the weight on bottom, and the higher up a weight was, the greater its potential to capsize us. When the *Flood Tide* finally paused in that terrifying roll, I wondered if that wave had hit us before we'd gotten the first seven pots off the top layer, would that extra two tons have been enough to make the roll unrecoverable, and instead of pausing for the longest time at the end, would we have rolled all the way over? The mighty *Flood Tide*, for what seemed like an eternity, paused and then she seemed to quiver a bit, like a dog shaking itself off after getting wet, and finally, oh finally, rolled back upright. Johnny gave me the nod again and I quickly unlashed the ties, and the last of the top pots slid away and quickly down to deck level.

Even then, the boat felt sluggish, and I looked down and saw that the main deck still had a foot or a foot and a half of water slopping back and forth as it slowly drained through the ports along either side of the hull. It must have been water that came in over the bulwarks when we had taken that roll.

Down a layer! Now, working on the tops of double-stacked pots, I felt so much more secure, even though I was just three feet lower. The wind still blew, harder if anything, fifty to sixty knots in the gusts, but I think the tide had turned in Unimak Pass northwest of us and was now ebbing, the current with the wind, and tending to reduce the height of the seas, so our motion was a lot easier.

When the last double-stacked pot was finally lowered to the deck, I climbed down to join the rest of the crew. I was aching all over and my sweatshirt was soaked from sweat and spray. What with the wind and the engine noise, it was hard to talk, but Bomba gave me a big welcoming slap on the back and, with his mouth to my ear, said, "Vas gud, Joe, is bad place on top ven rough, eh?" I nodded and slapped him back, and then the horn tooted, and the hanging pot slipped over the side.

About fifteen pots into the bottom layer, Russell suddenly shouted something and ran inside. A moment later, he and George were out on the back of the boat deck above us, pointing to something in the water behind us, a white blotchy shape. Then I got it: the buoys from the last pot were going underwater. The pot was "over its head," set into water that was too deep, or the buoy lines had tangled.

After a few minutes, Russell gave us the "coffee time" signal: raising an invisible coffee cup to his lips. We looked around at each other, surprised.

"Loran's down," Russell said, filling us in. We savored the totally unexpected treat of hot coffee and sweet coffeecake when we thought we were facing a long, nasty afternoon without a break. "The loran started to blink, but George was so focused on getting the boat up into the wind to set each pot that he didn't notice it." Russell nodded toward the outside. "There's an edge here, a real big drop-off, when the loran went out, the tide set us over the edge. Luckily, it was just the one pot. I watch all the buoys to make sure there isn't a tangle. I don't think it went down too far. We have big tides in two weeks; maybe we can find it then." The rest of us just nodded and drank.

Usually a blink or a bad signal lasted only a half hour or so while the technician at the loran station diagnosed the problem and replaced the faulty component. Whatever it was, we savored the break.

When I'd had my fill, I sat back. "Was that a dangerous roll, or did it just seem that way to me, up there on the pile?" I asked.

Johnny gave me a direct look. "Goddamn, George, I'm not leaving the dock triple stacked, not after that one. Yeah, it was bad, the rail went under and we had two feet of water on deck for a moment or two. I don't care what those engineers and marine architects say, down in their cozy Seattle offices, triple stacked for this boat is too much up here, period. They sit down there with their slide rules and don't have one fucking idea what the tide rips and the winds are like up here. Yeah, that was a god damned bad roll, and it was a good thing it didn't happen when we were stacked triple with the whole

load, or I'm not sure we would have come back. You get a couple of feet of
water on deck and it doesn't clear, that's another hundred tons moving back
and forth.

I'D FORGOTTEN ABOUT that part. Most big fish boats were built with heavy
bulwarks, about three feet high around the decks, with freeing ports
around the bottom, so that when a heavy sea came on board, it would be
able to quickly flow out the ports and not compromise stability. At sixty
pounds a cubic foot, it was important to get the decks clear as quickly as
possible. That much weight sloshing back and forth could definitely compromise stability.

In heavy weather, it wasn't uncommon to roll a rail under, bringing
many tons of water aboard, and in such situations a vessel's stability was significantly compromised until the water had cleared off. "Dipping a rail," as
it was called, was also hazardous because seas sweeping the deck were dangerous to the crew and gear. All that water could knock a man down, smash
him into a pot or a steel bulwark, or sweep an untied pot into the hauler or
a crewman. I'd found out the hard way that summer and had been lucky to
escape with just a broken rib.

Fortunately our deck wasn't that long, but in the big Cape Horners—the
300- and 400-foot-long deeply laden square-riggers that carried heavy bulk
cargos around the bottom end of South America, seas sweeping the decks
were such a problem that builders started constructing boats with a big full-
width deck house amidships to reduce the exposed area that the sea could
sweep in heavy seas. Those ships took so much water on deck in the big seas
that the crew would have to hold onto lifelines when walking along the deck
to avoid being swept overboard. Sometimes the crew reported that when they
were up in the rigging shortening sail, they would look down and see just the
masts sticking up out of solid green water washing across the midship decks.
These sweeping seas gathered so much power and momentum rolling down
the full length of the decks they could smash in deckhouses or rip off tightly
battened-down hatch covers.

Another bad situation was when you were heavily loaded and down by the stern and traveling in following seas. Vessels with a relatively flat sheer (the curve of the deck and bulwarks from bow to stern) were susceptible to taking seas over the stern, which would submerge the whole afterdeck of the boat before the remaining buoyancy of the vessel lifted the stern enough for the water to clear through the ports. When this happened, the stability of the vessel was instantly and drastically reduced until the rails had lifted clear of the water and the decks had drained. There were many tales around the fleet of vessel losses in such situations, and the storyline was usually something like this:

"I thought we were doing fine; we'd 'flattened her' [a fisherman's term for putting a really big load on] and were just cruising along, running downwind. There was a big swell, but nothing we hadn't handled before, when all of a sudden the boat started feeling odd, and one of the guys noticed we'd been pooped—a big sea had come over the stern, and the stern was underwater. She started to lay down to port, so I gave her full throttle and turned to port, figuring we'd just roll out of it, but then we rolled the other way, completely over."

Often in such situations, it was an unnoticed leak in the engine room or the lazarette that reduced a vessel's buoyancy enough for the stern rails to go under, but once they did, even for just a moment, that vessel's survival was in question.

"OK, GUYS," George suddenly said over the intercom. "Loran's up again. Let's get the rest of these pots off, and run up to the beach and drop the hook for the night. It isn't getting any better out there."

Instantly I perked up. Anchor for the night . . . wouldn't that be nice. It hadn't occurred to me that we might anchor. I thought that once we set the last pot, we'd go back and start picking a few to get a sense of where the crab were, and moving the empty ones to where there were crab.

After the coziness of the galley, opening the watertight door and going out onto the back deck was an abrupt change. The tide had turned so the seas weren't quite as big as before, but the wind seemed stronger, blowing the tops off the seas and filling the air with flying spray. We were lucky to just be setting gear: the guy at the crab block didn't have to lean out and try to see, and then throw the grapple to hook the buoys and bring them aboard. That would have been difficult.

By then we'd set about half our load, and having that 22,000 or so pounds off the deck made a noticeable difference. Occasionally we'd still roll a rail under, dipping tons of green water onto the deck, but it would clear off through the scuppers and freeing ports much more quickly.

I was working the back deck because I was tall. Bomba and Russell were both strongly built guys but were four or five inches shorter than I was. That extra height meant that I was able to reach the top of the pots and rock them forward, slamming them down flat onto the deck to be pulled forward to the rigging/setting area.

As we worked together in those very nasty conditions, it was almost impossible to communicate with words. Our field of vision was constrained by the visor of our hooded rain gear, our eyes were regularly blinded by stinging salt spray, and we were constantly battered by the motion of the boat, lurching into each other, into the pots, and into the steel bulwarks. Yet we still sought to achieve that smooth pattern of interwoven actions that was the mark of a really good crab crew.

When the pot was all baited, ready and hanging, the horn would toot and we'd all rush to get the next one ready. But George also was trying to set the gear in a pattern that covered the depths that the crab might be in, over a fairly wide geographic area, so that when he had hauled all the gear the next day, he would have enough information on the location of the crab to set our seventy-five pots in the most productive pattern. Occasionally it would mean that we might have to wait five or ten or occasionally fifteen minutes while he maneuvered us through that windy wasteland of dark heaving seas to just the spot that he wanted.

We would wait, getting chilled, as the steady rhythm of work was broken. Russell might light up a smoke, but the rest of us would just wait, and it was annoying to have the rhythm broken like that. Sometimes we would bitch at George in our limited exchanges of conversation. If he knew that he'd be ten minutes, we asked one another, couldn't he let us know so that we could go inside, and get a bite and a mug-up? But in that weather, it wasn't quite so easy. The skipper wasn't wearing rain gear so he couldn't just step out onto the back deck and call down to us. Up there, cozy and warm, he probably didn't notice the time as much as we did. To be fair to George, I knew that as he looked at his electronics—primarily the loran numbers and the sounding machine that gave him a bit of information about the nature of the bottom—it was like, "I'll know when I get there." Looking at the chart and the loran, watching for just the right places on the bottom, perhaps a shallow little basin just ten or twelve feet deeper than the bottom around it, he would set the pot when it felt right.

On the south side of the Aleutians, the landscape at the bottom of the ocean was very different from the flat, featureless, relatively shallow plain of the Bering Sea bottom. There you could set your gear in straight lines. Here we were setting our pots in 900 to 1,100 feet of water, and the bottom was like the edge of a cliff. To the south, the bottom dropped quickly down into 6,000 feet of water, and few miles south of that was the Aleutian Trench, one of the deepest places in the North Pacific, 23,000 to 25,000 feet deep—four miles, plus.

The current would push nutrients from the deeper water up over the edge and into, we hoped, the waiting crab population. But because of the lay of the land, that population could well be hanging out in one of these underwater basins or dips, and if George could find one of these little bonanzas, it could mean a huge fall season. We had to have patience.

The day died in the windy west, and our world became just that circle of rough water illuminated by the brilliant quartz-iodine lights over our heads. By then I was working at the very stern, among the last couple of rows of pots. When I hooked up the pot and it moved away from me up the deck toward the setting station, I'd stand there for a moment, one hand on a pot frame and the other on the steel rail, and wait for a break in the flying spray to get a glimpse forward.

When we nosed over the top of a big swell and headed down the other side, over the top of the pilothouse you could glimpse the next swell, with its top blown off far downwind, thirty or forty yards ahead of the boat. These weren't breaking seas, like those incredible ones in that unforgettable scene in *The Perfect Storm*, but they had gotten plenty big—probably thirty footers with an occasional bigger one thrown in. But seen like that, from our stern, in the circle of the brilliant lights on our mast, especially when we pitched down enough for them to be seen over the pilothouse, it was a spectacular sight. Just a glimpse and nothing more, and then I would pick my way carefully forward in that maelstrom of wind and noise and flying spray, ever vigilant for that quick roll to starboard that would bring solid water over the rail.

Finally around 11 p.m., the last pot went over the side, we gave ourselves big high fives all around, and the guys disappeared through the watertight door. I cleaned up the deck. As soon as I made the shelter of the back of the deck-house, George throttled up and steered hard over, throwing spray and heavy water far and wide as we went sideways to the big swells and the now building seas from the northwest. I got another couple of cases of frozen herring out of the freezer to thaw overnight, and just stood there, sheltered from the elements, looking out at the wild world beyond. Once, on the top of a big one, I thought I got a glimpse of the brilliant lights of a couple of other crabbers, working far to the east, but then they were quickly lost in the flying spray.

Inside, the guys already had the feedbag on. Bob had been working on a big pasta and chicken dinner in the moments he could snatch from the work on the back deck, and when I'd washed up, he set a steaming plate of it in front of me.

A hot meal after a long stint on deck was a comforting treat. But rather than savoring it one bite at a time, talking about how the day had gone and what was ahead for tomorrow, about all we could do was shovel it down quickly, eager to put our heads onto the pillow for a few hours before it would all start again. We knew we were facing some long round-the-clock days ahead.

It was my turn to drop the anchor, so I didn't undress, and just lay on my bunk, waiting for George to slow down. We must have been closer to land than I thought, for it hadn't seemed any time had passed before I could feel the motion of the boat ease noticeably. Groggily I got up and made my way up the stairs to the pilothouse to see where we were.

To my amazement we were entering what looked like a fjord, a bay so narrow and winding that already the motion of the sea had dropped away entirely. Our powerful lights shone out on steep hills dropping down to the water's edge and covered with what looked for all the world like green fur: the unmistakable treeless low ground cover of the Aleutians and the western Alaska Peninsula.

"Christ, George, what a nifty spot. Where the hell are we?"

"Udagak Bay," he said, stubbing his finger down on an indentation on the southwest side of Unalaska Island. There was a narrow passage between Unalaska and Sedanka Island to our west, and the bay was on the west side of the passage, looking secure enough to wait out a hurricane in. "This isn't like the eastern Bering Sea, where Amak's your only choice in a norther'. There's a bunch of little bays on the backside of Unalaska where a guy can sneak in when it starts to screech. Glad to be back in the saddle?" He lifted his head out toward the back deck.

"Oh, yeah," I answered. "Just loving it. Who wants to sail around in the warm sunshine when you can be doing this?"

The fathometer came up to about sixty feet, George turned us in a tight slow circle to make sure there wasn't any shallower water within our swinging radius, and said, "Okay, buddy," nodding out toward the bow.

I looked out. You could see ruffled places on the water where mild williwaws were eddying down from the high hills and from the winding strait behind us, but it wasn't raining. Wow, I could go out there in a sweatshirt and deck slippers. What a change from the booted, gloved, full woolies, and oilskins program of Amak and spring fishing. I ducked out the back door, around the corner and up to the bow, breathing in the rich, moist, land smells, wondering what that little cove would look like in the sunshine.

Probably it would be emerald and pristine, with streams coming down the steep hillsides to end in little waterfalls at the edge of the gravel beach. Before the green turned to brown and then white and the ice and snow came, I knew that the Aleutians had a certain beauty. It was, however, a quality probably appreciated by few crab fishermen, who, when they did see the land up close, it was through red, sleep-deprived eyes.

When I'd finished dropping the anchor and made my way back into the pilothouse, I could hear the distinctive rumble of the main engine stopping.

"Hey, George," I said, back inside. "Remember the old days when you anchored up for the night and shut everything down, and it was quiet?"

He looked up from writing something in the logbook. "I know what you mean. I touched on the subject when we were building this one, and the engineers looked at me as if I were nuts. They were so used to designing these new rigs with generator-powered all-electric galleys and electric heat, they couldn't conceive of doing it any other way."

"Ah, back on the *Sidney*," I said, "we were set up so that we could shut everything down at night. We still had 110 volts. We had a big battery bank and a rotary inverter to make AC. I just loved those quiet nights. Of course, sometimes I had to run the little 2-71 Jimmy [a small General Motors diesel] all night to chill the fish, but I'd say, at least three nights out of five, we'd shut everything off at night and have the quiet."

"Yeah," he answered, "and you had a oil stove in the galley that you could back up to and get some radiant heat and it kept the whole galley warm. Hey Joe, you're lucky you have those memories. That was the way it used to be in the whole fleet. Get the anchor down, get the booze out, and everyone would have a round or two before hitting the sack. Just sitting in the nice cozy galley, in the quiet of an evening. No big diesel generators pounding away all night long below where you were sleeping. Those were good days. We worked hard. We made okay money. It was enough."

He waved at the pilothouse full of electronics. "These big new rigs, they're great for catching crab. But once you got your name on the dotted line, they own you. Sometimes I look out there when one of the old wooden rigs goes by, and I miss those days. I wouldn't have one up here. For this fishery and the Bering Sea, a rig like ours is the only one I'd want to be on. But life was a bit simpler on those old rigs." He looked around again and went back to his writing.

"Yo . . . ANCHOR CRANKER . . . get up."

Already? I moaned and sat up. It was 5 a.m. I guess I had slept. Stiffly, I pulled on my long underwear and sweats, got my coffee, and went up to the pilothouse. George and Russell were studying the chart, cigarettes in their mouths. They just nodded, so I took a moment to savor my coffee before stepping outside.

Our brilliant lights illuminated the steep green hills ahead of us. I looked astern where it was still dark, and thought I could see a swath of stars through a fissure in the clouds. The chart showed a church and a Native village, Biorka, tucked into a cove behind us. I wondered, would people still be there? So many villages marked on the chart were abandoned now, the residents having moved to larger towns like Dutch. But if the village were still there, I knew it would be quiet. Few of the smaller settlements had community generators. The locals pretty much lived off the fishing, salmon in the summer and crab in the winter. They slept in their own beds at night, had a family and home life. What would that be like? And what would the big boats like ours do to their little fishery? The small boats could only fish the bays. Were we taking crab that they might be catching? Was there plenty for all?

"Okay, Joe, let's pick it," George said, breaking into my daydreams. "I'll jog along slow so you guys can get some food down. It's nice in here, but I think it's still pretty ugly out where the gear is."

 SORTING KING CRAB aboard the *Flood Tide* with Alaska Peninsula volcanoes in the distance, 1971. On occasion these volcanoes would blow out ash and lava, visible from many miles at sea.

20. The Hidden Canyons

OUT ON THE BOW, the wind was stronger than I had anticipated, williwawing down off the steep hills around the cove. It wasn't cold, but rather a moist wind, smelling of the land, of wet mossy hills and the low-tide shore. I looked around and savored that spot for a long moment before I engaged the winch and released the brake, thinking it might be the last peaceful moment we might have for quite a while.

And so the first pick of our fall season began, before six on a dark, rough morning, the boat heaving and plunging in the confused seas. We'd wolfed down a hearty breakfast: oatmeal, scrambled eggs, English muffins, and bacon, all you could eat. You never had to worry about gaining weight. This was just fuel against the calories you'd burn during the long day. I had a last mug up, hit the head, picked a pair of toasty rubber gloves out of the ever-tumbling dryer, and went out onto the back deck, just as George blew the horn.

Out there the wind was colder, wet, and raw; the trick was to keep moving. I hustled around to the overhang of the boat deck and started filling bait jars, staying warm, expecting any moment to feel the boat slow and see Johnny throw out the grapple to bring in the first buoys, signaling that the steady process would begin.

Instead, almost twenty minutes passed as we idled along slowly, and we began to get chilled. Russell stepped a few paces back along the rail until he could see up over the edge of the boat deck and into the back window of the pilothouse. He shook his head. "That cocksucker's yakking on the radio."

Finally it began again: the thunk of buoys coming aboard, the deepening whine of the spinning crab block, the rattle of the coiler, the thunk of the pot hitting the side, and all hands peering as the quick-release hook and then the safety strap were attached and the pot was hoisted awkwardly up into the frame over our heads, until the bag swung inboard and we could see what we had—a lot of crab, perhaps eighty or a hundred—but we quickly realized that most were sublegal males, too small to keep, and females.

"Give me a count," George hollered.

We sorted through quickly: fourteen big enough to keep, but just legal, no real size to them. George yanked his head toward the stern, and I followed the pot as it was winched toward the stern, bending over and keeping low so the motion of the boat wouldn't knock me over.

George stood above us with a fresh cigarette, peering down into the dark water as the crab block whined. Slim pickings again: maybe twenty crabs, but not much size to them. "Stack it," came the shouted direction.

The mental trick, I learned that summer, was to think one pot at a time. If a couple of pots came up dry and you were stacking them, it was easy to think, "Shit, we'll be stacking a whole fucking deck load," and right off I'd be working with a bad attitude. But it always changed, I had learned. Only rarely, in the thin days of early spring fishing, did we stack a whole load. More often we would stack fifteen or twenty, and then the tale of the pots emerging from the water would have given us enough information to start setting back what we had stacked.

What was different fishing the south side was the depth of the water. All spring and summer, we fished the eastern Bering Sea with just two shots of line totaling 300 feet. In the fall fishery, we were routinely fishing in 150 fathoms of water—900 feet, and occasionally deeper. Near the passes the currents were substantial, so we used eight 25-fathom shots or 1,200 feet of thick $^{13}/_{16}$-inch Esterlene buoy line on each pot.

He was right. In the summer having the coiler was no big deal. Often we wouldn't use the coiler, instead taking turns coiling the line as it came in, just to keep in practice. With just 300 feet of line per pot, it was easy once you got used to it. The line coiled naturally, and the pile at your feet was perhaps one or two feet high when the pot got to the surface.

However 1,200 feet of line was a coil chest high, and the higher the coil, the higher you had to lift your arms. The last fifty fathoms were a killer, with your arm and shoulder muscles screaming as you had to work higher and higher to keep the line on top of the pile. Not only that but you had to pat the pile down occasionally to keep it from falling over. Then, when you were done, if you were stacking the pot, you had to divide the tall coil up into four smaller coils, and tie each one off with a short piece of line, and then try to put them in the pot in the right order, so that after the pot had been pulled back to the stern, pulled upright, and the whole process reversed, the coils could be quickly untied, and readied to throw, without tangling in the process.

For smokers like Russell, who usually took the first bight in the line over to the coiler and got it started, running the coiler provided a perfect opportunity for a smoke break. Once the coiler was operating, he had three to four minutes with nothing to do but keep an eye on things and make sure the line was settling into a nice even coil—a perfect opportunity for a smoke.

At the bottom of the eastern Bering Sea, the population of crabs varied less dramatically than what we began to sense about the south side that first day. It seemed like the trick in the Bering where we were fishing more pots was to try to keep the bulk of your pots where the big males where, but not spend a lot of time placing each individual pot because the bottom was generally so uniform.

I'd studied the charts in the pilothouse and saw that on the south side, there were underwater gullies and ridges coming down from the islands to the north and extending all the way out to the edge, where the bottom drops off into the barely imaginable depths of the Aleutian Trench. I knew king crab were scavengers, feeding primarily on barnacles, small clams, fish when they could get one, and other species of crab. It was clear that in that bottom below us, infinitely more varied than the Bering Sea, there would be areas of greater abundance of all those things that crab feed on, as the microplankton

that the barnacles and clams fed on were swept by in the reversing tidal currents to and from the great depths beyond.

The seventh pot to come up that first day on the south side proved this
in spades: maybe eighty big keepers, averaging twelve pounds each—almost
1,000 pounds of crab in a single pot! When the bag broke the surface, we
stood back in awe and then started pounding each other on the back. We'd
found the mother lode! All we had to do was move the rest of our gear to
that little pocket and we'd load up, make that big season in a few big trips
that we'd all dreamed about for months. George went quickly back inside to
study the "paper machine," our recording depth finder, and the loran's reading against the chart to see if he could determine exactly what it was about
the bottom in that spot that had attracted all the crab.

"We'll set that one back, and pick a . . . more . . . we dump." The wind
had come on a lot stronger, so part of George's order was carried away, but
we got the gist, and Bomba and Russell pulled apart the tall coil of line in the
receiver of the coiler, and placed the smaller coils carefully on the deck next
to the rail. Next, Bomba, watching his feet, grabbed the first twenty-five or
thirty fathoms of line in his hands after we had baited the pot, and pushed it
over the rail.

In the Bering Sea, George would have tooted the horn, the pot would
have gone over, and we'd be onto the next spot. But on the south side, it
wasn't that easy. After we were ready and a few minutes passed while George
maneuvered the boat, it was obvious that George was trying to gauge the
current and our position for putting the pot, as it settled after its long trip to
the bottom, as close as possible to the spot where we had picked it. With the
wind blowing hard from the north, a big swell running up from the south,
and the current whipping down out of the passes between the islands, we
knew it was challenging.

Finally the horn tooted, the pot disappeared into the black water, and
Bomba did his usual smooth job: tossing the first shot of line into the water
as soon as the pot was dropped, then quickly picking up the next coil and
throwing it over the side, followed by the next and the next, and each time

making sure both to throw the coil flat onto the water with the line side leading down to the rapidly sinking pot on the bottom, and keeping his feet clear
of the other coils on deck. With the boat accelerating away from the pot and
the pot headed to the bottom, all this had to be done quickly and correctly. If
the coil was thrown upside down or got tangled on deck as it was being prepared, the chances of a snag were high, and in the deep water where we were
working, a snag likely would result in the buoys getting sucked down, and
losing that pot.

ANY NIGHT IN THE ELBOW ROOM, someone would invariably tell some version of the story about the green crewman, just up from south, working in
one of the crab processors, who in a stroke of luck, got onto a good boat when
a crewman broke his ankle stumbling around drunk in Dutch and had to be
flown out.

Few commercial fishing boats in those days had formal training for new
crewmembers. Essentially the safety of a new man depended on his own
smarts, and the ability and willingness of the rest of the crew to give him
the information he needed to perform well and stay safe. Skippers were busy
and not always able or willing to train a new man. That was usually the job
of the crew.

A new man, or an "in breaker" as he was called in some fisheries, often
was given a half share or some reduced portion of what a regular crewman would get. After a few trips, when the skipper and the rest of the crew
believed—sometimes there was even a vote—that the new man was contrib-
uting a full share of the work, he would receive a full crew share.

In this sad case, the new man didn't last long enough to get that full
share. According to the story, on the fourth day of their first trip, in some
rough fishing conditions with the boat double stacked, rolling enough for
green water to be coming over the rail and across the deck, somehow the new
man had stepped into an unseen bight of the line and had been yanked suddenly overboard, with barely time for a cry of surprise before disappearing
into the dark water.

Sometimes when a guy goes over the side tangled up in buoy line, he'll pop right back up, either having untangled himself or, carrying a knife in some readily accessible place, having cut the line. Getting back aboard a crabber in rough conditions was far from a sure thing. Without the now common inflatable vest under your rain gear, the survival clock is ticking. Rubber boots and heavy rain gear and sweatshirts weigh a guy down. The water is so cold that within a few minutes your muscles fail to respond to your commands. Your nervous system operates on chemistry, so as your body temperature drops, that chemistry—the nerve-to-nerve synapses firing and the muscles responding—simply slows down and eventually stops.

A federally sponsored education program for fishermen in New England had included an interesting demonstration. Fishermen were asked to place their arm in a fish tank of cold water and, after a few minutes, pick up a silver dollar from the bottom of the tank. None of those who tried was able to retrieve the dollar. This lesson got everyone's attention.

So, it was a huge challenge in the rough conditions of the Bering Sea and North Pacific to get a guy back on board, even if the guy in the water didn't have hypothermia. First of all, you had to find the guy. Unless he went over the side in calm conditions, a person in the water was a mighty hard target to find and track. Then maneuvering the boat close enough to grab and bring the person aboard was another challenge for the skipper.

Today there are many safety classes for fishermen and yachtsmen. In all the man-overboard sessions, the first rule is: Don't Fall Overboard. And the second and third rules are: Don't Fall Overboard.

The greenhorn in the story apparently never had a chance. He didn't have his knife ready, and his leg was too badly tangled. He never came up, and by the time the skipper got the boat turned around and the buoys back aboard, and hauled the pot back, the poor guy came up with it. He'd been at least a hundred feet down.

Just the fact that the story was out there making the rounds probably had saved lives. Every time I was working in the setting area when pots were going over the side, and I watched that buoy line, twitching over the deck and railing like writhing snakes, I knew that death lurked there, for the unwary and a careless moment.

OUR NEXT POT HAD only twenty crab. Welcome to fishing the south side. The Bering was never like that—if you had a good pot, most of the ones around it would be pretty good as well. And so it went. A ten, then a sixty, and an eighty again, even a blank once. After fishing the Bering Sea, this was unexpected.

The day grew darker and the seas grew rougher—short confused seas. A big tide was flooding north from the Gulf of Alaska to the Bering Sea, the current running into the northerly. We had to work carefully. When we winched the pots forward to set, the pots would lurch back and forth with the increasing motion of the boat, slamming heavily into the steel bulwarks a few times. This was a reminder, as if we needed it, of the danger lurking for the inattentive. It was especially tricky when a pot came out of the water and had to be guided tediously up into that rack over our heads so that the bag could be suspended over the picking bin and emptied. A pot banged heavily into the steel legs as it went up. Two seconds of inattention could result in a crushed hand or finger.

By now, I'd seen dozens of other crabbers, studied their deck arrangements carefully, and compared it to the *Flood Tide*. We were the only one using George's awkward system of the bags on the pots. I'd been open to our system in the beginning, seen the advantage of the dumping all the crab easily into the sorting bin rather than picking them out of the pot one and two at a time. But as time went on I became increasingly nervous. Each pot had to be hauled up in the air, I had to attach the safety strap as well as the quick-release device to each pot, and stand back as it went up into the "hayrack" as we called it. I knew that on board workboats, sometimes winches broke, lines snapped, safety devices failed. Sometimes when we were rafted up in Dutch and other crews crossed our decks, they'd ask me what in the hell the hayrack was. I'd explain about how the bags worked, dumping the crab into the sorting bin all at once. But all they could see was that hayrack and think about 700 pounds of steel suspended ten feet above their backs in the rough waters as they sorted crab.

I knew that if I went crabbing again, it would be on a traditionally rigged boat where the pot was lifted aboard and onto the dumping rack, low on the deck, where it posed no danger to the crew should the winch or rigging fail.

In mid-afternoon we found a good spot to dump the rest of the pots. I was glad to see them go. By then the motion of the boat made it challenging to move up and down the deck from the stern to the setting area. Seas were occasionally coming over the rail and sweeping across the deck. Breaking one rib that way was enough. So I just followed the pots closely as the boom winch pulled them forward, figuring if a big green one came over the rail, I'd just grab onto the pot.

It happened at the end of the afternoon, at the edge of day, when our crab lights high on the mast had begun to overpower the wan sun far to the west. All of a sudden, with a great roar, a huge plane appeared overhead, flying low and close to the water, a four-engine red and white Coast Guard C-130, trailing thin smoke from the engines that was quickly ripped away downwind. Seen, then gone, but in that glimpse we sensed that it was turning for another pass at us. It reappeared a few minutes later, even lower this time. We glimpsed helmeted figures peering intensely from small windows, searching the heaving sea below. Then they were gone.

A moment later, George was at the rail above us, yelling down. A crabber was in trouble to the west of us, somewhere farther out the chain, past Dutch. His distress call had been cut off before the skipper could give his position, so the plane was flying a grid pattern, trying hopefully to find the boat or a yellow life raft with the crew in it. We could go over to join in the search, but George pointed out that the boat was fifty miles away and that other boats were closer, already starting to search. Reluctantly we went back to work, but feeling fortunate. We prayed that the men on that crabber were still aboard their boat, that something other than a total disaster had caused the radio to fail. It had been intensely sobering to see that big plane, flying so close to the water, literally coming out of nowhere, its grim-faced pilots searching the heaving seas as the daylight died.

As we all knew, bad things could happen very fast on the water. As a crew, we talked often about exactly how an emergency might unfold, if someone went overboard, what each one of us should do. If there were a fire, what our jobs might be, and so forth. But there was always the unexpected, the unknown, the weak vulnerable spot that no one had realized was there. We knew that on a proven design like the *Flood Tide*, designed and built for the terrible winter conditions in the Bering Sea, the likelihood of some hidden flaw was slim.

Marco had built a successful series of ninety-four-foot king crabbers: the *Rosie G, Ocean Spray, Kevleen K, Olympic*, and others. The *Flood Tide* was simply a slightly scaled-up version of a proven design built with time-tested construction techniques and equipment selected for reliability. Except for some of the deck gear like the automatic line-coiler and the stacking winches, almost everything we used had been proven on other Marco boats in other crab seasons. So we had full confidence in our boat and equipment.

Yet safety standards that would have been considered normal and appropriate in any other industry were noticeably absent in commercial fishing in 1971. There were no requirements for crew or skipper training, no licensing standards or crewing requirements except for vessels larger than ours, and we were one of the biggest new crabbers yet built. Only modest safety equipment requirements, essentially life preservers and fire extinguishers, were required.

Anyone could take any kind of a boat up to Alaska and try to get in on the growing king crab bonanza. As a quick glance around Dutch showed, that was exactly what was happening. Some of the new boats were wood, seventy- to ninety-footers, looking like they might have had summer charters buying fish, and had then just unloaded the scales and other fish-buying equipment, put aboard a load of crab pots, and headed north. Others were steel, but older boats, with higher deckhouses and therefore higher centers of gravity. Even though I had been in the Bering Sea less than a year, it was clear to me that wooden boats could participate in the crab fishery safely only if they were rigorously prepared and equipped.

From what little we could gather, whatever had happened to the missing crabber had happened very quickly, which led one to suspect a sudden capsizing with no warning or some sort of structural failure.

To FIRST-TIME Bering Sea fishermen, having fished in places like the Washington coast or Southeast Alaska, where Coast Guard bases were closer, it was sobering to realize that a chopper, if they needed one, was so far away. The Coast Guard choppers based at Port Angeles in Washington State and at Sitka in Southeast Alaska were able to reach distressed vessels in those areas within a relatively short time with enough fuel to spend a good amount of time searching, lifting survivors, and returning to base.

In the Bering Sea, you would hear regular radio exchanges between the Coast Guard and vessels on mundane subjects—like a buoy's light not working. You might make the assumption because radio reception was so clear, that help was close at hand. But in reality, the nearest Coast Guard base was at Kodiak, 700 miles east of Dutch Harbor. It was the presence of a radio repeater on the Alaska Peninsula that allowed Kodiak to talk more or less easily on the radio to Bering Sea vessels.

The reality was that if your situation required help, a chopper was at least five hours away, and often would be low on fuel when it arrived.

The fast C-130 Hercules that flashed low over us that afternoon was a morale booster. But, once you were in the water, a C-130 couldn't do too much to help except alert other vessels to your position, or try to drop a raft, which was extremely hard to do accurately in rough seas. Fortunately, commercial fishermen everywhere are highly tuned to the safety of their comrades, and the first responders to most Bering Sea emergencies are usually other fishing vessels.

Before the Bering Sea crab fleet boomed in the 1970s, few American vessels worked those bleak waters except for halibut schooners. These were extremely seaworthy vessels, most often operated by professional fishermen, usually from Seattle's Norwegian community. They rarely needed Coast Guard help, usually taking care of problems themselves or with the help of other halibut vessels. It was only when crab began to boom and many more vessels began to fish the Bering Sea, some ill prepared for its rigors, that the Coast Guard was needed on a more regular basis.

Aboard the *Flood Tide*, we considered ourselves to be professionals. George, Russell, Johnny, and Bob had fished all of their adult lives, and Bomba since he was a child. We had regular crew talks about safety issues, and tried to operate and maintain the *Flood Tide* at high safety levels.

As the Coast Guard was to discover, some of the newer arrivals were less experienced than others. One well-known Kodiak helicopter pilot had an experience that quickly became legend among the crab fleet. A vessel had been in trouble south of one of the most rugged and remote parts of the Alaska Peninsula in terrible winter conditions. Launched from Kodiak, a chopper found the vessel with extreme difficulty. Conditions were challenging: visibility was barely above the wave tops, combined with blowing snow and powerful gusting winds. When the chopper finally found the distressed vessel, it had just enough fuel for only a few minutes over the sinking boat before it had to return to Kodiak lest it run out of fuel on the way back. Hovering with difficulty, the boat below them half hidden in the blowing snow and rising and falling dramatically in the seas, the winch operator lowered the rescue basket to start taking the crew off as the pilot struggled to keep the chopper stable. On the second or third try, the chopper was able to touch the deck with the rescue basket, which was loaded quickly and hoisted up toward the chopper.

As it appeared out of the swirling snow, the winch operator recoiled, stunned to see the basket full of boom boxes and big portable stereos. He lifted one side of the basket so that the equipment all tumbled over the side into the water, and thumbed the loudhailer to communicate with the crew on the stricken vessel:

"Last chance, assholes," he is reported to have said. Probably the crew couldn't hear him over the wind, the seas, and the chopper's rotors, but seeing their boom boxes pitched into the sea, they probably got the message. The next time the basket was lowered, it was a very eager crewman that got in.

Johnny had told us of a friend's experience in an eighty-foot wooden sardine seiner a few years earlier. They had been transiting one of the passes between the islands, struggling through the usual tide rip, where the tidal currents, working against the wind, heap up the seas into short, steep, nasty combers. They'd just finished a trip, had finished cleaning up the deck, and the whole gang was up in the pilothouse, watching soberly as the skipper worked the wheel back and forth, picking his way around the worst of the seas. It was a workout for the skipper, steering in conditions like that.

In contrast to the *Flood Tide* with its hydraulic steering and autopilot that allowed the helmsman to change course by simply turning a knob and dialing in a new course, this boat had the old traditional "Iron Mike" autopilot and cable steering: running from the steering wheel down through pulleys and steel pipes all the way to the stern and the big quadrant bolted to the rudder post. The Iron Mike was the autopilot unit, usually located on the floor near the helmsman. It had a bronze clutch lever that allowed the helmsman to engage or disengage it. To set a course, you hand steered until you were on the course you wanted, then you pushed the lever with your foot to engage it. To change course, you had to pull the lever back to disengage, hand steer the boat to the new course, and then kick the lever to engage it again. Once it was engaged, the steering wheel was turning back and forth constantly as the unit received sensing information from its compass. There was a steering wheel on the *Flood Tide*, but it was just for use in case the hydraulics and the autopilot failed.

So, as Johnny recounted, this boat was picking its way through the rip when the main engine suddenly slowed down, then speeded up again. The engineer quickly scanned the gauges in the pilothouse and disappeared down the stairs to the engine room to switch fuel filters, assuming that the engine was slowing because of a dirty filter. Large modern diesel engines used in big fishing boats are extremely reliable, but the chinks in their armor are fuel and fuel filters. As long as you change oil regularly and keep the fuel clean, these engines give their owners amazing service. To this end, most fishing boats over thirty-five or forty feet long have two fuel filters set up so that when one clogs, turning a few valves will switch over to a clean filter and the dirty or clogged one can be replaced as soon as convenient. It was common knowledge that rough weather will stir up the crud in the bottom of a fuel tank. Most savvy engineers had a couple cases of fuel filters stashed away.

In this case, the engineer switched over to a clean filter, expecting that to clear up the problem, but the engine kept losing rpm's and then speeding up again, in a cyclical rhythm. Thinking that perhaps the new filter was bad, the engineer replaced it with a new one and switched the valves again. The problem persisted. Stumped, he got a flashlight and a small adjustable wrench and started systematically checking the connections of all the little steel pipes and fittings of the fuel system, making sure every one was tight. Finding nothing loose, he began inspecting every exterior part of the engine.

As he worked his way around the back of the engine, something caught his eye back in the shaft alley, the narrow space underneath the fuel and crab tanks through which runs the long steel shaft from the engine to the propeller. On a boat the size of the sardine seiner, the shaft might be five inches in diameter or larger. The boat rose into a steep cross sea just then, the engine slowed down for maybe ten seconds, and he saw the problem. As the eighty-foot wooden boat struggled in the big seas, the whole boat was flexing noticeably, causing the long propeller shaft to bend and bind up enough in the three bearings that supported it to slow the engine for a few moments. He was shocked to realize that each time the boat flexed, water would flow from underneath the crab tanks, when the individual planks flexed and opened slightly as the boat struggled. He jogged up the stairs to the wheelhouse, and pulled the throttle back a third and explained breathlessly to the skipper what was happening.

He quit after that trip, Johnny said, saying he wouldn't work again on another wooden crab boat with steel tanks. The new quota system put immense pressure on everyone in the fishery, no matter what kind of boat they had. For boats like us and John Hall in the *King and Winge*, Jack Parks in the *Rosie G*, Sam Hjelle in the *Olympic*, Soren Sorenson in the *Ocean Spray*, Karl Kaldestad in the *Kevleen K*, Ole Hendricks in the *Sea Star*, and many others, boats that had already put in months of fishing in spring and summer, some of the financial pressure of having a big boat was off. But for the newcomers, with huge boat payments ahead and the very large costs of fitting out and gearing up, the effect of a shortened fall season was to make it imperative to "catch the last crab": fish in whatever the conditions, fish when boat and crew were all exhausted, fish when prudence dictated staying in.

THE DAY STARTED to die in the west, and George came out onto the boat deck in the windy dusk and told us to get something hot in our bellies because we would be fishing all night. Already cold and tired after just twelve hours on deck, we jumped at the chance, and gulped big helpings of hot stew. George slowed the boat to an idle and came down after a bite to eat with us, allowing the autopilot to just jog ahead slowly into the seas.

"I know they're there," George said. "I know you guys hate like hell when I got to jog around before I dump 'em. I know you're getting cold. But you saw those pots with seventies, and eighties, and nineties. They're in the little hollows and gullies, but it's so different from the Bering Sea, where a herd of big males might cover twenty-five acres of bottom. Here that same herd might be jammed thick into just two or three acres. With the tide running like a bullet out of these passes, you've got the challenge of not only finding where they are, but managing to drop your gear on them once you find them.

"Down here on the edges of the drop-off, we're trying to fish these little hidden canyons, maybe a couple hundred feet wide, and it's hard to set back on the same spot each time, especially when the current's running hard. When it's daylight and visibility's good, a lot of the time I'm using ranges to help me out too. You know, like in the old days. I can line up the south side of Tigalda Island with the peak of Shishaldin to make one line, and then line that up with the east side of Egg Island lining up with the west side of

Akuktan for another. That gives me a pretty good lineup for the edge here. But then when I'm setting the pots, sometimes I feel like a baseball pitcher in a big game—you just got a couple of narrow little edges around the sides of the plate that you shoot for. Too far off and it's either a big hit or a ball. That's why it just takes a while sometime . . . so you just have to get used to a little more time when I'm trying to set back. But take a break for a few minutes. I want to cruise around, get a better sense of the lay of the bottom before I start picking again. I'll toot when it's game time."

We assumed the "crabber's rest position"—boots on, bib overalls pulled down to our knees, and heads slumped forward on our arms on the table, asleep almost instantly. From somewhere far away, I thought I could hear the engine speed up or slow down, and then I was totally out, exhausted.

Perhaps an hour and a half later, the horn tooted and we rose with aching joints and muscles. It was wicked out there—wind, slashing spray, and cold. "Ohhhh," I said to myself. "Why couldn't I have picked an easier path in life? Why did I choose to be out here in these conditions?" For most of the time crabbing, we all got a certain satisfaction when things were really clicking. Your blood is flowing, your adrenaline running, all senses are tuned in to what was happening on deck and around you. That made the work almost . . . well . . . fun.

But, still, stepping outside on such a night was hard. Your body awoke slowly, your reactions weren't as quick, your mind wasn't as sharp. It had been a few weeks since we had worked together in the windy black, and we knew it was in this situation that we were most vulnerable to accidents. When George tooted, we moved into position, cautious and ready, each of us reviewing in our minds the moves we had to make.

A twenty: stack it, a thirty: reset, a thirty: reset. A twenty-five: a hesitation, an extra puff on the cigarette before it was flicked away, a red spinning dot in the night, and George's fist and thumb yanked toward the stern: stack it. And then some forties, and even a sixty: reset, reset, reset. Then a ten, stack, and then an eighty, reset, and a few minutes while George cruised back and forth, no doubt studying the trace on the depth-recorder And there on the back deck, in the roaring, windy black, too noisy to communicate except by shouting, I felt the thrill of the chase. Somewhere beneath us the crab lurked. I could sense that there was a substantial body of crab. These were short soaks. Some of the pots had been in the water barely thirty-six hours and already had sixty big crab—big numbers compared to our longer, two- to four-day soaks in the Bering Sea. Of course, we were fishing 150 pots in those days.

While we waited on the back deck for the toot and the next set of buoys to come thunking aboard, in the shelter deck area by the big resistance heaters to soak in a bit of the heat, I thought about George up there in the pilothouse. For us, the challenges were straightforward: stay safe and keep the deck operating smoothly. George was warm, up there in that electronic world of radar display, scrolling depth-recorder chart, and the little lighted numbers in the loran tubes. But I didn't envy him. Each time a pot came up blank or poor, you could see the frustration and worry lines on his face. Plus, in such conditions as we were fishing, he would be getting thrown about the wheelhouse as well.

I'd been up there sometimes at night in the Bering Sea when we were working the gear. A skipper was very much like an aircraft pilot, flying on instruments on a black stormy night, buffeted by the wind. Only by concentrating on the information that the multiple instruments were presenting and by integrating them into a three-dimensional picture in his mind could George maneuver the *Flood Tide* where he wanted it.

Today's crabbers have a mind-boggling array of electronics in front of them that eases the challenge of finding the crab. The GPS gives a vessel's position with startling accuracy, within fifty feet. Coupled with color plotters, the GPS displays your position as a little ship icon on a detailed moving color chart in real time. A cross-track feature shows you how fast the tide is running and its effect on your course. Units called scanning sonars, sort of like underwater radars, display the bottom under and around your vessel in a graphic almost three-dimensional rendition on a big color screen as well. Those little gullies and canyons that a crabber from our era would find so elusive are presented in all their glory.

That fall of 1971, George relied primarily on just three instruments—the radar, the fathometer, and the loran. The radar, a Decca forty-eight-mile unit, showed our position on the familiar circular CRT-style display, but simply as light colored land masses and sea clutter against the dark sea. However, in the typically rough conditions of the Bering Sea and North Pacific, the big seas reflected the radar signals to create a lot of smaller targets, like snow on a TV screen. The fathometer only showed a line that represented the depth and, to a much lesser degree, the quality and texture of the ocean floor directly under the boat. The underwater detail on our chart was only good enough to use as a rough approximation of what the lay of the bottom was.

Essentially George had to create in his mind a three-dimensional map of the bottom, based on the loran numbers and the trace from the recording fathometer. Occasionally, he told me later, he might do a little sketch with a cross-hatching of lines that represented the loran lines with the locations of the underwater canyons and gullies where he believed them to be.

But the biggest problem was simply the tide and the currents. Even though we were fishing some twenty miles south of Akutan Pass, there was still a considerable current where we were. Part was from the action of the tide and part was from the action of the Japanese Current as it pushed up from the 20,000-foot depths of the Aleutian Trench just offshore.

Even though our pots were heavy, their substantial areas of nylon mesh slowed them on their way to the bottom. If the pots landed directly underneath where you set them, George's task would be a lot easier. Unfortunately, in 900 to 1,000 feet of water with the current running, a pot could travel several hundred feet laterally before it finally hit and settled on the bottom. Nor is the current easily predictable. If there were no other influences, the current would set toward the pass in the flood and out toward the deeper water on the ebb. However, the wind greatly influences the direction and strength of the current, as does atmospheric pressure, high- or low-pressure systems, and the rotation of the earth as well. Plus the underwater landscape sets up unpredictable currents.

Once George had set the gear, typically twenty-four to thirty-six hours would pass before it was hauled up, so there was no way of telling if the herd of crab that had been attracted to the pot were still there. As we had learned in the Bering Sea, the herds were frequently on the move.

All this calculating and strategizing took place in the confines of a pilot-house, perhaps eight by twenty feet, while being tossed and thrown some-times violently about, with the only thing seen out the windows being the heaving seas brilliantly lit by the lights. No wonder George had become a chain smoker.

We worked through the night. We'd started out warm and dry, but with the wind blowing and the air full of spray, it was hard to avoid getting that occasional shot of frigid water in the face that eventually worked its way down under our collars and wicked down the front of our cotton sweatshirts. This was before the wonderful microfleece garments available to fishermen today, made of light synthetic fabric that will keep you warm even when it is wet.

Two or three times that night, George was thoughtful enough to come out to the back of the boat deck to yell down to us to take a break while he felt his way around the bottom, and we'd hit the galley to wolf a big slice or two of cake and some hot coffee and rest until the horn blew, and then it was up and out into the cold and the wind again.

What I had learned that summer working in Southeast Alaska was that inevitably deck work involves some waiting: it isn't like a factory or agricul-tural job where there is almost more work than the time available. Rather, the pace of deck work varies from intense to laid back to nothing, depending on the weather conditions, the style of gear, the timing of boats coming in to unload, and so on. In a typical situation the crew fills in these slower peri-ods with talking among themselves and sharing experiences. This was part of the excitement of working on a fishing boat—the camaraderie that devel-ops among folks working together for common goals in challenging circum-stances, and the sharing of truly fascinating stories.

Unfortunately the *Flood Tide*'s deck was a very noisy one. Her die-sel engine had an air compressor that spun at several times engine speed, imparting a particularly annoying whine to the exhaust, and the exhaust exited almost directly over our heads. Added to the noise of the wind and the seas, and the fact that we were wearing wool hats and often sweat shirts and rain-gear hoods pulled over our ears, the effect was that except for important communication which often had to be shouted with mouth close to ear, we quickly learned that to share a story with your buddies on deck was almost impossible. Only one person at a time could even hear it, and if you did try to tell the group, inevitably someone would miss an important part of the story. So in weather like this, we rarely spoke to one another on the back deck.

WALTER "BOMBA" KUHR, with a growing deckload of crab on the *Flood Tide*, October 1971. After crab tanks are full, we would keep fishing until the deck was full of another 20,000 to 30,000 pounds, and then go into a sheltered bay, drop anchor, and pump down the level of the water in one of our big holds maybe three feet, then load the crabs on deck one by one into the sides of the hold. King crab are hardy, so they can stand being overcrowded on the last day of two of a trip.

21. Putting Your Winter Money in Your Ass Pocket

THE NEW DAY, when it finally came, was gray and grim. Temperatures were in the low forties—too warm for icing. And the fishing was better. We were still resetting a lot of gear, but now we were stacking pots that had gleaned thirties and even forties to move to areas where we'd pulled steady sixties and seventies—big numbers compared to the Bering Sea.

What with all the water flying and all that required our attention on deck, you don't look around much in such situations. But occasionally when there was a break between pots, I'd stand up straight, put my hand on something for support, and look around. Another "Pacific disturbance" was obviously getting ready to move through with its attendant rain and wind, but occasionally through a crack in the low, racing clouds, the sun would break through and shine full and bright on the volcanoes that were the tops of all the islands north of us.

And something else in those fleeting moments when we were bow up into the wind and sea and you could look out without getting hosed: I could see our pots, the buoys in little clusters, spread along what must have been the edge of the drop-off. In the Bering Sea, the way we had been fishing, having our pots close together meant maybe 600 feet apart. You would rarely if ever see more than two sets of buoys at one time. But that day, I could see a dozen sets of our buoys, close together on the shoulder of a sea. Then when it rolled away, another cluster of buoys could be seen a few wave sets farther away.

Suddenly, the wind grew stronger from the southwest, and unexpectedly George was out, calling down to us, but it took us a moment to get what he was saying, over the noise. "Hawaii," he yelled down to us. "Can't you smell it? That system's come all the way up from the islands and you can smell them on the wind. Smell it! The guys on the radio have all been talking about it." He waved off to the southwest and then was gone, back into the pilothouse.

We stepped into the wind and over to the windward rail, wrinkling our noses and concentrating. He was right! The wind was noticeably warmer, almost sultry for a moment. There something almost sweet in it, a faint smell of gardenia, or jasmine, maybe even a trace of sandalwood. Truly thrilling, in an odd way. Then the rain came, moving across the water like a curtain, flattening the chop on top of the seas, and then the smell was gone. We went back to work.

We hauled seventies, eighties, nineties, then in mid-afternoon the first hundred, and George came out to get a count. He knew it might be a big one, when we hoisted it up; giving us the thumbs up when we gave him the count: 106 really nice big males, hardly any discards. That would be 1,400, maybe even 1,600 pounds of crab in a single pot. It was stunning fishing. Giving ourselves a quick high five, we went back to work. If we hadn't been fishing almost thirty-six hours with little rest, we might have been more excited.

And still they kept coming. George was homing in on the herd, and now when we got a thirty or even a forty, instead of stacking it, he'd tell us to just hang on to it, and he'd steam five or six minutes and we'd drop it. Thank you, George, this was way better than stacking and resetting.

Our first totally full pot broke water around 4:30 p.m., when the light in the sky was almost gone. When we got it up on the sorter, we just stared for a long moment, not fully realizing what we were seeing. The bag was full, up into the pot itself, and the meshes were bulging. When we opened the bag, the crab filled the sorting bin, and sixty or seventy big males overflowed onto the deck. These were all big legal males, with not a single female or small male in the bunch. It was clear that something more than just the smell of herring was bringing the crab into the pot. It must have been some facet of crab herd behavior that made them, once they started, push their way blindly into the pot. And keep on pushing, even when the pot was crowded. This one pot contained over 160 big crab weighing 2,200 pounds.

Around 8 that evening the forward hold appeared to be full, so we closed the hatch, turned on the lights in the engine room, and started to put the crab in the after hold. At 10 p.m., we quickly downed some food. No one spoke. George said he'd give us an hour or so, and we fell instantly asleep at the table. But he must have relented, or overslept his own alarm. When the horn blew and we jerked awake, the clock said 2 a.m. But if we had rested, I couldn't feel it, my muscles and joints complaining as we suited up and stumbled out once again into the windy black.

It was even nastier than before, the rain slashing sideways across the deck whenever we had to turn across the wind. And still big pots came up: seventies and eighties, occasionally a hundred or more. We reopened the forward hatch. The light had fooled the crabs into moving forward, and we were able to keep filling it again for a couple of hours. We were doing about eight to ten pots an hour, depending on volume. When we got a rare thirty or a forty, we could pick out the crab quickly, but then we usually had to steam four or five minutes with the pot in the sorter or launcher before we dumped it, so that slowed us down. And when we got one of the full ones, that slowed us down as well. I figured we were catching 10,000 pounds an hour.

This was the big fishing that we had heard about, and now it was finally our turn.

I'd heard that sometimes when salmon or halibut boats make some big score, the crew would high-five each other and talk about what they might buy with the money. That day we were into the biggest fishing we'd seen all season. But we'd been up almost forty hours, and any enthusiasm or excitement had been overwhelmed by the difficult conditions. If there hadn't been a fresh pot at the rail most times within a minute of dropping the last one, we would have fallen asleep standing up.

The dawn came, mean and gray with heavy spray, filling the air with flying water. We'd started in on the aft tank; the front one was completely full. We could see the end of the tunnel; when the smaller aft tank was full, we'd have to go in, we figured. Then around dusk, George gave us the word.

"That's it," he said. "We're heading in to unload. The plant called for us to bring in what we had, either that or wait another five days for our unloading slot."

We all just stood there for a moment, stunned. Finally, in what seemed like drunken slow motion, we cleaned up. The rest of the guys went inside, but I stayed on deck for a bit just watching the scene. George throttled up and we surged forward, toward the northwest and the entrance to Amalga Pass, twenty-three miles away. The seas were from the southwest, on our stern quarter, and I could watch them from where I stood under the shelter of the overhanging boat deck. Probably twenty-five footers, but with a long period between them, and as they slowly overtook us, first we would slowly accelerate as the shoulder of the sea moved under us, then pitch up as it passed beneath us. I could look back and see our wake, a wide streak of white against the dark sea, as another swell loomed up in the distance. Once a big roller slewed us briefly around to port, so our stern was facing more to the east, and in a break in the clouds I got a brief glimpse of mighty Shishaldin Volcano, its smoke blown to leeward. Was there a bleaker, more godforsaken place to fish? I didn't think so.

I DON'T REMEMBER MUCH about the trip in. I don't remember tying up. Maybe George called up to the crab plant when we were still a mile or two out, and they sent a crew to come aboard and tie up and even do the tedious job of unscrewing the big flathead bolts that held the hatch covers on. That would have given us a few extra hours of sweet uninterrupted sleep. I'd heard of kind skippers doing that.

"OK, guys . . . we're done. We'll bring your bait over in five." A strange voice at the door.

I swung my legs around and sat up, peering at my watch. It was 8 a.m. I'd slept almost fourteen hours. My joints and muscles complained painfully when I stood up. I dressed and went outside to low, racing clouds and spits of rain. Our two big hatch covers sat on the back deck, the yawning holds revealed. The holds were clean, hardly a crab leg to be seen. The unloading crew had gone the extra mile. Usually, in summer fishing, they would leave a hundred pounds or so of crab parts in each hold, which had to be picked up and then the hold washed down and pumped out. I hadn't even heard the pumps running.

I got a coffee and sat down at the galley table, still savoring the night's unbroken sleep. I could have used a few more hours.

"Yo, *Flood Tide*, here's your bait." A voice rang out, and that sweet dream disappeared.

I didn't make it up to the Elbow Room that turnaround. I could have, I suppose. But even after those fourteen hours, all I wanted to do was sleep. Johnny changed the oil, Bob went up to the Alaska Commercial Company to see if by some remarkable coincidence there was any fresh produce, and Bomba and I went up to the crab plant to borrow a forklift and bring down a few more loads of buoy line in case George decided to fish in even deeper water. Russell was tasked to get the latest scuttlebutt on who was doing what and where.

Too soon, we were on our way again, all of us up in the pilothouse as we swung around Priest Rock, rising and falling in the swell.

"No big slams yet," said Russell, filling us in on the news. "From all I heard, we're right in there with our load. Of course there are a few big boats still due in anytime, and the plant's pretty closed-mouthed about what they're bringing in."

I felt no emotion, no real pride or satisfaction at having just delivered our biggest trip yet. All I felt was exhaustion and the numbing realization that in a few hours it would start over again.

The first few pots revealed a grim reality: the crab had moved. Once again, the cigarettes cast to leeward, the chin jerked to the stern. The heavy coils tied off and carefully thrown inside, the pots followed to the stern and tied off. Jogging forward across the deck, and always, warily watching the sea. The days blurring, one into another, the weather uniformly bad. George talking on the radio, the guys waiting on deck. The equinox—September 21—came with its trademark storm. Hoods up, pucker strings pulled tight. The whine of the hauler, the slam of the pot into the rail. Dinner was just a time to get the food down fast so you could doze for just a few precious moments before it was time to go out again.

Now and again, far in the distance, we'd glimpse the mast or hull of another crabber, or at night the glow of a boat's crab lights reflected off the clouds. As far as I could tell, each vessel in this relatively small fleet that fall was working within the little circle of water and sea floor that it had claimed. If we even saw a pot that was not ours, it was something to be remarked upon. For the most part, we worked in a block of sea floor maybe ten miles east and west, but just a mile or two north and south.

The bottom was rugged and jumbled with peaks and valleys, narrow underwater canyons, and little hidden basins through which the crab crawled. Those 400 or 500 acres that George had explored so thoroughly on the first trip proved more complex than he had thought. Valleys that had yielded steady fishing before came up blank. Underwater hilltops that George had thought barren yielded surprising catches. With the moon full in the middle of the trip, the biggest tides of the fall and the strongest currents for months, George couldn't be sure if he was landing the pots were he thought he was. Sometimes we'd set, the buoys would go under, and we'd think the wind or the current had carried us to the edge and the pots into the abyss that lurked so close. George would circle back and the top of one of the buoys would appear just below the surface, an eerie red or white blob in the gloomy chop, and we'd see that the current was running so hard it was sucking the buoys under.

When the tide ran like that, picking gear was harder than usual. Even if Russell or John got the grapple over the buoy line on the first pass, some-times he couldn't pull the buoy up enough, and George had to swing the boat around into the current to take some of the strain off the line.

On the day when the moon was full, two strings couldn't be found. The buoys had been pulled completely under by the current. A couple of days later, when the tides were smaller, there they were.

Nine days blurred one into the other. Not a single one that we didn't stack almost a full load. Not a single day that the wind didn't blow and the spray didn't fly so mean and hard that looking to windward was almost impossible. We all rotated at the rail, throwing the grapple at the pots, our faces red and burning.

The crab teased us. Occasionally we'd get one of those big ones, a pot so full that the meshes were bulging, and George would swing the boat around and around, as we hung on, while he tried to make some sense of what the fathometer and the loran were showing him, trying to find what must have been a target less than an acre, a tiny hollow, some corner in some under-water canyon where the crab were hiding. But between them and us were a thousand feet of tide-churned water.

From my perspective it seemed to be random. You'd look out and see the buoys just a few boat lengths apart at times when George thought he'd found the hot spot, and then you'd get a blank next to a big one again.

Once a day, we'd stop for a few hours. We never even hit our bunks. We just jammed something quick and hot into our stomachs and slumped onto the galley table until it was time to go out again. At the peak of the equinox storm, we crept into Udagak Bay again and dropped the anchor for what was left of the night, and we actually got our clothes off and slid into our bunks.

WHEN WE FINALLY MADE Dutch for our delivery date, with just half a load in our holds, we moved like dead men. Fortunately, although George was anxious to get out and fish again, the autopilot had been acting up and he needed some parts from Seattle. But the weather was keeping even the weather-hardened pilots of Reeve Aleutian Airlines grounded on the Peninsula, unable to fly into the fierce turbulence and poor visibility of the last 200 miles out to Dutch. And so we had the treat of a whole day to sleep, to give our bodies the very minimum that they needed to keep functioning. And then we hit the Elbow Room—just to get the news, of course. Fishing was spotty. Some boats had big smashes; others, like us, were coming in with half a load or so but with the crew worn down and exhausted.

In the bar's restroom I got a glimpse of my face and barely recognized it: drawn and gray even after twelve hours of sleep. Someone had said that a year in the Bering Sea shortened your life by five, which I felt wasn't an exaggeration.

A couple of greenhorns at the bar, workers from one of the crab plants, were nursing their drinks, trying to pry whatever information they could get out of us. They let on that they had just arrived a few days earlier and hadn't met any crab crews yet. I could tell from the way that they looked at us that we weren't exactly what they were expecting. Maybe we should have rung the bell—a signal to the bartender that you're buying a round for the house. Probably that was what they expected: some guys, eager to share their good fortune after an outing on the crab grounds, slapping each other on the back, and shucking C-notes out of fat wallets. Instead, what they saw were some guys with the thousand-mile stare in their eyes, looking like something that a raccoon had drug out of a trashcan. We hadn't done laundry since I don't know when; we were just wearing our greasy insulated coveralls.

"So what's it's like out there?" A fellow with a brand-new red-checked Filson wool shirt said. I didn't say anything. Sucking down a rum and savoring the feeling of sitting down in a warm place with no diesel engine pounding away a few feet under my feet was about all I could handle.

He asked again.

Russell finally turned to him, taking a moment to focus his eyes. "What's what like?" He slurred his words and indicated to the bartender that he and I wanted another round.

"You know," the fellow stammered, taken aback by our brusqueness, "crab fishing."

The bartender set another double in front of each of us, and Russell downed half of his in a long, determined pull.

"If somebody offers you a job on a crab boat," Russell said, lighting a smoke and taking another long pull at his rum, "hit him in the fucking mouth."

After two missed approaches, the Reeve Aleutian DC-6 found a hole in the clouds and set down hard, unloaded, took on a few passengers, and got the hell out before the visibility dropped below minimum again. The parts the autopilot technician needed were on the plane, unfortunately, and four hours later we were headed out again, taking green water over the bow in the tide rips as soon as we turned the corner and entered Akutan Pass against a hard southerly.

First pot was just a twenty, and that after almost a four-day soak. My heart sank as we tied off the coils and threw them in, and I tried to keep my footing as I chased the pot back along the lurching deck to the stern to tie it off. We'd had, by fall crabbing standards, a lot of rest between trips, yet the thought of stacking another deck load was almost too much to bear. "One pot at a time," I told myself. "Just one pot at a time, and at the end you'll have put together some sort of a trip."

The second pot had even less. We stacked almost sixty pots and moved them east, toward the Krenitzin Islands that form the south side of Unimak Pass. George had gotten a tip from someone at Dutch that pickings were better in the slightly deeper water.

Then on the afternoon of the third day, after we had begun to accept that this was to be a pisser of trip, stacking and moving every day, George found the herd. They were in deeper water than the first trip, almost 1,100 feet down, and we lengthened the buoy lines as we moved the gear.

By dusk we were into them, thick, most pots coming up with eighty to a hundred. We went back toward the edge south of Sedanka Island and picked and retrieved the rest of our gear, and brought all the pots to where the action was. It was apparent the herd was jammed into a tiny space on the bottom, two or three acres at the most, so we just set the pots closer and

closer together. Pretty soon we had them as close together as we could physi-
cally set them without their buoys tangling when we hauled.

We worked in a little circle of heaving green-gray seas. Once, after daylight came on the fourth day, I was standing up for a moment, working a
kink out of my back, and a big sea passed under us without breaking, and
high on its backside I could see almost all our buoys, a remarkable sight.
All seventy or so pots (we'd lost a few) were in the distance—maybe sixty,
seventy yards at the most—between the big seas. I could see it was a challenge
for George to get some of the pots set in the middle of the group without tangling buoy lines from the others in our propeller. Fortunately the current ran
strongly through there, keeping the buoy lines taut with no slack or bights to
cause tangles.

Up they came, bag jammed full and meshes bulging, pot after pot.
Heads down we worked, pulling crab out of the sorting bin, tossing them
gently into the holds. If there was a break in the action, we'd grab a piece of
coffee cake through the porthole on the bulkhead, stuff it in our mouths, and
keep going. Sometimes Bob would duck into the galley and bring us all a cup
of coffee. And if the wind wasn't blowing too hard and the spray flying, we'd
peer down into the dark water beside the rail.

And wonder in amazement what it was like down there. How many feet
thick was the herd of crab? How many were being crushed by our pots? We
were constantly moving the pots that produced the least crab—forties and
fifties—as close to the more productive middle of the herd as we could bring
them. It was eerie that such a volume of crab could come out of such a small
area.

Two hours before dark, both holds were full and we were deck loading—
just tossing the crab on deck—and their crawling and the motion of the boat
would more or less distribute them evenly. When George felt like we had a full
load, we'd go up into the shelter of the land to get away from the wind and
the seas, to open and pump down the hatches and try to fit the deck load in.

It was strange beyond imagination. Working in that brilliantly lit circle
of sky amid heaving hills of dark water, with the wind howling and the spray

KING CRAB ON DECK aboard the *Flood Tide*, 1971. To be out there working the deck in the rough seas when it was covered with this mass of slowly moving, grasping king crabs, especially after dark, was a scene as weird as any in a science fiction movie.

flying and inky darkness beyond, our entire deck was covered deeper and deeper with this mass of slowly moving, crawling, grasping, big red spider-like crab. No science fiction movie I'd seen came with a scene as weird as our deck that black and windy night.

This finally was what we had all come to Alaska for—finding in that desolate land and seascape the crab and the money that would make what we had been through worth it. We were tired beyond words. Yet there was the deep satisfaction of seeing those pots come up bulging full. We were fishing almost around the clock then, rarely stacking gear. When we came to the last pot, number seventy-one, we'd just start again on number one, probably twenty or twenty-five hours since we had last picked it. It too, would be full!

After midnight, George set the autopilot to jog up into the wind and surprised us by coming out on the boat deck. He surveyed the scene with a rare smile on his face—the whole back deck a foot deep in places with crawling crab. When the bow lifted on an especially steep one, the entire mass of crab on deck would slide toward the stern, and then when we nosed down after the sea passed under us, they'd slide forward again. We huddled around so we could hear him over the noise of the generator and the main engine.

"That's it. We're plugged. We'll run up to Udagak Bay again. It's the only shelter in this southerly. We'll drop the hook and lay in there to get these crab below decks. I'm waiting for the plant to get back to me to see if they can fit us in to unload early. Otherwise, we'll have to wait three days for our slot, and I don't want to miss this kind of fishing."

We just nodded, already feeling our muscles starting to unwind.

"It'll be a couple hours running to get up in there."

Ten minutes later, we were all slumped, heads on our arms on the galley table, thinking maybe we'd get a day off; that we could actually sleep for twelve or eighteen hours if the plant couldn't take our crab right away. Sure, we'd miss a little fishing, but what a sweet thought.

What seemed like ten minutes later, George rousted me out to drop the anchor. Up there on the bow, I was away from the noise of the engines, so I could hear the sea beating on the shore of Udagak Strait and the wind in the hills around the bay. It was a good thing we'd gotten our load, I thought. It was starting to get nasty out there again.

AFTER JOHNNY PUMPED OUT seawater so the level in the tanks dropped about two feet, we unbolted and lifted away the big hatch. Then a half sheet of plywood, kept tied to the forward bulkhead for just that occasion, was placed on top of the pile of crab and I, as the youngest once again, jumped down onto the plywood and as the rest of the crew was throwing the crab from the deck gently onto the pile, Bomba would pass me crab, one at a time and I would toss them as far back as I could, into the corners and the sides of the tank, the areas under the deck.

It took hours to get the crab all put below.

"Hey, Joe, give me a hand up here for a bit, will you?" George stuck his head into the galley just as I was finishing up a big wedge of chocolate cake and dreaming of my bunk. The other guys were already in theirs.

"Here's the deal," George explained, when I got into the wheelhouse. "The plant can just squeeze us in, but only if we get in there within the next three hours. In a hard southeaster like this and a big tide ebbing out of the Bering Sea. I wouldn't dare take us through Akutan Pass, but I think if we're careful we can just squeeze through Unalga Pass.

"It's not a huge tide, but it's big enough to make it pretty shitty in there. Normally I'd wait until it turned, but that would mean missing this chance to unload and get out here again maybe while the crab are still in that little spot. But there's a little back eddy, in along the beach, so I think we can sneak along there and stay out of the rip. So here's what I want you to do: stick your head in the radar, I've set it down to quarter mile range, and set the inner ring to about a hundred yards. I figure as long as we stay a hundred yards off the beach, we're okay, so you just tell me to go right or left to keep that ring just on the shore."

I studied the chart for a bit, comparing it with the picture on the radar screen to get oriented. About three miles long by maybe a mile and a half wide, the pass is the channel between Unalaska and Unalga Islands.

Priest Rock and the entrance to Dutch Harbor was just on the other side of the pass: so near and yet so far. We passed out of the shelter of Sedanka Island and into the force of the wind and the sea from the southeast. We began to roll heavily. The seas were probably twenty-footers, steep, their tops blown downwind but not breaking. But in the few minutes that I studied the chart and the radar, the motion of the boat changed as the effect of the tide pouring out of Unalga Pass to our north made itself felt, bringing the seas closer together and steeper.

I was uneasy. There were plenty of stories around Dutch and the Elbow Room about boats getting their pilothouse windows blown out by tide rips in the passes, how your cozy, warm pilothouse could be transformed in an instant into flooded chaos, killing all your electronics.

I always believed in what I called the Prudent Mariner Strategy. When I had my little gillnetter, or even back on my Dad's thirty-one-foot sailboat back in college days, taking it up to Maine in the summer, there were occasionally situations when the weather or the visibility would require you to make a choice that sort of boiled down to: do I leave the harbor and continue my journey in marginal conditions or do I wait it out for the weather to improve? To resolve it, I would pose the question to myself, "What would the prudent mariner do?" In most situations, the answer would be: wait.

Unfortunately the decisions crab fishermen had to make, forced by pressure of time and money, had little to do with the prudent mariner. This night was a perfect example. There we were, anchored in a great anchorage. A hurricane could ravage the Aleutians and we'd be perfectly safe in Udagak Bay. Unalga Pass was a bad place when the tide ran against the wind. There it was in black and white in the *Coast Pilot*, the official guide to Alaskan waters:

> Under exceptional circumstances, currents and tide rips of
> unusual magnitude may be encountered, and treacherous seas,
> particularly in the narrow part of Unalga Pass, caused by wind
> opposing the current, often sweep a vessel without warning. These
> have caused severe damage and men have been washed overboard
> with resultant loss of life. There are temporary anchorages, easy of
> access, at either end of Unalga Pass, where better conditions may
> be awaited.
> — *United States Coast Pilot, Vol. 9: Pacific and Arctic Coasts*
> *of Alaska from Cape Spencer to the Beaufort Sea*

The only thing between us and this fate was the craftsmanship of the Marco welders, ship-fitters, and designers. I hoped they'd truly considered what their creation would be facing when they put her together.

"Okay, kid," said George, tersely. "Here we go. Keep us safe."

In 1971, almost all crabbers' radars used a CRT—a cathode ray tube—display mounted almost vertically with a big viewing hood over it with a rubber mask that your face fitted onto when you leaned over to look into it.

I fitted my face into it. The shore of Unalaska Island to our west was a clearly visible, brightly glowing shape as we traveled parallel to it. The variable range ring was set to about a hundred yards, close to the minimum setting.

"Okay," I said, "come left about ten degrees."

George moved the jog stick and I could feel the boat swing slightly beneath my feet, and in a few minutes the range ring grazed the shore.

"That's good. Now slowly right about ten." We were approaching a place where the shore swung to the east, so we had to turn slightly to follow it. After a few commands and seeing how the boat responded, I got the hang of it, and when we came to a reasonably straight stretch of shore, I lifted my head from the hood briefly to steal a glance out the windows.

Just as quickly, I dropped my head again. The sight was sobering. As is often the case where powerful currents push through narrow channels, there is a back eddy along the shore where the current runs in the opposite direction of the main current, and it was along this back eddy that we were picking our way. Because the back eddy was traveling in the same direction as the gale force winds funneled by the mountains on either side of the pass, the seas were almost calm.

But the back eddy was narrow and ended just a few boat lengths east of us. And it was the brief sight of what was happening beyond the eddy that so chilled me. It was total chaos: a tumbling, churning, maelstrom of violent seas in which no boat our size would possibly survive.

"Shit," said George, his voice anxious.

I chanced another glance to see what was up, and quickly saw the problem. Dimly seen, at the very edge of vision ahead of us was a point of land extending out into the pass. For some reason, the back eddy was weaker there and the tide rip extended much closer to the land than the hundred yards I was giving us.

"Check the chart," George said, his hand already on the throttle slowing down. "See if there are any rocks off that point."

I looked, and it seemed clear. "Looks okay," I said, but with a note of caution in my voice. Both of us knew that in places like the passes, only the middle of the channel was surveyed and charted accurately . . . that the prudent mariner always stayed in the deepest water . . . that the dotted line along the shore, the ten-fathom line, was only an approximation.

George slowed down until the engine was at little more than an idle. But I could tell from the radar and my glimpses of the shore as we approached inside of the hundred-yard ring, the tide was still pushing us fast toward the point.

"Probably too late to turn around," George said.

I didn't say anything. Any decision had to be George's, and his attention was focused on the mass of churning water to the east that was moving visibly closer as we approached the point. I looked over toward the land. There wasn't any possible way we could turn around by swinging east; we'd be in the rip before we got halfway around. And inside of us, a boat length or so, well within the lighted circle that our crab lights created, I could see the tops of kelp fronds, lying on the surface and streaming parallel with the beach from the tide. Kelp usually meant rocks close to the surface.

"There's kelp a couple boat lengths inside of us," I said. "You can scooch over a little, but not much."

Then the tide pushed us out to the point, and there was no more time. A dark glistening wall of water seemed to rise out of nowhere and loom suddenly over our bow. I saw it and as quickly looked away, pushing my face into the radar hood, for protection more than anything else. I felt us start to rise, and then we were slammed hard enough that I thought we had careened into a hidden wall of rock.

Fortunately the radars back then were big, solid units, bolted to the floor and heavily built. Otherwise, I'm sure ours would have been ripped from its mounts. Everything loose in the pilothouse and on the chart table hit the floor—books, charts, mugs. I heard dishes crash in the galley below.

But we were dry! Amazingly, the pilothouse windows had held, thanks to the Marco staff and their careful design—thicker windows than some would think necessary, and in smaller frames, to make them even more resistant to attack by a sea. And we were through. That one sea was the end of it. Beyond the point, the land fell away to the west, the point sheltering us from the wind, and the seas lengthened out. In the thin first light that was just coming over the land, I could make out the familiar shape of Priest Rock marking the outer entrance to Dutch Harbor, and in the distance, faint steam from Makushin Volcano.

"Smoke?"

I looked over at George. He was extending a cigarette to me. I thought I could just see a tremor in his hand. I wasn't a smoking man, but I took it. He lit both our smokes, and we surveyed the mess on the floor for a moment.

"You know," he said, "that was just the edge of the rip."

So much for bunk time. I got to slump over the galley table for an hour or so, and then it was time to get out the tie-up lines.

WHILE THE PAN ALASKA unloading crew worked, we took a few more hours of bunk time. But then it was time to take on bait, water, and fuel, and head out again. On the trip back out, Russell took the helm, and George and I finally had a chance to sleep for five hours.

And so, on that windy, heaving plain, with the grim shape of the smoking volcanoes always in the distance, from those hidden underwater canyons where the coastal shelf falls away into the lightless depths of the Aleutian Trench, we made our season and put that legendary Alaska money in our ass pockets.

The best of it was that big trip when we finally plugged the boat, when we spent that amazing night with that slowly moving mass of crab covering the whole deck. We had a couple of good trips after that, but not the huge fishing that left us amazed and in awe at the herd of crab that must have been on the bottom below us.

In our new, state-of-the-art Marco, we weren't high boat in the fleet by any measure. But we'd caught our share and maybe a little more, thanks to our perseverance, and the fish and weather gods. If we didn't have quite the huge crew shares that we'd hoped for, we had enough to be very satisfied.

And then there was this: 1971 was my second season in the Alaska fishing industry, and at the end of our season, even stronger than at the end of my first season, I felt filled up, almost with a sense of triumph, at having wrested a season, a good year's pay, from such a place.

At the end of the season, we let prudence dictate that we bring our pots back to town in two loads instead of one. That bad roll we took that first day setting gear was too close for comfort, and we took the lesson to heart.

WITH THE BOOM LOWERED and chained securely down, in early November, we slid through Akutan Pass and headed to Seattle via the more direct, but still prudent route, across the Gulf of Alaska to Cape Spencer and then down the Inside Passage.

Sure, we could go straight from Akutan Pass to Cape Flattery on the Washington Coast and save maybe a day, but it was early November and the big fronts were starting to march across the North Pacific. Besides, for me at least, there was something deeply satisfying about sitting up there on my wheel watches as we wound our way among those hundreds of thickly forested islands that soon would be covered with snow.

We spent three days in winding waterways and narrow channels, coming around some point, and seeing another channel, and another one after that, deep through the mountain heart of British Columbia. After all that we had been through in the Bering Sea, as much as anything else, it was a wonderful way to decompress.

We passed through the Ballard Locks and into Seattle's Fishermen's Terminal to tie up at the Marco shipyard on a drizzly, cold November morning. The Marco boys took our lines and paused, looking at our bow where the gravel and pebbles from Uyak Spit had sandblasted away most of the paint.

In the old ships with a bridge telegraph that signaled to the engineer what to do, like "full speed ahead," one position was marked "finished with engines." And so, almost eight months after we'd started up our generators and disconnected shore power that winter morning, we were finished. In the wonderful quiet that suddenly filled the boat, we heard the noise of a grinder in the shipyard and the low rumble of traffic over a nearby bridge.

Just like that, our season was done. We said our goodbyes, shouldered our sea bags, and walked up the dock to our winter lives.

I'd gotten a "Dear Joe" letter a month before, so there wasn't much of a welcome back. I caught a cab up to the house where I kept a room, and packed some camping gear, and called my folks back on the East Coast to check in and get the news.

I started my car and went down to the ferry terminal downtown, crossed Puget Sound, and drove until finally there was a lake and a campground. Setting up my tent on the shore I built a cozy fire and the sparks and smoke rose still and straight into the evening air. And then I slept, without the deck heaving, or the thrum of a diesel engine pounding away beneath me. It was exquisite beyond words.

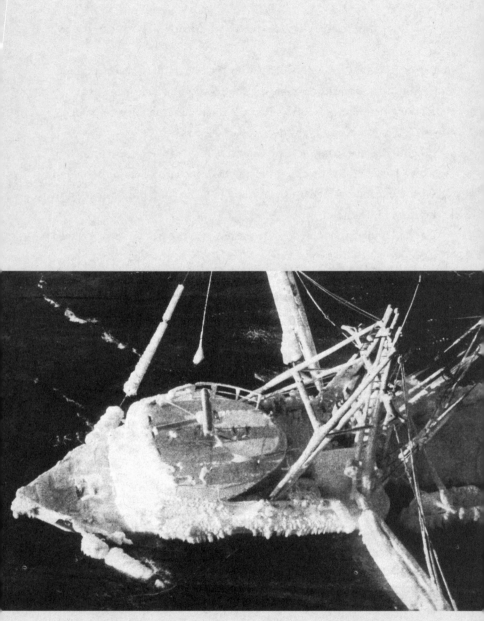

The *John and Olaf*, Puale Bay, Alaska, 1973. In winter, a number of bays on the north side of Shelikof Strait become wind tunnels as dense and bitterly cold air flows down river valleys into the heads of the bays. The wind picks up the sea even in the sheltered waters of the bay, creating a sort of ice fog that freezes instantly on any surface that it touches. The loss of the *John and Olaf* was a sobering reminder to all Alaska fishermen of how quickly a strong and well-managed vessel can be overwhelmed by heavy icing. U. S. Coast Guard photo

22. The *John and Olaf*

S OMETHING WOKE ME early that March morning, three years after leaving the *Flood Tide*. First I thought it was the dog, and climbed down the ladder from the sleeping loft in our one-room cabin. But he was snoozing peacefully by the wood stove, and the wind and snow that battered us all night had eased a bit.

It came again and I recognized it: the sound of a big diesel engine, coming across the wind from far away. Then I saw it, beyond the cove, in Sumner Strait: a big crab boat headed out toward the ocean. I got the binoculars off the driftwood table and studied it. It was big one, maybe a Marco.

They'd started building 108 footers: the *Sea Rover* for John Johannessen, the *Silver Dolphin* for Karl Kaldestad, the *Norseman* for Kjell Fjortoft, and the *Pacific Viking* for Kaare Ness. Maybe it was one of those. It was triple-stacked, and the heavy railroad boom was in the fishing position, high in the air. It was blowing harder out there and they were starting to plunge and rear in the seas driving up from the ocean.

I poked the fire to life, let it warm yesterday's coffee, and sat for a moment with a cup, feeling the room start to warm up. Then I realized what had struck me as odd: Why was the crabber headed westbound in Sumner Strait in early March? The regular route north for crab boats traveling through Southeast Alaska was via Wrangell Narrows and past Petersburg, about fifty miles to the east of us. The only reason you'd see a crabber headed west in Sumner Strait would be if it were headed out across the Gulf of Alaska from

Cape Ommaney, forty miles west. He was obviously going that way instead of carefully following the coast as we had on our terrible trip north. I looked at the thermometer: twenty degrees.

Sometimes we could pick up a station with our little battery-powered radio and get the weather, and I knew that a big arctic high covered the Bering Sea and the Alaska Peninsula, and was moving south. If that crabber wasn't making ice now, he surely would be once he got out in the Gulf and into that frigid high. And I thought of the crew inside, maybe reading in their bunks, or up in the impressive pilothouse of their big, brand-new crabber, feeling oh so secure.

I wanted to get on my insulated coveralls, boots, and gloves, row out to my salmon boat, get on the radio, call them up, and warn them about what they were getting into. Tell them that they should pull into the shelter of the land, get out of the wind and the building seas while they still could. At least lower their heavy railroad boom down onto the top of the stacked pots; just to reduce their center of gravity in case they got into bad icing conditions. Because once they were out in the Gulf and it got rough, it would be awkward and dangerous to lower it.

But I knew they'd just laugh: their boat was powerful, so big, so new. It was built to take whatever Alaska could throw at them. Why shouldn't they head straight across the Gulf and save a day and a bunch of fuel?

Yet just a few months earlier, the fishing newspapers had been full of the story of one of the most dramatic tragedies to yet befall the Alaska fishing fleet, a story so sobering that fishermen began calling the region where the boat got lost "*John and Olaf* country."

The *John and Olaf* was a new eighty-foot shrimper, operating out of Kodiak, owned by two popular fishermen, John Blaalid and Olaf Welzien. It was fishing in the Puale Bay area of Shelikof Strait with four on board. This was near where the sand and gravel picked up by the wind off Uyak Spit had sandblasted the bow of the *Flood Tide*. This was where after we'd been out in the wind and the sea for just twenty minutes before turning around, it took us forty-five minutes to beat enough ice off the winch to drop the anchor.

The shrimper had radioed a mayday. They were icing badly, feared they were about to capsize, and were abandoning ship.

The Coast Guard contacted a nearby vessel, the 170-foot *Shelikof Strait*, a small tanker converted into a crabber, to proceed to Puale Bay. But when skipper George Johnson came around the point and made his turn up into Puale Bay, his ship was assaulted by winds that he estimated at 150 knots, which quickly blew him out again. He tried again and again, but each time, the wind pushed the bow of his powerful boat sideways.

Above him a Coast Guard C-130 also was trying to find the *John and Olaf*. The pilot reported encountering heavy freezing sea spray 700 feet off the water, and the big aircraft turned back. Forty-eight hours later the wind eased and a Coast Guard cutter finally made its way into Puale Bay. They found the *John and Olaf* on a reef, totally encased in ice but still more or less upright. An unspilled mug of frozen coffee was still on the table. Her crew was never found.

The picture of that ice-encased shrimper, looking more like an iceberg than a boat, was splashed across the front page of every fishing newspaper in the Northwest. It was an eye-catcher, instantly frightening to anyone who was thinking about traveling Northern waters in winter.

Yet less than two months after the *John and Olaf* was lost, here was this brand new, triple-stacked crabber heading out into a cold front in the Gulf of Alaska. If you hadn't yet iced up bad, as we had, hadn't felt that terrifying slow roll, it was easy to be seduced by the size of your boat, and place great confidence in all its equipment and electronics. Those crabbers felt so big, tied to the dock in Seattle. I knew. We had. But then the farther north we got, the smaller it seemed.

A MONTH LATER, my wife and I packed our little thirty-two footer with bait and groceries and headed to Noyes Island on the outer coast of Southeast Alaska to troll for king salmon. It seemed like it was still winter out there. When the wind blew, we could hear trees falling in the woods around our anchorage. Each morning we'd screw our courage on tight and head into the

OUR CABIN in Southeast Alaska, with our boat out front, summer 1975. After a long season in the Bering Sea, building a waterfront cabin and gillnetting and trolling for salmon in the calmer waters of Southeast Alaska was a huge contrast. We didn't make the big money the Bering Sea boys were making, yet it was good and it was enough.

swells and the seas pouring around notorious Cape Addington. At night, exhausted, our little diesel-oil stove fighting to keep our cabin warm, we'd eat a quiet supper and go to bed early with our dog sleeping on the bunk between us. But there were a few fish, and other friends in their boats, and every four or five days, if the fish-buyer was in a kindly mood, the rare treat of a hot shower.

When summer came, we switched to our gill net, setting it out among islands forested dark and thick and winding channels. Where except for fishing boats, the hand of man was nowhere to be seen. Sometimes we'd come ashore to our cabin for a few nights, enjoying the wonder of the late high-latitude sunsets over the straits out the window.

A couple of humpback whales hung out in the tide rip out past our little cove, and at night, if the wind wasn't blowing or the tide running hard, we could lie in our bed and listen to them breathing when they surfaced. It was magic.

In the fall we took our boat 250 miles north to an inlet overhung by glaciers so close that sometimes you would hear a noise like distant thunder and look up to see chunks of ice the size of trucks tumble into the forest below. There was a big run of ten-dollar-a-fish dog salmon, or chum, and in four hectic weeks, we doubled our season.

Finally, on the nastiest kind of night, with snow and sleet swirling around us and the diehards still fishing, we called it a season. My wife was asleep in her cozy sleeping bag, the dog snuggled close. I picked our way into the shelter of the anchorage with radar, dropped the hook, took off my sweats and rain gear, and sat for a moment with a cup of hot tea before turning in. Occasionally through the swirling snow outside, I saw the shapes of other small boats, snow-blasted white like us, a figure on the bow, dropping the anchor, then quickly retreating inside to huddle by the stove.

In the morning, we sold our fish and headed south, eager to get out of that wind tunnel before another Pacific low trapped us. That night we anchored up in a remote cove, and the next day we saw just one other boat. On the late afternoon of the third day of hard traveling, we navigated through narrow Rocky Pass with surprised flocks of ducks rising around us, crossed Sumner Straits, and with the last of the light, tied to the little home-made log float in the cove below our cabin.

We'd been away six weeks, and except for the skiff being full of water, everything was as we had left it. We bailed it out and rowed the skiff ashore. Our dog took off to sniff around his old haunts, and I built a fire in the woodstove, my wife put away our things, and we found the rum bottle.

Outside the wind came on again, shaking a loose shingle like a dog worrying a stick. But our boat was secure, the cove sheltered, and the two of us looked out at the wild night, feeling the heat of the rum and the fire. We'd made our winter money, and our lives seemed filled up . It wasn't the big crab money that the Bering Sea boys were making, but it was good, and it was enough.

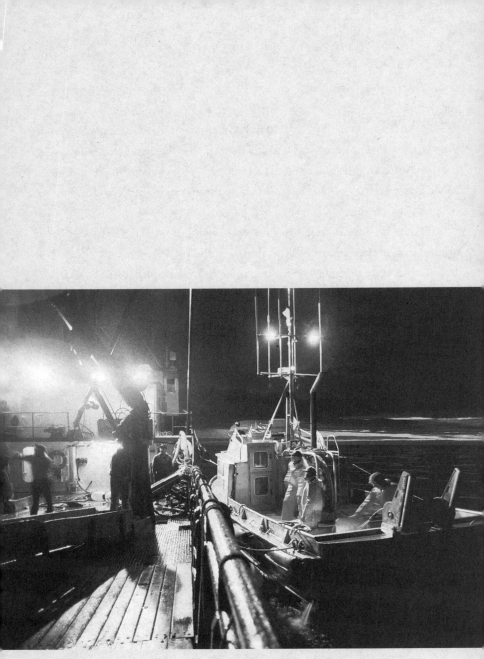

My SALMON gillnetter, *Katie Anne,* making a night delivery to a king crabber, Egegik River, Alaska, 1993. Many king crabbers invested in refrigeration systems to enable them to work as tenders or fish buyers in the summer salmon fisheries all over Alaska. On the crabber's deck you can see the pot launcher and the crab block just on the forward right.

Epilogue

O F COURSE, had I taken George up on his unusual offer, I could have been relief skipper in 1972, and possibly, with a very uncomfortable level of debt, part owner of a shiny new crabber the year after. And I might have joined the many crab fishermen who became very wealthy during the amazing 1970s.

Those were the glory years of king crabbing. Even though the Bering Sea fleet went from a congenial fifty-two crabbers in 1971 to 236 boats in 1980, a five-fold increase in a decade, the catch went up ten times: from 13 million pounds in 1971 to 130 million pounds in 1980.

Fortunes and legends were made. Sam Hjelle, who had the first Marco crabber, the ninety-four foot *Olympic* built in 1968, was having such great fishing that he took delivery of a much bigger boat, the 110-foot *American Star* barely two and a half years later. In the 1976 crab season, legend has it that he stayed up for twenty days straight to catch half a million pounds of king crab.

Fishermen who borrowed heavily paid off their boats within a decade and built fine homes, often in the Sunset and Richmond Beach neighborhoods of Seattle, a few miles north of Fishermen's Terminal, where much of the Alaska fleet spent the off season.

And remember: this was in the Northwest before the high-tech boom and Microsoft created so much wealth. In the 1970s, wealthy crab fishermen became a recognized part of the Northwest social and economic scene.

A few owners, such as Chuck Bundrant, went on to create American fishing empires. A Tennessee Boy, as he likes to remember himself from those early days, Bundrant had hardly ever seen a fishing boat before he arrived on the Seattle waterfront in the early 1960s. Within a few years, he rose from deckhand to skipper, and then had the *Tugidak* built. After some great seasons with that boat, Bundrant was one of the first to see the advantage of having processing capability aboard—you don't have to waste time going in to town to unload. He had the big 135-footer *Billikin* built eight years later and went on to found a small crab- and fish-processing company, Trident Seafoods, in 1973. Again his timing was right: the Japanese appetite for Alaska seafood was booming. Within a decade, Trident became the largest seafood company in the Northwest and one of the largest in the United States.

Prudent crewmen, who refrained from ringing the bell at the Elbow Room too often and stayed away from cocaine, could retire, buy some nice shoreside business, or maybe even invest in their own crab boat after a few years. On a top boat, an annual crew share might edge up beyond $75,000— huge money in those days. Many fishermen wore watches, rings, bracelets, and necklaces festooned with gaudy gold king crabs.

The boats kept getting bigger. In 1978, Magne Ness converted a navy freighter into the high-tech trawler-crabber-processor *Northern Aurora*. A Navy oiler (small tanker) was refashioned into the *Northern Endeavor*, able to carry 400 pots. Biggest yet was the *Winchmann Command*, a 176 footer built in the Gulf of Mexico for Tor Olsen, Olav Sola, Peder Nornes, and others.

Even with the rapidly growing fleet, there was no sign of overfishing. Sometimes in heavy fishing, when crabbers pulled yet another pot jammed full of big keepers, maybe a ton of crab in a single pot, they would peer over the side in amazement and wonder at the seemingly endless herd of crab on the bottom beneath them.

Then in the fall of 1980, when the Alaska Department of Fish and Game conducted its annual crab trawl survey to determine the appropriate harvest quota for 1981, the results were far from what anyone had anticipated.

DEADLIEST CATCH crabber *Cornelia Marie*, working as a summer fish buyer, or tender, anchored in the Naknek River, Bristol Bay, Alaska, around 1994. With almost 1,800 32-foot salmon fishing boats and an intense, short, five-week season peaking around July Fourth, salmon companies needed a lot of tenders. They would anchor and unload fish from the salmon boats into their holds, which were filled with refrigerated seawater. Such jobs allowed many crabbers to keep their heads above water after the Bering Sea king crab population collapsed in 1980.

The 1979 survey, conducted by towing a net along the bottom for specific distances, yielded forty to sixty legal king crab per mile. But the 1980 tows brought up only one to three crab per mile, a stunning decrease. All over the Bering Sea, the yields were the same: totally unexpectedly, the king crab population had crashed. As one biologist put it, "King crab appear to have undergone about as violent a transition as I know of for a fishery." Fishery news reporter Chris Blackburn put it succinctly: "Did thirty million king crab simply walk away into the tide, never to be seen again?"

When the season opened in the fall, it became evident that the surveys had been correct. The fishery that had produced 130 million pounds the year before only yielded 30 million.

Some biologists thought the cause was some unknown disease. Others believed that the dramatic decline could have been caused by a slight warming of the water in the bottom of the Bering Sea. A third theory blamed the handling of the sublegal and female crab in the sorting process, which weakened the survivors. In 1980, the 236 big boats of the Bering Sea fleet may have handled fifty or sixty million crabs to order to catch the fifteen or sixteen million. Many of those sublegals were probably handled multiple times. Crabs, like lobsters, but unlike fish, are unusual in that normally they can survive the trauma of being brought up from a thousand feet of water in just a few minutes, dropped on the deck of a crabber, and kept out of the water until being thrown back. But in the stress of high-production, fast-paced fishing, many of the smaller and female crab may have been possibly thrown over the side with enough force to injure or make them susceptible to disease, so the theory goes.

The results were devastating to the industry, especially to the newer boats with the biggest mortgages. Some of the huge boats quickly got in trouble. The *Northern Aurora*, launched with such fanfare just four years earlier, went bankrupt, as did many others. The joke around Alaska was that instead of giving you a toaster for opening a new account, the banks were handing out crabbers.

Most crewmen, for tax purposes, were treated as self-employed contractors, meaning no withholding or Social Security payments were taken from their paychecks. Many fishermen had gotten into the habit of paying last year's taxes with this year's crab earnings, so when the crab population collapsed, they were left without funds to pay the fifteen or twenty thousand dollars they owed. In the boom years, some crab crewmen simply didn't file at all, hoping that the government wouldn't catch up with them.

I employed a crab fisherman as crew on my salmon boat during that period. One year I got a notice from the IRS. When you get a letter from the IRS, your eyes immediately go to the bottom line. It said I owed some $123,000 in back taxes and penalties! Only when I got my breath back and sat down and read it a little closer did I realize it was my ex-crewman who owed the taxes. He hadn't filed for the previous four years. He had a family, lived pretty high with a nice house out in the Sun Valley area. Now I knew why.

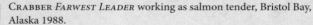 CRABBER *FARWEST LEADER* working as salmon tender, Bristol Bay,
Alaska 1988.

The 1981 season wasn't a fluke. The poor catches continued into the
1980s, and crabbers scrambled to find ways to survive. Fortunately, several
opportunities provided just enough cash flow to keep some of them afloat
financially. The Bristol Bay salmon fishery in the eastern Bering Sea was
having a major comeback after the 200-mile limit had eliminated Japanese
from fishing on those salmon runs. The canneries and processors needed big
tenders or fish-buyers to bring the fish in. This required the crabbers to be fitted with refrigerated sea water systems for their holds, a major expense.

Another big development was the joint ventures between big foreign
fish-processing vessels and American fishing boats. The idea of the 200-mile
limit established in 1977 was that the resource then would be harvested,
processed, and marketed by Americans. However, in the beginning, there
were neither enough American processing facilities nor American catching-
processing ships to handle the volume of fish, primarily cod and pollock,
that the foreign fleets had been catching.

So, the joint ventures, or JVs, evolved, essentially pairing American catcher boats with foreign processing ships. It was a wonderful deal for the American fishermen. Traditionally the most tedious part of trawling—towing a net along the bottom for fish—is handling the fish. Most had to be cleaned and then carefully iced in layers in the holds. But in the joint-venture arrangement, the Americans never touched the fish. The nets were designed with detachable cod ends—the end that holds the fish—so the American catcher boat just towed the net until it was full, then steamed up behind the waiting foreign processing ship, picked up a heavy line, hooked it onto the net's cod end, and cast the net free. While the processor hauled the fish up an inclined ramp in its stern, the American hooked up a new cod end, and went back to fishing.

It was also an eye-opening experience for the U.S. fisherman. At that time, the American offshore finfish trawl fleet was concentrated between Boston and Rhode Island, primarily fishing Georges and Grand Banks at a time when the resource in those areas had been depleted by foreign fishing. Their catches were small. After a decade of bringing home maybe 60,000 to 80,000 pounds of fish from a week-long trip to Georges Bank, transplanted East Coast fishermen who made their first trip on a JV boat working the Bering Sea could hardly believe that it was possible to tow a net for a couple of hours and come up with 40,000 pounds of fish. One well-known New England skipper was sent by his company to crew on an Alaska trawler in preparation for taking his company's boat to Alaska to trawl. When the bag came up and 20,000 to 30,000 pounds of fish were dumped on deck, a few hundred pounds started to flow overboard through the deck scuppers. The New Englander hustled over to recover the fish before they were lost over the side. But the deck boss stopped him, saying, "That's okay, this is Alaska. We have plenty."

Before the JVs, trawling for ground-fish along the West Coast had been a relatively modest enterprise consisting of mostly wooden boats in the fifty to seventy-foot range making short trips and delivering to fresh markets. Most of these boats were unsuited to the rigors and heavy gear required by high-volume fishing in the Bering Sea. The big crabbers, however, with the addition of several hundred thousand dollars of winches and nets, and sometimes a more powerful engine, were perfect for it, and many grasped at the chance.

This was a new kind of fishing for Americans. Even the toughest New Englanders had never seen the kind of conditions that the big converted crabbers were experiencing in the Bering Sea. Sometimes the big foreign processors would plow through miles of ice to get to where they wanted their American partners to fish.

At the same time, American crab-processors who had prospered in the boom years were expanding the markets of the previously lowly tanner, or opilio, crab. By clever marketing, renaming the meat as snow crab, they were able to receive and pass along prices so that opilio slowly became a significant income producer for king crabbers.

After the sudden collapse of the king crab population in 1981, the Bering Sea crab fishery evolved into a number of smaller fisheries. The "Pribs" (Pribilof Islands) might open for a two-week king crab season, then Adak in the far western Aleutians might open for another short period. What had been the gravy train for almost two decades—the Bristol Bay king crab fishery—might open for two or three weeks. And then there would be an opie (opilio) season as well. The glory years never returned, but a good crabber, between perhaps some JV work and hitting all the short crab fisheries, could still put together a respectable season.

Had I stayed in the crab fishery, there was another very real alternative to getting rich: getting killed.

During my first summer working in Southeast Alaska, I developed the impression that fishing boats that were lost or on which injuries occurred were often older, perhaps less well maintained, and that you could judge your risks on a boat simply by looking at it. At the time, it was a fair assessment.

The crab fishery and the Bering Sea were very different. Except in the early years when there were many smaller and older wooden boats in the fishery, the fleet was generally newer, well built, well equipped, skippered by experienced men, and manned by experienced crews. Yet vessels and crews were lost regularly. The event that epitomized this kind of loss happened in February of 1983 and became known as the A-Boat Tragedy.

On February 3, a crowd of some 200 well-wishers gathered at the docks in Anacortes, Washington, to wave goodbye as two of the town's newest and best boats, the crabbers *Americus* and *Altair*, left for the Bering Sea king crab grounds. Aboard were fourteen men from town, experienced crab fishermen plus a few greenhorns feeling lucky to have landed such plum jobs.

In Anacortes, a crew position on one of owner Jeff Hendricks's four state-of-the-art crabbers, the A-fleet, was a young man's dream. Instead of a modest wage job at the local cannery or sawmill or at the nearby refinery, a crewman might make $50,000 or even $80,000 in three or four months if they hit it big, which was huge money for a working man in those days.

And probably more than any other West Coast town, residents of Anacortes felt a special bond to these boats. Not only were the five boats one of the biggest single-owner fleets fishing in Alaska, but three of the boats had been built in the local boatyard, Dakota Creek, which specifically built crab boats for the booming fishery. Hendricks was known as a man who spared no effort to make his boats not only safe but also comfortable and even elegant in some ways, with well thought out touches to give crews an incentive to go the extra mile for him.

In 1983, there were very few safety regulations and requirements for fishing boats the size of the A-boats: 123 feet by 34 feet by 14 feet. Essentially the boats were required to have flares, fire extinguishers, and life jackets for every one on board, a bell, and a placard warning not to pump oil overboard. Although survival suits and life rafts were widely available and proven lifesavers, the Coast Guard did not require them on crabbers. But Hendricks, like most crab owners who were aware of the dangers of fishing the Bering Sea, provided his boats with all of the extra equipment. Furthermore, his captains, George Nations on the *Americus* and Ronald Beirnes on the *Altair*, regularly had their crews practice emergency drills.

Despite traveling across the Gulf of Alaska from Dixon Entrance to Unimak Pass during winter, the weather gods had smiled, and the two crabbers arrived at Dutch Harbor during an unusual period of light winds and moderate temperatures.

The other two boats of Hendricks's fleet, a sister ship, the *Alyeska*, and the smaller *Alliance*, had traveled to Dutch Harbor a few days earlier. Upon arrival and before they loaded themselves six layers high with crab pots stored on shore, the *Americus* and the *Altair* each pumped out some 28,000 gallons of fuel— approximately seventy tons—to lighten their boats so they could better receive their roughly eighty-five tons of crab pots and gear. By traveling up to Dutch Harbor loaded with fuel purchased in Anacortes and then off-loading that fuel to the processing ship to whom they delivered their crab, to use at a later date, they were able to save about eight cents a gallon.

As part of Hendricks's safety program, he also had required that his vessels undergo stability tests when they were built. These steps were tedious and expensive, essentially putting specific weights at specific places on the vessels and measuring the distance that the vessel heeled, which allowed the vessels' designer, Jacob Fisker-Andersen, to calculate how many crab pots the vessels could safely carry.

However, after the vessels were built, several additions and modifications had been made to allow them to trawl—tow heavy nets along the bottom. These changes added significant weight. To compensate for the weight, the operators reduced the number of crab pots they carried, making the decision essentially by guesswork and by how the vessels felt under various conditions.

A year earlier, the fifth boat in Hendricks's fleet, the *Antares*, caught fire and sank. Fortunately the crew survived, thanks to their rigorous training. The loss of the vessel put an extra burden on the remaining vessels to put in a good crab season in 1983.

That February, as the king crab season was about to begin, the A-Boat skippers concluded that their best shot at getting their pots on productive fishing as soon as possible was to start fishing in the area southwest of the

Pribilof Islands, a two-hundred mile steam from Dutch Harbor. Given the distance, each skipper knew that the more pots he could carry out to the grounds in his first load, the better his chances of putting in a big season, since typically the best catches were in the first two or three weeks of the ever-shorter seasons.

Nations loaded 228 pots, Beirnes 225, and Brian Melvin, on the *Alyeska*, whose trawl conversion included heavier gear, loaded 208. By any standards, these were very big loads. The big 700-pound pots were stacked six layers high, and were tightly chained down to avoid any shifting as the boat moved through the seas toward the Pribs. In addition, to balance the weight higher up on the boat from the pots, each vessel flooded at least two of its crab tanks, putting an additional sixty or seventy tons of weight aboard.

The *Altair* was the first to leave Dutch, throwing off her lines about 2 a.m. The skippers of the *Alliance* and the *Alyeska*, Glenn Treadwell and Brian Melvin, watched as she slid out of the harbor. They observed that she was sitting very deep in the water and water was rolling out of her scuppers, a sign that some of her crab tanks were pressed full by the circulating pumps, spilling the excess water overboard. The weather was light; winds were from the northeast, and there was perhaps a two-foot sea running, which were mild conditions for the Bering Sea.

About seven hours later, George Nations finished up the last-minute details on the *Americus*, the crew made their last phone calls home, and they headed out. An hour or so later, they were over the horizon, headed, like the *Altair*, for the Pribilof Islands and what they hoped would be a short, intense king crab season with big shares for skipper and crew.

Around noon that same day, a 750-foot freighter, the *Neptune Jade*, was headed to Asia via the Great Circle Route, which took it through Unimak Pass and parallel to the Aleutian Islands on the north side. About twenty-five miles northwest of Dutch Harbor, it noted an odd target on her radar, what appeared to be a small crabber but not moving. Thinking the vessel might be in distress, the freighter called on VHF channel 16, a universal ship bridge-to-bridge channel, but without any results. The skipper turned his big ship toward the target, thinking perhaps he could offer help.

Three hours later, they came upon a stunning sight—the radar target was the upside down hull of a fishing boat, perhaps eighty feet long. Taking a risk by coming within a hundred feet, he observed that the hull was undamaged, and despite circling the vessel several times, the freighter saw no sign of survivors or debris. Were there men trapped within the hull? The bridge staff of the *Neptune Jade* could only wonder. But in their huge ship with limited maneuverability, with the wind increasing and another Bering Sea storm forecasted, they couldn't do more than announce their find over the radio.

Unable to reach the nearest Coast Guard station at Kodiak almost a thousand miles away, the *Neptune Jade* announced its find on a general calling frequency to anyone who might be listening. Eventually another big freighter, the *Aleutian Developer*, over 500 miles away to the southwest, was able to successfully relay the information to Coast Guard Kodiak. Having done all they could, the *Neptune Jade* resumed its course to Asia.

Amazingly, just forty-five minutes later, another big Asia-bound freighter, the *Ocean Brother*, also reported coming across an overturned hull three and a half miles southwest of the first sighting. The freighter made its call to Coast Guard Hawaii.

Meanwhile, two crabbers, the *Alaska Invader* and *Pacific Invader*, several hours away, heard the startling radio conversations. Knowing that if crewmen were trapped in the hull, time was of the essence, the two vessels headed over to the last reported position of the hull.

Were there two overturned hulls? Or were the two reported sightings, three and a half miles and forty-five minutes apart, one and the same? It is unlikely that an overturned hull could have drifted three and a half miles in less than an hour. So it is very possible that the two freighters had seen two different hulls.

Unfortunately, the *Ocean Brother* had a delivery schedule to meet, and after circling several times without seeing any sign of life, the vessel also headed off to Japan.

Dark comes early that time of year, and there was nothing to be seen by the time the *Alaska Invader*, and a Russian factory trawler that also heard the radio calls, arrived at the last reported position.

Back at Dutch Harbor, the word of a possible vessel loss was spreading around the waterfront like prairie fire. But there hadn't been a mayday, and after reflection, most concluded that what the freighters had seen was the hull of another fishing boat that had been abandoned after a fire a week earlier and had been reported to be drifting toward Dutch.

Meanwhile, not particularly alarmed, the crews of the other A-Boats, the *Alliance* and the *Alyeska*, got under way around 8 p.m. They altered their course so as to pass close to the reported position of the hull, but saw nothing, and kept on their way.

With the nearest Coast Guard station so far away, it often fell to the Dutch Harbor police chief, Loni Sullivan, to act on his own with whatever resources he could marshal before the Coast Guard arrived. Knowing that the last reported position was just twenty-five miles away, and that sometimes fishermen could stay alive while trapped within an overturned hull for many hours, he decided to do what he could to reach the scene, just in case the overturned hull wasn't the burned and abandoned one many assumed it to be.

Finding a friend, Buster McNabb, in town with his crabber, the 100-foot *Golden Pisces*, and willing to help, Sullivan contacted diver Bill Evans, gathered up essential gear, and headed out to search for the hull. If they found it, the plan was for Evans to enter the water, climb up on the overturned hull, bang on it, and listen for signals from within. They carried a cutting torch to open up the hull if it came to that.

Around 4:30 a.m., the Russian processing ship *Svetlaya* also looking for survivors, came upon the capsized hull and reported its position.

With the hull sighted again, the Dutch Harbor rescue team in the *Golden Pisces* was able to home in on its position quickly. When they arrived, skipper McNabb took one look and was stunned to realize that it wasn't the burned-out boat that they had assumed it would be, and that it also was much larger than the eighty feet earlier reported. By the look of it, it was probably larger than his own 100-footer.

By then the brief calm that had settled over the Aleutians for a few days was over, and a storm was approaching from the northeast. The seas quickly grew to fifteen feet, washing over the hull, and making it too dangerous for diver Evans to enter the water and swim over to it.

Helpless and sick from the tragedy they were witnessing, the men from *Golden Pisces* circled the hull and watched as the building seas occasionally submerged it entirely. Then it happened: a sea larger than the others lifted the bow briefly and the men saw the American flag emblazoned across it and gasped as they recognized it as one of the mighty A-boats. They quickly radioed the information back to Dutch.

About 120 miles to the north, the *Alyeska* was about halfway to its destination near the Pribilof Islands. Skipper Brian Melvin was in the pilothouse, listening to boats talking to each other on the radio, when a familiar voice, Chuck Beach, the manager of the processor that he delivered his crab to, the *Sea Alaska*, broke through the chatter with a terse question: "Which one of the A-boats is out?"

Having followed the events around the submerged hull, he was instantly alert as a voice he didn't recognize said that all the A-boats had left Dutch on their way north.

Beach came back on the radio to announce what the *Golden Pisces* had seen: that the overturned hull had the big American flag on the bow, a trademark of the A-boats. The information hit Melvin like a blow. It had to be the *Americus*, skippered by his friend George Nations. He knew the whole crew.

It got worse. The sea conditions coming out of Dutch had been very mild. The hull of the *Americus* appeared to be undamaged. Yet the boat had capsized, and apparently with so little warning that whoever was on watch didn't even have time to grab a microphone and make a frantic call. The radios were always on and warmed up; in five seconds, ten at the most, a hand could reach one of the mikes, push the button, and shout. Whatever happened had been stunningly swift and totally without warning.

A suspicion that the *Americus* had capsized because it was overloaded and top-heavy must have flashed through Melvin's mind. It was the first explanation that came to mind given the evidence—no radio call and no indication of a collision.

Melvin knew that his boat, the *Alyeska*, sister ship to the *Americus*, had been trimmed and loaded more or less the way the *Americus* had. He, too, had unloaded some 28,000 gallons of fuel. He, too, flooded his crab tanks before he left. Suddenly, he worried that his vessel might be a time bomb ticking down to the same mysterious catastrophe that had suddenly and inexplicably overwhelmed the *Americus*.

He called the crew up into the pilothouse and explained to the grim faces what had happened. Next, he headed to the nearest patch of water shallow enough to drop thirty pots, and then swung off toward the *Americus*. Dropping the pots accomplished two purposes: it gave them room on deck in case a survivor was sighted and lowered their weight by ten tons to increase their stability.

About midnight on the fifteenth, a day and a half after the *Neptune Jade* had discovered the capsized hull, the *Alyeska* came upon the grim sight of her sister ship, with their friends likely trapped inside, dead or alive. By then the first edges of the new storm were pounding the hull, and the wind was increasing, so there was nothing the men could do but look on helplessly.

Meanwhile, Brian Melvin on the *Alyeska* had been trying to radio his friend Ron Beirnes and the crew of the *Altair* to give them the terrible news. When his first calls went unanswered, he thought Beirnes was probably busy setting his gear in the worsening weather. But as the hours passed with no answer, the men on the *Alyeska* and the *Alliance*, which had by then arrived on scene, began to have a terrible and growing fear that whatever had claimed the *Americus* had also befallen the *Altair*. That one of the newest and best-equipped and crewed crabbers in the whole U.S. king crab fleet could capsize without time to make a radio call was beyond belief. That it could happen to two vessels in calm weather, within maybe an hour of each other, had to be impossible.

By dawn on February 16, Coast Guard aircraft were circling the area and searching the nearby beaches where survivors might have drifted ashore. Around noon, as the stunned crews of the *Alliance* and the *Alyeska* watched, the bow of the *Americus* hull rose for the last time, clearly revealing the ship's name, and disappeared into 4,200 feet of water.

A couple of hours later, the Coast Guard, after trying and failing with their more powerful radios to reach the *Altair*, reluctantly radioed Melvin to tell him that they were considering the *Altair* lost as well.

The news hit Anacortes like an earthquake. Many of the families were at a high school basketball game, and were pulled off the bleachers to get the terrible word that quickly spread to all corners of the tight-knit community.

The families of the seven *Altair* crewmembers kept their hopes alive, yet most knew that in the unforgiving Bering Sea, "missing" becomes "lost" all too quickly. The families hoped that skipper Ron Biernes had stumbled onto a crab bonanza and was loading up, too busy to talk. When the Coast Guard suspended the search without finding the *Altair*, relatives hired a plane on their own, but with the same result.

The apparent simultaneous loss of two seemingly well-equipped and capable crabbers, indeed, by any standards some of the best in the fleet, stunned and stumped the Coast Guard, which took the unusual step of convening a Marine Board of Investigation with subpoena powers. The investigation quickly focused on the way that the vessels were loaded, with officers interviewing the crews of the remaining A-boats as soon as they arrived back at Dutch after the ordeal of searching for their friends.

A critical problem was the lack of a witness, someone who could give any insight into those terrible last moments. Theories were floated but quickly discarded. Some suggested one or another of the foreign trawlers in the Bering Sea had sunk them somehow. But the lack of a radio call made this unlikely. The designer suggested the boats might have rammed each other, yet the hull of the *Americus* had appeared undamaged. One particular area of interest was the huge amount of fuel that was unloaded in Dutch Harbor, roughly seventy-five tons from each boat, and what effect that might have had on stability.

Stumped, the board hired an expert on vessel stability, Bruce Adee from the University of Washington, who often worked with models to try to recreate the conditions a vessel was in at the time of its capsizing.

Another issue was the weight of the equipment that had been installed aboard the lost A-boats to convert them to trawl as well as crab. Hendricks had asked designer Fisker-Andersen to determine the exact weight of the new winches and other equipment. The numbers were sobering. On the *Alyeska*, a slightly smaller boat than the vessels that were lost, the added weight amounted to thirty-five tons more than her stability letter had been issued for. Yet, even after Adee rigged his eight-foot model to simulate the added weight that Fisker-Andersen had determined that the trawl conversion added and drove it full speed with the rudder turned hard over—it was a remote-control model—it refused to capsize. All indications were that even with the heavy load of pots and the added trawl gear weight, the boats should not have rolled.

Then Adee and the Coast Guard took the unusual step of persuading the owner of an A-boat sister ship, the *Morning Star*, that was already in for shipyard work, to allow them to strip the vessel to determine what the actual weight of it was, suspecting that Fisker-Anderson's numbers were somehow in error. What he found simply didn't make sense: the *Morning Star* weighed some fifty-six tons more than the baseline numbers that the designer had used for the stability tests. Such a huge discrepancy was too large to accept. Yet, with the A-boats on the bottom, there was no way to establish what their actual weights were when they were lost.

Then by a fluke, the key clue to the puzzle came in the mail—a series of photos of the *Altair* showing her clearly in profile while traveling in calm water. When Adee compared the photos to some taken of the *Altair* leaving Anacortes less than two weeks before she was lost, he made a startling discovery. Her boot strip—the top of her waterline—had been repainted a foot higher than in the earlier photos and higher than indicated on the designer's blueprints. He already knew that it took roughly seven tons to submerge the lost boats an inch. The added foot meant that the boats were almost seventy tons heavier than the weight on which their stability letter had based its calculations.

When Adee plugged in the new data with the weights of the crab pots, the trawl-gear, and the effects of probably having their double-bottom fuel tanks empty or partially empty, he instantly understood what had happened. In reality, when they left the dock, they had so little stability left that if a swell had been running into Dutch Harbor or if they had made a hard turn, they would have rolled over right as they left the dock!

And so, as they steamed along, the crew probably trying to get some sleep after the frenzy before the rigorous crab season began, something sinister was happening belowdecks. As fuel was consumed by the 1,200-horsepower diesel from tanks deep within the hull, the vessel's center of gravity rose. The skipper may have been just relaxing. Likely, the boat was rolling subtly slower and slower, giving no indication of what was about to happen, until at the end of one of the rolls, it simply kept on going, capsizing before the startled skipper could even speak on the radio.

A much more detailed account of this tragedy is the excellent *Lost at Sea* by Patrick Dillon.

That 1983 season was a wake-up call to the whole industry. Three other crabbers were lost as well: the *Sea Hawk*, the *Arctic Dreamer*, and the *Flyboy*. Fortunately there were only two fatalities from the three boats. But capsizes continued to take lives. In the summer opilio season that year, there were two more obviously stability-related vessel losses. First, the *Ocean Grace* capsized so quickly there was neither time for a radio call nor for the crew to put on their survival suits and four were lost. Subsequent investigations revealed a safe load of pots would have been around seventy-five, whereas she was carrying around a hundred and twenty. A few weeks later the big *Golden Viking* capsized in mild weather as she was making a sharp turn with a full load of pots, and two men were lost. Again carrying too many pots was the prime suspect.

As one of the investigators in the A-boat tragedy put it, "A fisherman is only interested in one thing: getting fish aboard. God knows we've tried to educate him. He just doesn't understand that freeboard is a fisherman's best friend."

In 1984, just three years after the Bering Sea king crab fishery had yielded 130 million pounds, eighty-eight vessels showed up for what turned out to be a fifteen-day season. The total catch was 3.5 million pounds. The average haul was five king crab per pot. A year later, 127 boats showed up for a seven-day season; the harvest was 5 million pounds.

But if the seasons were shrinking, the price was booming: in 1987, 300 boats headed out for 17 million pounds at an unheard of $4.25 a pound. At least one big boat, word had it, caught 250,000 pounds. On that boat an 8 percent crew share would have been maybe $70,000 after expenses, for maybe three weeks work. By then opilios were starting to replace the income that king crab had once provided: in 1992, 285 boats harvested an amazing 330 million pounds of those small brown crabs at around fifty cents a pound.

By 2000, the fleet size either had been or was in the process of being limited in many Alaska fisheries. The problem was that as the fleets grew larger, their harvesting capacity dictated in some cases ridiculously short seasons. For example, before the size of the halibut fleet was limited in 1995, the season had been reduced to just a few short forty-eight- or seventy-two-hour openings or fishing periods. Generally fleets were limited either by giving participants with the most history in the fishery a limited entry license or an individual vessel quota based on their catch history. Such management schemes inevitably shut boats and fishermen out of the fishery (but they can always buy someone else's license or quota shares), and because of this, they are very controversial.

After the expected controversy and opposition, the size of the crab fleet was finally limited by what was called rationalization in 2004. Boats received a quota based on their past participation in the fishery. In some cases, vessel owners had an opportunity to sell their fishing rights to the government—the crab buy-out program—in exchange for an agreement that the vessel would never participate again in commercial fishing.

Quota shares could be bought and sold. Many boats that received small shares elected to sell their shares. The effect was dramatic: 251 boats left port to fish Bering Sea crab in 2004. After rationalization (some called it limited entry), eighty-nine boats fished the Bering Sea for crab in 2005. The reduction didn't take the danger out of crab fishing. As one crabber said, "You still have to get the crab and get back to Dutch." But it did reduce the level of competition, and by allowing crabbers to elect to stay in port if the weather was particularly bad, it kept the fleet out of the kind of weather that they would have had no choice but to fish in just a year earlier.

Now, each winter, the remaining smaller fleet sets out to fish crab in the exacting conditions of the Bering Sea. The popular TV show *The Deadliest Catch* highlights the challenges of this fishery. But watchers should view the show with a grain of salt. The Bering Sea will always be a challenging and at times deadly place to fish. But today's fishermen, with their much smaller fleets and larger quota face significantly less challenges than they did, say just after the king crab collapse of 1981, when crabbers had their backs against the wall financially and fought for a much smaller resource against a much larger fleet during a much shorter season.

For myself, if there was a single event that epitomized the vicious conditions of the Bering Sea, always probing the defenses of any boat, it was what happened to the big 120 footer *Vestfjord* on an October evening in 1981 and shocked the entire Bering Sea crab fleet.

Skipper Jens Jensen was up in the bridge jogging slowly into heavy seas and winds while his crew was below in the galley. As Bering Sea storms go, it wasn't a really bad one, but around 9 p.m. the vessel slammed into a particularly nasty sea, and a few moments later, the crew was startled by water pouring down the stairs from the pilothouse. They ran up to find Jensen stone dead on the floor.

At the moment of impact, he apparently had been standing directly behind the so-called spinner, a circular section of the pilothouse window

PATHS WE TAKE. I could have stayed in the crab fishery, and perhaps become very wealthy (or died). But I was always drawn to the fisheries with smaller boats, ones you could take your children on when they were young. This is our son Matthew, on the flying bridge of our gillnetter, *Katie Anne*, off the mouth of the Ugashik River in Bristol Bay, Alaska, in 1993. Sometimes caribou would stand on the top of the bluff in the background and look down curiously at the fishing boats.

with an electric motor, a little fist-sized brass unit, which spun the glass in the middle of the circle. In icing conditions, the circular motion made it difficult for ice to accumulate on that area of glass, giving the skipper at least one place with an ice-free view.

Apparently the wave that hit the *Vestfjord* blew her pilothouse windows inward with enough force that the brass motor of the spinner drove directly into Jensen's head, killing him instantly. The water also shorted out most of the radios, the automatic pilot, and all the electronic navigation equipment. Only after a fierce struggle with the wind howling through the shattered pilothouse windows was the crew able to get the manual steering operating, the crabber turned away from the wind, a radio operating, and start back to Dutch Harbor.

It was a tragic reminder to the whole crab fleet that even in the apparent security of the pilothouse, the Bering Sea is capable of striking a fatal blow.

AUTHOR'S NOTE: I lost track of Bob, Russell, and Johnny Nott after the 1971 season. They stayed crab fishing, and I entered the very different world of salmon trolling and gillnetting. But George and I stayed in touch, and he filled me in on Bomba (Walter Kuhr) as well. Both were extremely experienced and innovative trawl fishermen before the crab boom, and were well positioned to take advantage of those skills after the U.S. imposed the 200-mile limit in 1977. George had the 123-foot crabber-trawler *Storm Petrel* built in 1980, and the next boat out of the Marco shipyard just a few months later was the almost identical 123-foot *Dona Genoveva* for Bomba. Their timing was perfect: they were there just as the crab fishery was collapsing and there was a premium on capable trawlers and skippers. Both rode the next boom—Bering Sea ground-fish—becoming successful and well-known skippers and boat owners.

I had a new aluminum 32-foot salmon gillnetter, the *Katie Anne*, built for the booming Bristol Bay fishery in 1989. And each year, I'd see a number of the old crabbers from the 1971 season, including the *Flood Tide*, renamed the *Sea Venture*, working as tenders.

VIEW FROM THE FLYING BRIDGE of my gillnetter, *Katie Anne,* as we wait to unload our catch to the *Silent Lady,* Bristol Bay, 1993. She is buying salmon from boats on either side and we are tied up waiting our turn. Tied to our stern were another four or five boats, also waiting to unload. The *Silent Lady,* like the *Shelikof,* had been converted from a so-called mud boat, or oil rig supply boat, which were built to supply offshore drilling rigs in the Gulf of Mexico with supplies, particularly long lengths of drill shaft and drilling mud. When oil prices slumped in the late 1980s, these vessels could be had cheaply and many found their way into the king crab fleet.

Index

PORT UPTON evening, Southeast Alaska, 1973. We called our unnamed cove Port Upton, and built a floating dock where we would work on our nets and store our gear. Friends would often tie up there with us in the evening after fishing.

About the Author

AFTER THE 1971 SEASON on the *Flood Tide*, Joe Upton purchased a thirty-two-foot salmon gillnetter-troller to pursue his dream of fishing in the sheltered waters of Southeast Alaska. He and his wife built a waterfront cabin on a small island near the roadless fishing community of Point Baker, and traveled throughout the region fishing for salmon. The community had a floating bar–general store, floating post office, and conveniently, the bar tender was also the fish buyer and you could sell your fish for bar credit! Upton wrote about those years in the award-winning book *Alaska Blues*. When salmon fishing in Southeast Alaska went through one of its cyclical slumps in the mid-1970s, Upton headed to the coast of Maine, purchasing a 1917 seventy-one-foot sardine carrier to operate in the lobster bait business. But Alaska always called Upton, and in 1981, he and his new wife, Mary Lou, returned to Alaska to operate a fish-buying vessel, the *Emily Jane*, in Southeast Alaska for several seasons.

Returning to Maine to start a family, Upton began fishing mussels in Maine during the winter, and gillnetting for red salmon in Alaska's Bristol Bay in the summertime. After eleven years in Bristol Bay, Upton retired from commercial fishing in 1998 to start Coastal Publishing, to produce a guide for Alaska cruise passengers, the *Alaska Cruise Handbook*, and the *Alaska Cruise Companion*. In 2010, Upton teamed up with fisherman-moviemaker Dan Kowalski to produce volume 1 of *The Alaska Story Project*, to acquaint viewers with some of the dramatic stories that Upton had heard over the years.

Upton lives with his wife in Vinalhaven Island, Maine, and Bainbridge Island, Washington.

READING RECOMMENDATIONS

for readers who enjoy Alaskan memoirs & biographies

ALASKA BLUES: A Story of Freedom, Risk, and Living Your Dream,
Joe Upton, $14.95

ARCTIC BUSH PILOT: From Navy Combat to Flying Alaska's Northern
Wilderness, James Anderson & Jim Rearden, $17.95

BOOM TOWN BOY: Coming of Age on the Lost Frontier,
Jack de Yonge, $14.95

COLD STARRY NIGHT: An Artist's Memoir, Claire Fejes, $17.95

ESKIMO STAR: From the Tundra to Tinseltown,
the Ray Mala Story, Lael Morgan, $17.95

GOING TO EXTREMES: Searching for the Essence of Alaska,
Joe McGinniss, $17.95

IN SEARCH OF THE KUSKOKWIM & OTHER ENDEAVORS:
The Life and Times of J. Edward Spurr, Stephen Spurr, $14.95

NORTH TO WOLF COUNTRY: My Life Among the Creatures of Alaska,
James W. Brooks, $17.95

SISTERS: Coming of Age and Living Dangerously in the Wild Copper
River Valley, Samme & Aileen Gallaher, $14.95

SURVIVING THE ISLAND OF GRACE: A Life on the Wild Edge of America,
Leslie Leyland Fields, $17.95

These titles may be found at or special-ordered from your favorite bookstore or ordered
directly from the publisher by visiting www.Epicenter Press.com or phoning 800-950-6663.

Alaska Book Adventures™
EPICENTER PRESS
www.EpicenterPress.com